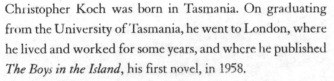
Christopher Koch was born in Tasmania. On graduating from the University of Tasmania, he went to London, where he lived and worked for some years, and where he published *The Boys in the Island*, his first novel, in 1958.

He has been a full-time writer since 1972, having worked for a total of twelve years as a radio producer for the Australian Broadcasting Corporation. One of his novels, *The Year of Living Dangerously*, set in Sukarno's Indonesia, was made into a film directed by Peter Weir and starring Mel Gibson. The screenplay, co-written by Koch, Weir and David Williamson, was nominated for an Academy Award, while the novel won the *Age* Book of the Year in 1978, and the National Book Council Award for Australian Literature in 1979. Other books include: *The Doubleman*, which won the Miles Franklin Award in 1985, *Highways to a War*, awarded the Miles Franklin in 1996, and *Out of Ireland*, winner of the Victorian Premier's Literary Award in 2000.

In 1995 Koch was made an Officer of the Order of Australia – one of the nation's highest honours – for his contribution to Australian literature.

ALSO BY CHRISTOPHER KOCH

The Boys in the Island
Across the Sea Wall
The Year of Living Dangerously
The Doubleman
Crossing the Gap: a Novelist's Essays
Highways to a War
Out of Ireland

CHRISTOPHER KOCH

THE MANY-COLOURED LAND

A RETURN TO IRELAND

PICADOR

First published 2002 in Picador by Pan Macmillan Australia Pty Limited
St Martins Tower, 31 Market Street, Sydney

This edition published 2003 by Picador
an imprint of Pan Macmillan Ltd
Pan Macmillan, 20 New Wharf Road, London N1 9RR
Basingstoke and Oxford
Associated companies throughout the world
www.panmacmillan.com

ISBN 0 330 48727 2

1 3 5 7 9 8 6 4 2

A CIP catalogue record for this book is available from
the British Library.

Printed and bound in Great Britain by
Mackays of Chatham plc, Chatham, Kent

In memory of my cousin Wendy Knoller (née Hurburgh),
brave spirit,
who discovered the stories of our Irish great-great-grandmothers,
but did not live to see them told.

The black potatoes scattered our neighbours,
Sent them to the poorhouse and across the sea;
They are stretched in hundreds in the mountain graveyard,
May the heavenly host take up their plea.

O God of Glory, save and answer us,
Loose our bonds and right our case,
Give us life from out your heart again
And level the poorhouse in every place.

MICHAEL COADY, *Na Prátaí Dubha* (from the song of the
Great Famine attributed to Máire Ní Dhroma of Ring, Co
Waterford, c. 1850)

After this Earth there is the world of the Shí. Beyond it again lies the Many-
Coloured Land. Next comes the Land of Wonder, and after that the Land of
Promise awaits us. You will cross clay to get into the Shí; you will cross
water to attain the Many-Coloured Land; fire must be passed ere the Land
of Wonder is attained, but we do not know what will be crossed for the
fourth world.

JAMES STEPHENS, *Irish Fairy Tales*

Contents

ONE

The Pass-holder

I

I HAD TWO Irish great-great-grandmothers who settled in Tasmania: then the British penal colony of Van Diemen's Land. This was in the 1840s, at the time of the Great Famine.

One of the two was Jane Devereux, a gentlewoman from Green Hills in County Cork, who paid her own passage to the colony, in 1840. She was from an Anglo-Norman family whose ancestry in Ireland went back to the Norman invasion of the twelfth century. Sir Philip Devereux had served in Strongbow's expedition of 1169, and the Devereuxs were rewarded with much land in Wexford. Later, they would acquire more land in County Clare.

But Jane's branch of the family, like so many Anglo-Irish families, had lost its substance – in their case, an estate called 'Deerpark', near Sixmilebridge, in Clare. Jane was single. Her parents were dead, two of her brothers had emigrated to America, and her sister Eliza had come to Van Diemen's Land six years earlier. Now, at twenty-nine, Jane was following Eliza, probably seeking a husband, and no doubt looking for protection from more fortunate relatives in the colony: her cousins Robert and William Carte. Robert was a lieutenant in the 63rd Regiment here, while William was Principal Superintendent of Convicts at the Port Arthur penal station. It's a familiar Ascendancy story: the estates lost; the descendants of once powerful landowners scattered; impoverished gentlewomen forced to seek husbands and shelter where they could.

Eliza Devereux had come out on the *Strathfieldsay*. This was one of the vessels known as 'girl ships'. They carried young women described as 'respectable female immigrants' to a colony with an acute shortage of females, the women being seen as potential wives for free settlers. But not all of them turned out to be as respectable as expected. The Governor of Van Diemen's Land, Colonel George Arthur, divided them into three groups: 'the very respectable, quite respectable, and abandoned'. When the *Strathfieldsay* docked, it was besieged by a crowd of some two thousand men. The *Colonial Times* recorded that 'disgusting scenes ensued', with vile language directed at the women. A Ladies' Committee, set up by the Governor and Mrs Arthur to look after the women, hurried them away to the shelter of the Orphan School – many of them weeping and in distress. Eliza Devereux was quickly taken care of, however, being employed as a housekeeper by Mrs Arthur at Government House.

By the time Jane arrived, Eliza was married to a property owner in the rural district of Sorell, near Hobart. Jane joined her there, and soon succeeded in finding a husband. She was married in the following year to my maternal great-great-grandfather, Captain James Hurburgh, in the Church of England at Sorell. Hurburgh was a native of Greenwich: a British merchant navy officer who had settled in Van Diemen's Land, commanding a number of vessels for the Colonial Government. For many years, he was pilot on the Derwent estuary, taking sailing ships arriving from overseas up to Hobart Town. Prior to this, he had commanded the Government schooner

Eliza, one of whose tasks was to pursue any convicts attempting to escape the island by boat.

My other maternal great-great-grandmother, a servant girl from Tipperary called Margaret O'Meara, arrived in 1845. She did not pay her passage to the colony. Convicted of larceny, she had been sentenced to transportation to Van Diemen's Land for seven years. I thus combine in my ancestry the two opposite ends of the Irish spectrum: the Protestant Ascendancy and the Catholic peasantry. I might also be said to descend from the gaolers and the gaoled.

All through my childhood, and for long afterwards, Margaret O'Meara was successfully hidden. My mother led us to believe that her family tree contained no convicts – those ancestors whom Tasmanians most dreaded to discover. I asked her several times if she could be sure of this; after all, convict ancestors were to be found in a great many families that had settled here before 1850. Her eyes would widen, her lips would purse, and she would deny it with the same indignation she would have shown had I suggested she was a criminal herself. *No!* Her family was entirely respectable.

She probably believed it. That she knew of her great-grand-mother's origins I'm inclined to doubt; but if she did, she took her secret knowledge to the grave, like so many others in her generation. She was always happy, however, to talk about her other great-grand-mother, Jane Devereux – whom she referred to as 'Grandma Hurburgh'. She spoke of 'Deerpark', the estate that the Devereux family had lost, and of Jane's two brothers, Robert and Ringrose, who had gone to America, never to be heard of again. Their portraits, which Jane had brought out with her, sat on our mantelpiece in oval brass frames; and my mother presented me with a history of the Devereux family going back to the Conquest. This had been compiled and printed privately by her late great-uncle, the Reverend Walter

Hurburgh – son of Captain James Hurburgh and Jane Devereux.

Great-Uncle Walter, a Church of England clergyman, had been Rector of the rural district of D'Entrecasteaux Channel. The Channel was where the sailing ships passed between Bruny Island and the mainland, on their way up the Derwent to Hobart – often in the care of Walter's father, the old pilot. Walter was said to have been the first white child born on Bruny Island. When my mother was a girl, she told me, Great-Uncle Walter would gaze fixedly at her across the dinner table and say: 'You have the peculiar nose of the Devereuxs.' He remained a bachelor, and his two chief interests were flower painting, and the production of a set of genealogies. These were devoted to families in Tasmania, including his own, who were descendants of nobility and gentry. In a stirring passage at the end of his monograph on the house of Devereux, Walter speaks of the spirit of *Noblesse Oblige* continuing to survive in the colonies, and of those families scattered about the Empire who by birthright still represented 'the *Ancienne Noblesse*', and the age of chivalry.

'The *Ancienne Noblesse*' had clearly been a grand obsession with the Reverend Walter Hurburgh, bordering on a mystical passion. His photograph shows him posed in his priestly cassock, Bible in hand. His bearded face might well be Don Quixote's: innocent, solemn, with bereft, pale eyes that gaze into an irrecoverable past; into vanished and mythical splendour. His father James was a simple merchant seaman whose own father, Joseph, had been a private in the Royal Marines: an illiterate Prussian emigrant to England originally called Haarburg. Joseph, serving on the *Fox* in the Napoleonic wars, had been wounded in the arm, entitling him to send his two sons to Greenwich Naval College as charity boys, to be trained as officers. Nothing aristocratic about the Hurburghs; but Walter's mother's family was another matter. Around the Devereuxs were woven all his dreams of ancient nobility. It mattered so much, in his day, this music that's no longer heard.

The title page of the Devereux monograph carries the sub-title:

Some County Families, or Men of Coat Armour of the United Kingdom, Represented in Tasmania. By a Representative of One of the Families. And it bears the epigraph: *Unless the Lord keep the city, in vain watch they who guard it.* It tells how both the English and Irish branches of the Devereux family were descended from Robert D'Evreux – an earl who was a cousin of William the Conqueror. Robert had fought at Hastings, and his name derived from his place of origin: Evreux, in Normandy. The English branch included among its luminaries Walter Devereux, first Earl of Essex, who carried out appalling massacres in Ulster in the sixteenth century on behalf of Queen Elizabeth, and his son Robert, the second Earl, who was Elizabeth's favourite before she had him beheaded for treason. But Great-Uncle Walter's obsession does not stop with the family tree. At the end he deals with 'Deerpark', whose loss he clearly mourned – as his mother had no doubt done.

Did she speak of it often in his youth, sowing the seeds of his monomania? Very likely, since she may well have known the great house as a small child, and would have grieved over its loss. And almost certainly, she would have spoken of the dubious and tragic circumstances which surrounded the selling up of the house and the estates. The culprit in this affair, according to Walter's account, was Jane's aunt, Averina Massy Devereux. Averina's husband Robert, Jane's uncle, was a Dublin barrister. As eldest son, Robert had been the heir to 'Deerpark'. He had married his cousin, Averina Massy, and had died childless. Jane's father Ringrose – Robert's younger brother – then became the heir; but Aunt Averina induced him to sell the estates to pay off debts, and to distribute most of what was left among his six sisters as dowries. Why Ringrose Devereux did this was surrounded by mystery, and by ancient family bitterness. And Walter informs his readers that the family disputed the legality of what had been done, 'though not in a court of law.'

Ringrose was a wine merchant, whose business was in the city of Limerick; his family was a large one, and he died when Jane was thirteen. Her mother died when she was twenty-one. A long letter has survived, dated July 27th 1835, which was written to Jane Devereux when she was twenty-five, before she left Ireland. It comes from Aunt Averina in Dublin, and parts of it are both cryptic and self-justifying:

Well, my dear Jane, you at last took it into your head to allow me the pleasure of hearing from you . . . A traitor to my deepest enemy I thank God I have never been, nor my enemy would I willingly deceive. Somehow my character seems with you all to be overshadowed by doubts, mistrust, and unbelief, but in God's good time he will show you all . . .

From this out I shall receive the rents myself . . . I hope I shall pay you better than I have paid you heretofore.

But for all Aunt Averina's promises, there was presumably very little income available to Jane when she embarked for distant Van Diemen's Land, as a spinster of twenty-nine.

II

Tasmanians can generally learn much more about their ancestors in the colony if those ancestors were convicts than is possible if they came out free. The only published details to be found about Jane Devereux are her name on the passenger lists of the ships that brought her to Melbourne and Hobart, and a mention of her arrival in a Van Diemen's Land newspaper. ('A Miss Devereux arrived at Hobart Town from Port Phillip on the *Jean*.') But the records of the Convict Department in Van Diemen's Land were very complete, and remain pretty much intact; and Margaret O'Meara steps out of them with some vividness.

Many years after my mother's death, the truth about her convict great-grandmother has emerged, as a result of a search in the Tasmanian Archives.

A good deal more has turned up, as well. The maternal side of my mother's family tree, far from being respectable – as her paternal Hurburgh side had been – has proved in the end to have more than one convict lurking in its branches. That my mother did not live to be confronted with this is probably just as well, since she could not have faced it without deep distress. Today, a felon in one's past has become almost a matter of pride, in Australia. Not so in my mother's day – or in my childhood. Convict ancestors were either hidden, or given false occupations and backgrounds. Anything to hide what was then called the Stain.

Little is recorded about Margaret O'Meara's background in Ireland. But there is a good deal on her convict record concerning her activities in the colony, since she kept on getting into trouble. She was clearly a rebellious, passionate and perhaps flighty woman, whose morals, in that century, would have been described as 'loose'.

She is sometimes listed as 'O'Meara' and at others merely as 'Meara' – since the British officials were casual about the 'O' in Irish names. A newspaper report of her conviction – in the *Tipperary Free Press* for 12th April, 1845 – shows her simply as 'Mara': a frequently used variant of the name. She is five feet four and a half inches tall in some convict records, and four feet eleven and a half in others. She had dark brown hair and eyebrows, blue eyes, a fresh complexion, a short nose, a 'full' forehead, and what the records call a 'medium' mouth and chin. Her occupation is given as 'country servant', or housemaid. She was single, a Roman Catholic, and could neither read nor write. Her place of birth is given as Limerick; but she was living in Tipperary at the time of her conviction – probably in the town of Clonmel, since this was where she was tried, and where she committed her crime. She was twenty years old.

The *Tipperary Free Press* reports in some detail the cases dealt with at the Clonmel Quarter Sessions on that Friday in April. Michael

Costello was convicted of stealing potatoes, and was sentenced to two months' gaol; Thomas Power was sentenced to a year's imprisonment for stealing a cloak; and Margaret Mara was convicted of stealing clothes from Mrs Forristal, of Stephen Street. Since Margaret was a servant, it seems likely that Mrs Forristal was her employer – although this remains uncertain. Her convict record shows that she had a prior conviction for drunkenness, and had been previously charged with stealing clothes, but had been acquitted. On this occasion she was convicted. This being her third offence, she was sentenced to transportation for seven years.

The only relatives shown on Margaret's convict record are her father, Matthew, and a sister, both still living in Limerick – probably in the parish of Doon, just across the Tipperary border. Local records show that in the mid-1820s, when Margaret was an infant, Matthew Meara rented a plot of land in Doon from Lord Clonmel – but he is no longer shown as doing so in 1845. Perhaps he had been evicted. Margaret's birth certificate shows that her mother's name was Nancy Moloney, but no marriage certificate for Matthew Meara and Nancy Moloney can be found. Nothing is said about her mother on her convict record. Probably Nancy was now dead.

Margaret committed her theft in the first year of the Famine. I would like to believe that she was driven to it by the Famine itself; but this is unlikely. Early in that year, the Famine had not yet taken hold; the first signs of the potato blight had appeared, but only in a sporadic way, while crops remained good in other areas. The horrors of mass starvation were yet to come. But even before the Famine spread, the poverty of many rural people was extreme; and this may well have been the case with Matthew Meara and his family. Overpopulation, and the division of farms into smaller and smaller plots, spelled ruin for the people eventually, even without the Famine. Without a patch of land on which to grow potatoes, they starved; and those who were ejected from their land faced a virtual death sentence. There were women, as

8

well as men, particularly in the countryside, who committed crimes such as arson in order to be transported – since conditions in an English penal colony were so much better than those they were enduring. Some even asked to be transported.

Irish women convicts were regarded by contemporary commentators as less vicious than those from the stews of London and elsewhere in England. They were mostly young, illiterate country girls, driven to their offences by want, whose conduct in the penal colony proved better than that of the English or Scottish women. John West, the nineteenth century clergyman who is the author of the best history of Tasmania written in that period, had this to say about Irish female convicts:

In many instances the Irish courts must have been influenced rather by a vague notion of humanity than of punishing offenders. Such are often young creatures: not a few could scarcely be considered depraved.

Larceny, Margaret O'Meara's crime, was not an offence generally committed by country servants – yet Margaret is shown on her record as a country servant. Petty theft – usually of clothing or household linen – was mostly a town crime. Even so, a number of country servants in Tipperary in this period did steal both food and clothing out of want, and were transported. Which was Margaret O'Meara? A country girl driven to stealing through want? A dishonest servant in the town of Clonmel? Or simply an unemployed town thief? I will never know. It is not even clear whether she lived in the town of Clonmel or in the country.

She embarked for Van Diemen's Land on the female convict transport *Tasmania* – the new name that the notorious penal island would soon adopt officially – together with one hundred and forty other Irish women, one of whom was put ashore before the ship sailed 'on the score of insanity', and another of whom died on the voyage. The women also brought with them thirty-seven children. They were travelling in style, by the standards of the day: the *Tasmania* was a new, fast, Sunderland-built barque of 500 tons, and conditions for the prisoners were much improved on those of the older vessels in the service. The ship sailed on September 2nd, 1845 from Kingstown Harbour (now Dun Laoghaire), the port in the south-eastern tip of Dublin Bay.

The period yields up many accounts of the departures of these transports, as well as of conditions on the voyages. In 1842, three years before Margaret O'Meara's departure, Thackeray had described a boat race at fashionable Kingstown Harbour, and a transport lying there:

> . . . the beach and piers swarming with spectators, the bay full of small yachts and innumerable row-boats, and in the midst of the assemblage a convict ship, lying ready for sail, with a black mass of poor wretches on her deck, who too were eager for pleasure. Who is not, in this country?

The year before that, the *Limerick Reporter* had described the departure of the *Mexborough*, a female convict ship also bound for Van Diemen's Land. The women were visited by an Irish Catholic priest, the Reverend Bernard Kirby, who was the chaplain who had attended them at the female penitentiary. He regularly saw convicts off in this way, both men and women, and regarded them as his brothers and sisters; it seems likely he would eventually have addressed the women on the *Tasmania* as well. It was he who had to explain to such women that few of them would ever return to Ireland, even when their sentences were served, since few would ever earn the money to pay for so long a voyage. They must resign themselves to marrying in Australia, and staying there. The women are described by the newspaper's reporter as crowding about Father Kirby as though about a parent, weeping bitterly. Speaking from the poop deck, he told them that this was the last time he would address them as an Irish priest, and did his best to comfort them. He assured them of their salvation, and told them that their crimes were no worse than that of the good thief on the cross at Calvary. Finally, he distributed gifts of rosary beads and medals, amidst their tears and prayers.

When the *Tasmania* sailed, the hatches would have been battened down on the women's quarters. But they would no doubt have crowded to the scuttle holes along the side for their last sight of Ireland: the great sweep of Dublin Bay, and the pier-wall and villas and spires and smart terrace houses of prosperous Kingstown. Did Margaret O'Meara weep? Surely she would have done, as the others did. An illiterate girl from rural Ireland, probably Gaelic-speaking, with a shaky grasp of English, with no conception of the vast global distances she would now cross – or of the nature of the grim British penal colony that lay waiting for her in the remote southern hemisphere, in the latitude of the Roaring Forties she was being torn from her family and her country and everything she knew, to enter a blank hole in the wall of the world. I see her there, in her brown prison serge, her face probably resembling my grandmother's: wiping away her tears, wide-set blue eyes staring with a fixed expression from under her high-arched, strongly-marked eyebrows, her small, pugnacious jaw set at an angle – ready to defy whoever might assail her.

What my great-great-grandmother's personal experience of life on the *Tasmania* may have been is closed to me, since she doesn't begin to make her entrances into official records before her arrival in Van Diemen's Land. But a good deal of general detail concerning the voyage is to be found in the official report of the surgeon-superintendent in charge, Dr Jason Lardner. A strict daily routine was enforced, he says, and this was conducive to the health of the women, which improved greatly on the voyage. Most of them gained in weight. The sole woman who died did so from dysentery; she had been 'desponding', seldom spoke to anyone, had been weak when she came aboard, and refused food.

The *Tasmania* took just over three months to reach Van Diemen's Land: a reasonably fast trip, in those days. There have been many reports of the conditions on female convict transports, and there is no reason to suppose that those on the *Tasmania* would have varied from the norm. Margaret O'Meara would have been issued with a brown serge jacket and petticoat, a couple of linen shifts, a linen cap, a neckerchief, stockings and a pair of shoes. She would probably have found the food more varied and wholesome than any she had eaten in her life: beef or pork daily; gruel with sugar or butter in it; biscuit; red wine and lime juice to combat scurvy. Dr Lardner's report also says that fresh potatoes were brought on board, and were issued daily instead of flour, to enable these Irish women to become used to a gradual change in their diet. In addition, the women in each mess were issued with tea, sugar and a kettle. When damp and cold caused illness, extra clothing was issued, and stoves lighted below.

The situation on female transports was in many ways scarcely rigorous. In fact, it was well-nigh permissive – even though this had never been the intention of the penal authorities. Fraternization with the crew, including sexual relationships, went on all the time, in the face of every effort to prevent it. Perhaps this was inevitable, when one considers the implications of placing hundreds of young women on ships whose men were separated for months from wives, sweethearts, and the consolations of dockside whores. Of all this, there is no hint in Dr Lardner's report – but such discretion, apparently, was standard practice among ship's officers, surgeons and crew: there seems to have been an agreement between all concerned to say nothing of the sexual relationships with the women.

It was notorious that female convicts gave more trouble aboard ships than male convicts, and were much more difficult to control; and only on this matter does Dr Lardner's report, which otherwise is blandly positive, give a hint of dissatisfaction:

> The behaviour of the Convicts was on the whole very good, they were very ignorant and made but slight improvement in their education during the Voyage, none were found capable of teaching, and but few inclined to learn – their principal offences were against discipline.

The punishments for women were naturally not as heavy as those for male convicts, and there was a reluctance to use violence – although very occasionally they were caned, or put into a special confinement box for a couple of hours. Such punishments had little effect, and complaints over the years dwell on the 'insolence' of the women, and their uncontrollable, even 'demonic' behaviour: their quarrelling, shameless language, and thieving; and above all, on their trysts with the sailors. There are stories of gifts of rings and money; of a convict woman pimping for the crew, and arranging meetings with young women in the water closets; of the first mate merrily pulling the bedclothes off the women in the mornings; of hatch doors left unlocked so that women could spend the night in the cabins of the officers. On some voyages, in fact, convict women were in a relationship with the surgeon-superintendent himself, and even with the captain: a fact which says more about the delinquency of those gentlemen than that of the women in their care. Many of the women had defacto 'marriages' with crew members; some arrived in Australia pregnant. Others actually married their partners after arrival. It all sounds – though it can't really have been so – like a somewhat rougher version of the situation on board the old, cut-price passenger liners on which young Australians of my generation went to visit Britain, in the years before cheap air travel pushed these ships into history.

The higher authorities had tried, since the earliest female convict ships went out, to prevent the licentious doings on board; and many a committee looked into the matter. But to no avail; in the 1840s, there seems to have been little if any improvement. Following advice from Elizabeth Fry, a matron had now been appointed to sail on the female transports, to assist the surgeon-superintendent in charge of convicts; but one matron was apparently powerless to deal with the situation. In 1849, four years after the *Tasmania* made its run with Margaret O'Meara, the Reverend R.W. Gibbs travelled as pastor on a similar transport: the *Cadet*. After this experience, the Reverend recommended that two assistant matrons be appointed as well, in order for there to be any hope of preventing the women from engaging in sexual relationships with the sailors – as well as with each other.

The past is a mysterious place, and full of paradoxes. The images on the screen flicker; cancel each other out; seem to contradict each other. Not all the convict women participated in the sexual carnival that some of these glimpses conjure up; and not all arrived at their destination in a happy condition. Many grew ill, from dysentery and bronchitis and other ailments; and it is not hard to imagine the effects of the long voyage, with its often terrifying seas, and of the misery that life must have presented on board to those women who were sensitive or weak: the overcrowded messes; the persecution by female bullies; the endless squabbling; the theft by fellow-prisoners of their few precious possessions.

Colonel George Arthur was one of Van Diemen's Land's sternest governors; yet we owe to him this compassionate glimpse of female prisoners arriving in 1837, given to a Select Committee on transportation:

I am sure it would excite the sympathy of any person to see them on their arrival. I have gone aboard the transports to see the women; the state of depression and agony they are in is scarcely to be described.

Not all the women on these transports were troublesome; some were rated 'quiet'. But it seems unlikely, from her escapades on Van Diemen's Land, that Margaret O'Meara was one of these.

When the *Tasmania* arrived at Hobart Town, the island's capital, my great-great-grandmother took her place under a regime of convict discipline known as the Probation System – administered from on high by the Comptroller of Convicts.

Peculiar to Van Diemen's Land, it had been introduced six years earlier, in 1839. It was high-minded: an experiment aimed at the reform of the transported convicts. And this was desirable, since more than half the penal island's population consisted of felons. The system was much criticised at the time, and has generally had a bad press: like so many penal systems, it often proved less happy in practice than in theory. But in quite a few cases – perhaps willy-nilly – it did produce the results it aimed at. Many convicts, coming out of lives of want and vice in their native lands, managed in the end to emerge into freedom, making use of the rare opportunities to acquire a home and land of their own that the new country presented. A good number of them reared law-abiding families in conditions of security and plenty they could never have known in Britain or Ireland; and a number grew wealthy, and founded some of the colony's leading businesses. Their highly respectable descendants would carefully hide or disguise their origins.

The Probation System was one of planned rewards, taking the prisoner through various levels of a sort of Purgatory, where the punishment grew less painful at each successive stage – bringing the convict eventually to the Paradise of a pardon, and freedom. The magic certificate which testified to this was the ticket-of-leave. Any ill behaviour, however, meant slipping back a level – or beginning all over again. There were three levels.

First, a convict must serve time in a probation gang. This was the hardest, especially for male convicts. The men were sent to one of the probation stations scattered about the island, or else to the penitentiary in Hobart Town, to spend their days cutting timber, or breaking stones on the roads – often under sadistic overseers, who were much given to flogging. The females arriving in the capital in 1845 did their period of gang probation on the prison hulk *Anson*, moored in the Derwent River to the north of the town.

In the next stage, with good behaviour, the prisoner would be given a probation pass. Such a pass-holder, who initially went to a hiring depot, was free to take service for wages, in a private household. Pass-holders had a sort of relative freedom, in their spare time: they could even slip into one of the city's many taverns (though this was officially frowned on), provided they were back before curfew. But even at this stage, there were various levels: the convict became a pass-holder of the first, second or third class, with varying degrees of privilege at each stage. Beyond this lay the ticket-of-leave.

Very soon after the *Tasmania* docked at the New Wharf in Hobart Town, the officials of the Convict Department, accompanied by constables, would have come on board, with their documents and registers and red tape. The women would then have been mustered on deck, to answer the roll and to be processed: their physical descriptions taken, their personal details noted. It was then that Margaret O'Meara's record – a copy of which lies in front of me – would have been entered into the Convict Department's all-embracing registers.

It was the 3rd of December: summer, here in the Antipodes. The *Tasmania* had been piloted for some thirteen miles up the estuary of the River Derwent – probably by Captain James Hurburgh, who had been appointed pilot the year before, and who would have boarded at the head of the D'Entrecasteaux Channel. Coming up this calm, extensive estuary, with its wooded hills and many little bays – a panorama which the free settlers regarded as one of the Empire's finest – the women must surely have felt relief, after the huge, icy rollers and fearsome gales of the Southern Ocean. Now, as they gathered on deck, they found themselves in a setting of unusual beauty: but a beauty which had a certain Gothic sombreness.

They had entered one of the world's best harbours, running deep all the way to the wharves and quays of Hobart Town: then a city with a population of some 23,000. The port was crowded with ships – many of them whalers. They flew flags from all over the earth, since at this time Hobart rivalled New Bedford as one of the world's great whaling ports. On Battery Point, above the New Wharf and its long stone warehouses and ordnance buildings, a red flag fluttered, to announce the arrival of a prison ship. Directly behind the city in the west rose dark blue Mount Wellington, with its fluted volcanic peak. It loomed like a rampart, seeming to brood, and gave the little city a forbidding air. Beyond it lay untouched wilderness: range after range of bush-covered hills and mountains.

Soon after being processed, those women who were sick were sent to the Government Hospital. Margaret O'Meara was not among them; her name does not appear on the surgeon's sick list for the voyage. She and her companions would have been escorted onto a small steamer, to be taken north up the Derwent to the *Anson*, which was moored on the river's western shore.

The hulk lay in Prince of Wales Bay, near a place called Risdon, on the northern outskirts of the city. There were a few small farms here, and a solid, stone-built hostelry called the Derwent Inn. A ferry, rowed by a set of oarsmen, took travellers across the big river to the distant eastern shore. Over there, another mountain rose, more modest and less oppressive than Mount Wellington: double-humped Mount Direction.

The *Anson* had once been a 74-gun ship of the line: now, having acted as a transport, she was reduced to this. The hulk had been established with worthy aims, as part of the grand, well-meaning plan that lay behind the Probation System. The British Government's penal regime on Van Diemen's Land is constantly vilified in Australia today – often by people who know it only through the distorting glass of folk mythology. And certainly there is much to vilify where the punishments meted out to male convicts are concerned – particularly in the harsh period of early settlement, before the 1840s. But the system was constantly changing, and the British zeal for reform, by the time of Margaret O'Meara's arrival, had done much to reduce the old horrors. Looking at the reports and the regulations that were drawn up in this period, one is struck by the fact that many of the authors of the system genuinely wished to reform the convicts, and to deal with them justly – even humanely, by the standards of the time. But between the conception (which often took place in London), and the execution, many of these perfect plans were undone by muddle, neglect, and the human factor. The case of the *Anson* is typical.

Previously, newly arrived women convicts had served their six months of gang probation in one of the female penitentiaries known as 'female factories'. These were principally used as places of punishment for women who committed new offences in the colony, and the reformers now wished to keep the new prisoners separate from these old offenders, many of whom – a tough crew known as 'the Flash Mob' – had a corrupting and brutalising influence. A special prison for gang probation was planned; meanwhile, the *Anson* was established as a stopgap, and was placed under the control of a surgeon-superintendent and matron: a married couple called Bowden, who were highly-qualified professionals and genuine reformers, believing in modern methods of prison discipline. Six female nurses and a schoolmistress formed part of their staff. But the special prison was never built, and the *Anson* experiment was seen in the end as a failure – largely because of the restricted space, and lack of sufficient employment for the women.

Even so, a journalist from the *Hobart Town Courier* who was shown over the hulk wrote glowingly of its cleanliness, and of the general health of the women. And a glimpse of the ideas that motivated the authors of the Probation System can be gained from looking at the regulations concerning the management of the female convicts, drawn up in the year of Margaret O'Meara's arrival. One example:

> *Reproachful or harsh language can never be attended with advantage, and must be carefully avoided. Kind treatment and mild language are perfectly compatible with strict and systematic discipline.*

For Margaret O'Meara and her fellow-prisoners, once they were taken aboard the *Anson*, Van Diemen's Land remained a mystery. They had simply been removed from one ship to another: the only difference being that this ship didn't move. They had glimpsed the city and its port and its mountain; now, from the decks of the hulk, all that they could see close at hand were the traffic on the road on the western shore, with its few houses and stone inn, and the passing and re-passing ferry and other river craft. To the east, across the broad reaches of the Derwent, wilderness began: enigmatic, round-bosomed Mount Direction, and the island's endless, olive-green hills and valleys, with their strange, ragged gum trees.

So they conjured up fears concerning the life that lay in wait for them when they were sent out as servants. After all, terrible tales were told about Van Diemen's Land, and songs were sung about its cruelties. John West, who also visited the *Anson*, spoke to Mrs Bowden about their mental state:

This lady . . . found the women generally submissive and docile: they were haunted with all kinds of terrors, and had less than the ordinary courage of women. Mere children in understanding; some, such only in years; but their actual reformation . . . remained an object of confident expectation, while their true tendencies were repressed.

Two years later, in 1847, a young gentlewoman called Caroline Leakey came to Van Diemen's Land for the sake of her health, and spent five years there, living with her married sister. When she went back to London, she published a novel set in the colony entitled *The Broad Arrow*, taking the pen-name Oliné Keese. It is the story of a female convict; and its style and plot are those of the typical Victorian melodrama. But the portrait it paints of Hobart Town society, from the dining rooms of the gentry to the kitchens, slums and prisons which were the natural habitation of the convicts, has a documentary accuracy, drawn from personal experience. Miss Leakey visited HMS *Anson*; and she details the fears of the female prisoners with a novelist's insight:

Strange and vague are the mental picturings of the prisoned female form of the land of her exile, which she knows lies little further than a stone's throw from her. Some think, on leaving the Anson, they are to be turned adrift to all the horrors of an unexplored region; others that they will be driven to market for sale. The cunning and malicious amongst them delight in filling the minds of their less gifted associates with the most terrible apprehensions of the barbarities awaiting them on their departure from probation. It is with a thrill of cruel suspense that such prisoners first place their foot on Tasmanian ground.

Whatever her fears or sorrows at this point, Margaret O'Meara would have found the conditions on the *Anson* a great improvement on those of the *Tasmania*. The food was of a standard that neither she nor any of her companions could ever have experienced in Ireland. It included fresh meat and vegetables served daily, bread, and oatmeal; and meals were served three times a day now. She would probably have been put into a ward on the orlop deck, the lowest in the ship, where she would have slept in a hammock; the bedding was aired on the deck each day, and the ward cleaned. The day's routine included schooling, prayers, and exercise on deck. The labour consisted of spinning, carding, knitting, dying and shoemaking.

The glimpse of the *Anson* given in Caroline Leakey's novel, taken direct from the life, reveals that although 'harsh language' may have been avoided, there was a good deal of schoolteacherly nagging by the female warders, perhaps for the benefit of visitors:

'Mary Gull, tie your cap. What, Mary Pike, yours off! The next offence, you'll go downstairs.' Mary understood the allusion, and hastily put on her cap.

'Sarah Gubb, you are talking there. Jane Dawson, where's your curtsey? Why don't you rise, Ellen Brackett? Muggins, I shall complain of you.'

From Caroline Leakey's account, my great-great-grandmother would now have been clad in a brown serge skirt, a jacket of brown and yellow gingham, a dark blue cotton kerchief, a white calico cap, knitted blue stockings, and a masculine pair of half boots that Miss Leakey calls 'clownish'. I see her in this outfit, standing on deck in some moment of respite, perhaps in the late afternoon: a small, brown-haired figure in her white cap and clumsy boots, staring at the far silver reaches of the river, and at the looming double hump of Mount Direction, smoke-blue in the east: that same eastern mountain at which I gazed all through my childhood, from a point just a mile or so from here. I see her there, this bereft Irish peasant girl from Tipperary, as she tries to guess what threats the sullen, olive-green landscape might be hiding, and what pleasures might be found under the roofs of the scatter of

English buildings beside the river: buildings that are both familiar and queer. No doubt she also tries to decide whether the fearsome stories that some of the women have told her are true: whether she will be bought and sold like a slave; whether she will be raped by brutal convict constables; whether she will get into trouble, and be put in a prison worse than this – or whether she may somehow get free and find friends here, and even a man to love her.

I see her there. It isn't so very long ago.

There is nothing on her record to show that Margaret O'Meara committed any offence against discipline on the *Anson*. Perhaps she found some sort of contentment there – or at least, security. But once she had completed her six months of gang probation, her life was destined to be stormy: and the storms would continue remorselessly.

She had now become a probation pass-holder of the third class, eligible to be hired as a servant in a private household. Most of the women from the *Anson* would have been taken by prison van to the Brickfields hiring depot in Hobart Town, to be billeted there until local householders selected them as servants. However, some were hired directly from the *Anson* by settlers from elsewhere on the island, as well as from Hobart Town, and Margaret O'Meara was one of these. Her record shows that on the 16th of June, 1846, she was hired by people called Mills, from the city of Launceston – a married couple, presumably, since the regulations prohibited a bachelor from hiring a female convict.

Van Diemen's Land had two small cities: Hobart Town in the south, and Launceston in the north. Hobart, the larger of the two, was the administrative centre and seat of government. Launceston, with its port on the River Tamar, was essentially a commercial town: an outlet for much of the island's pastoral wealth, and a supplier of goods and services to the whaling and trading ships, with an establishment of prosperous merchants, bankers and ship-owners. At this time, it already had all the features of a town in the other hemisphere: counting houses, ship's chandlers, mills, breweries, libraries, an excellent local newspaper, churches, charming villas for the well-to-do, temperance societies, comfortable inns, warrens of squalid little houses for the less prosperous, exceptionally sordid taverns for the poor, and rookeries that harboured the local criminal class. It had a poor Irish section in South Launceston, where many of the worst of the taverns were located.

No doubt when she was allowed time off by her mistress (a freedom which was limited by the eight o'clock evening curfew), Margaret O'Meara discovered these taverns, and fell in with other pass-holders – her fellow-countrymen in particular. As the charge of drunkenness in Tipperary shows, she was a young woman who was fond of a jar or two. But for a time, she did not get into trouble. For a year and three months after her entry into the Mills household, the record of convictions is silent: this bald, harsh document which gives me the only clues I have to the rest of my great-great-grandmother's short life. Then, on September 20th, 1847, she is charged before a magistrate with being 'absent without leave'.

She had absconded from the Mills household for an unstated period. Whether she was found and arrested, or whether she voluntarily gave herself up, is not recorded. But what seems likely – from the various other records through which her progress can be traced – is that she had been with a man. He was a man very much older than herself: an English ex-convict called Joseph Smith. And what the authorities probably did not know at this stage was that Margaret O'Meara was three months pregnant.

Joseph Smith had been transported on the *Isabella* from London in 1833, at the age of forty-seven. Born in 1786, he was now sixty-one years old. He came from the market town of Trowbridge in Wiltshire, and was a widower; he had left four children in England, now grown up. Sentenced to fourteen years for receiving a case of stolen glass, he had served his term and been granted his certificate of freedom the year before meeting Margaret O'Meara. He was five feet seven inches tall; no other physical description appears on his record. He was illiterate. His conduct sheet as a convict is rich with the usual lapses, such as being in a public house after hours, and making a false statement; but he clearly behaved well on the whole, since at one stage he was made an overseer, and at another, a 'Javelin Man'. A Javelin Man had the responsibility of guarding prisoners being taken to court for trial, and an interesting entry appears on Smith's record at this point: 'Allowed Thomas Davis, a prisoner under Sentence of Port Arthur, to escape when on duty.' For this, Smith was stripped of his position as a Javelin Man. Now that he was free, he was working as a labourer.

The official response to Margaret's escapade was swift and to the point. Tersely, the record states: '14 days solitary' – and she was sent to the Launceston Female Factory to serve her sentence. This institution, otherwise known as 'the house of correction', served both as a prison and a hiring depot, and from here Margaret would eventually be sent to new masters. The Factory stood in Paterson Street, on the northern edge of the town, close by the Tamar and its port. The bottom end of Paterson Street must have had a chilling appearance, in those days: next to the Factory was the city gaol, and beyond that, the treadmill. All are vanished now, their memories purged and obliterated by a high school and a car park.

In the Factory, there were a good many women of a different kind from those whom Margaret O'Meara had encountered on the *Anson*: hardened old lags who had been in the system for many years, revolving on its wheel. Cheerfully unrepentant, they went from one household to another, always committing new offences (disobedience, drunkenness, insolence, theft, conceiving illegitimate children), and always returning to the Factory. Margaret would presumably have had little contact with them on this occasion, since she must serve out her fortnight in one of the solitary cells.

Punishment through isolation was commonly used in the factories: in normal cells for less serious cases, like Margaret O'Meara's, and in dark cells for the most intransigent women. This sounds forbidding; but nothing was quite how it was intended to be, in penal Van Diemen's Land. There are interesting glimpses of cracks in the system – even for those women doing solitary. This was because of the large amount of illegal trafficking that went on in the factories, through illicit links to the world outside. Food, letters, clothing, tobacco and many other goods were smuggled in through prisoner turnkeys, whom the women bribed with such currencies as tea and tobacco. Some women boasted that they could get these goods – and rum and brandy as well – not only in the solitary cells but even in the dark cells. In some cases, the turnkeys even let them leave their solitary cells to go visiting one another. Not surprisingly, the women considered the colonial female factories much more lenient than the English gaols; and some servants committed offences to get back in, since they preferred the life there.

Whatever my great-great-grandmother's experiences in that fortnight, she was soon available to be hired again, and went to the household of a Launceston family called Innes. She did not last long there. On the 29th of November, she was convicted of the theft of unspecified goods – presumably from her masters – of a value below five pounds. For this, her sentence was extended by another twelve months, and she was sentenced to another six months in the Launceston Factory.

On her return, Margaret O'Meara would have been placed in the crime-class category – as distinct from those women who were merely waiting to be hired. Clad in a white mobcap and a dress of coarse grey duffle, she would have been put to work at the washtubs. The women did laundry for the townsfolk of Launceston, up to their elbows in suds; being 'sent to the suds' was a common term for being sent to the

Factory for punishment. She might also have been given needlework to do – from which she could earn money, if she had the skill – or carding and combing wool. How onerous was her situation? Again, the images from the past flicker uncertainly, and its distant voices argue with one another. But a general answer would seem to be that, although some women did better than others there, life in the Launceston Factory was usually not too harsh, and even had its enjoyments. In fact, the tougher women laughed at being sent there as punishment. One of them is reported as jeering at the magistrate who gave her four months, saying: 'I'll soon bowl that out!'

Easy or not, it was a life which clearly had its compensations for many of the women – and perhaps for Margaret O'Meara. She would now have been initiated into the Factory's underground culture, and would have found herself exchanging stories with women in the same plight as herself, and with a similar past. The work was carried out communally, and there was a rough vitality, humour and mutual sympathy here which no doubt lightened her days. There were also fights; but the details on her record in the years to come show her to be a woman of spirit, and I suspect that she would have dealt with bullies in a typical Irish manner.

Many contemporary reports tell us in outraged tones of the coarseness and rebelliousness of the women: of their singing songs of their own composition that mocked the authorities; of their telling lewd jokes and stories; of their drinking and smuggling; and of the fact that they were very often idle in the exercise yards, and carried out a sort of play-acting together, dressing themselves up. In the Launceston Factory, it was said, telling stories and dancing took up a good deal of the women's time; and evidence was given to an 1843 committee of enquiry that at the Cascades Factory in Hobart, a group of women had been spied through a window dancing naked together, 'singing and shouting and making use of most disgusting language', and imitating men and women in sexual intercourse. A few years earlier, the *Colonial*

Times of Hobart Town had published a piece about the Cascades Factory, complaining that 'the wash tub affords an opportunity for the merry laugh, the song and the joke, and this punishment is laughed at, absolutely laughed at'. It also went on to complain about that alarming group of women known as 'the Flash Mob'. The management of these women, the paper said, 'produces more trouble to the prison disciplinarians than that of any other class'; and their tricks and manoeuvres and misconduct, it went on, 'have baffled the exertions of every person appointed to control and correct them'.

There was certainly a Flash Mob in the Launceston Factory. Only a few years before Margaret O'Meara's arrival, they had organized a riot there of such ferocity that it took fifty male convicts, sworn in as special constables, to subdue it. Margaret would now have had dealings with the Flash Mob, and is likely to have been approached sexually by some of them – since a good many were lesbians. In fact, there was an entire lesbian culture in the factories, in which women took regular lovers, sometimes attempted to rape those who were unwilling, and carried out jealous feuds. How extensive it was will never be established; but certainly it preoccupied and horrified the authorities, so that the reports made to their official enquiries carry constant references to 'unnatural practices', and to 'extraordinary and unnatural links between the women.' This in an era when Queen Victoria, told what lesbianism was, flatly refused to believe that such a phenomenon existed.

I am now in the area of conjecture, but I doubt that Margaret O'Meara would have taken a female lover. Men were her downfall; she loved them too well, as her subsequent history will show. It seems likely that she would have carried on communication from the Factory with Joseph Smith, since she was carrying a child that was ultimately presumed to be his, and since letters to lovers outside were easily delivered though the smuggling system. True, she was illiterate; but one of her literate fellows would have drafted a letter for her.

Perhaps she was happy for a time, growing heavy with her child, and anticipating a reunion with Joseph. The baby was born on March 1st, 1848, and her conduct sheet now states: 'delivered of an illegitimate child named John'. No birth or baptismal certificates survive. She would have nursed him herself, joining the many other single mothers in the Factory's communal nursery.

Three months later, the newspapers published a statement that the Convict Department had given its consent for a number of convicts to marry, including 'Margaret Meara, in the House of Correction, Launceston, and Joseph Smith, free, residing in Launceston'. They were married in June, at Trinity Church; Smith was a Protestant, and this was an Anglican church. She was twenty-four; he gave his age as forty-six. He was lying: he was now sixty-two. Had he lied to Margaret as well? Whatever the case, he must have been a vigorous man.

Soon after this, the newly wed Margaret Smith was discharged from the Factory. Surprisingly, she was also granted her ticket-of-leave, not having served her full sentence. The likely explanation for this is that she gained her freedom on the condition that she would live with her husband in Launceston – and that Joseph guaranteed that she would be of good behaviour. In the following November, 1849, she bore him another son – named Joseph after his father. She must have insisted that the child be given her faith: he was baptised a Catholic, in St Joseph's Church.

There is now a silence of a little over eighteen months. Then, in the middle of June, 1851, my great-great-grandmother breaks out again.

Her Convict Department conduct sheet, resuming its remorseless record, makes a terse announcement. She has been charged with 'absconding and being in open adultery with John Nadin'. For this, her ticket-of-leave is revoked, and she is sentenced to eighteen months at hard labour.

There is no way to discover what the circumstances of her desertion were. Her motives, too, can only be guessed at. But the bare facts are clear. At the age of twenty-six, Margaret had deserted her two young children and her sixty-five-year-old husband – a man old enough to be her grandfather – for a man close to her own age: a thirty-year-old English convict from Huddersfield. John Nadin had been given his certificate of freedom the previous year. His convict record shows him to be a Protestant, and able to read and write. A professional burglar, he had been transported for ten years for housebreaking, using a pick-lock. Once made a convict, he was smart and self-controlled enough to keep out of trouble; except for some lapses into 'insolence', his conduct is described as 'very good' and 'orderly', so that no extra time was added to his sentence. His description makes it seem likely that he was physi-cally quite attractive: dark brown hair, dark brows, light hazel eyes, an oval face, clean-shaven, with a medium nose, mouth and chin. He was of average height for that period: five feet six inches tall.

That Margaret fell in love with him I have little doubt. She had left her home, her husband and her infant sons for a man who could offer her neither wealth nor even increased security: his occupation is given as 'labourer'. And in deserting Joseph Smith she had thrown away her ticket-of-leave and called down official wrath on her head. What did she and Nadin hope for, when they set up house together? A miracu-lous exemption from penalties? Or did they hope for nothing, the world well lost for love? Whatever the case, the hand of officialdom soon reached out, flinging Margaret into the Ross Female Factory in the Midlands. And when she arrived there, history had repeated itself: she was pregnant again – this time, presumably, to John Nadin.

The Midlands village of Ross, on the highway that links Hobart and Launceston, stands on the 42nd parallel of latitude. In 1851 it was an important garrison town and stock market. Today, mercifully preserved from modern debasement, it remains one of the prettiest colonial villages surviving in Australia. Its grey Georgian buildings are constructed from the fine local freestone, and a graceful, convict-built bridge of the same stone crosses the Macquarie River. Ross is at the heart of Tasmania's richest pastoral country. The local graziers produce the finest Merino wool in the world, getting record prices year after year; and in the nineteenth century, their ancestors there were just as prosperous. With plenty of cheap convict labour, they were able to create a near-perfect replica of England. Outside the town, though, the round, lonely, tawny-grassed hills, dotted with dark clumps of eucalypt and she-oak, could never have been English: they have a faintly forbidding air, as though leading to some country of dubious dream.

Stand in the main street of Ross, and you are standing in much the same town as Margaret O'Meara was brought to. Side by side with the tearooms, gift shops for tourists, and today's little stores and garage, are the old barracks building she knew, and the Man O' Ross Hotel, and the Ordnance Office. But the Female Factory is gone – or almost gone. All that remains, in a paddock beyond a rise on the south-eastern corner of the town, are some grassy mounds and stone footings. Why? How to explain this? There are prosaic explanations, such as the structures being allowed to fall into disrepair. But this won't do: these were very solid buildings. No: they were deliberately destroyed, as the chief penal station of Port Arthur was destroyed.

Two years after Margaret arrived here, in 1853, Van Diemen's Land's free settlers would at last get their way with London, and the transportation of convicts from Britain would end for ever. Under its new name, Tasmania would cease to be a penal colony; and the evidence of the hated convict past was not wanted, in the virtuous new Tasmania. So the penal buildings were deliberately torn down, and the materials used by building contractors for other constructions. This was what was done at Port Arthur, which now stands in ruins; and it was done at the Ross Female Factory.

Wandering there recently, among those quiet mounds, I thought of my reckless and foolish little great-great-grandmother. The voices of a group of nearby tourists faded and grew unreal; and a loneliness and sorrow that were not entirely my own enclosed me like a wave. The dead are not really close, as we sometimes like to imagine; it is their pain and annihilation that hang so near in the air.

The complex at Ross that Margaret O'Meara was brought to had only been in operation for three years. It was smart, and very well-planned. On the left as you entered were the crime-class wards, to which Margaret would have been sent. The pass-holders' wards were on the right, and the solitary confinement cells were set below the chapel. In the middle of the Factory were the nurseries for the newborn babies of the inmates – soon to be joined by Margaret's latest child.

In that same year, the Factory was inspected by a Lieutenant-Colonel G.C. Mundy – who wrote a detailed account of his experience. He described the cleanliness as 'dazzling', and the discipline as 'fault-less'. He also noted that during the inspection the place was dead silent: the women made not a sound. The matron of the Factory was in charge of forty-nine women and almost as many babies, Mundy says. 'Never was I in so numerous a nursery'. He calls it 'a rather pretty sight for a father' – the infants sleeping two or three to a crib, 'stowed away head and tail like sardines in oil'. But most of the women, he remarks, 'were not even tolerably nice-looking'.

The Colonel also reported an encounter that obviously shook him. He came by accident on one of the punishment cells:

I found it to be completely darkened. It seemed empty, so I passed within the door to examine its construction and almost started back when from the extreme end I found a pair of bright, flashing eyes fixed on mine. The owner arose and took a step or two forward. It was quite a young girl, small and slight – very beautiful in feature and complex-ion – but it was the fierce beauty of a wild cat. At no period of my life would I for a trifle have shared for half an hour the cell of that sleek

*little savage . . . As the door slammed in her face and the strong bolts
slid into their grooves, the turnkey informed me that this was one of the
most refractory and unmanageable characters in the prison . . . Justice
would have to be doubly blindfolded when dealing with her.*

Despite its well-conducted appearance, all was not as well at the
Ross Female Factory as Colonel Mundy thought. Mr and Mrs Imrie,
the Assistant Superintendent and Matron, were eventually accused of
misconduct, and dismissed. Smuggling went on here, as it did at the
Launceston Factory; and there were accusations of connivance between
staff and convicts, and of unauthorised male visitors who may well
have been responsible for a good many of the pregnancies. The historian Kay Daniels, in her book *Convict Women*, gives a detailed and
innovative account of the female 'houses of correction' in Van Diemen's
Land – and her research uncovers the fact that there was an extremely
active Flash Mob at the Ross Factory. It also reveals that the problem of
'unnatural practices' among the women was, if anything, even more
worrying to the authorities at Ross than at Launceston.

A good deal of this concern is revealed in a detailed letter, written by
Dr N.J. Irvine, the Superintendent of the Factory, to a visiting magistrate. This was just a year before Margaret O'Meara's arrival. Dr Irvine,
a member of the Royal College of Surgeons in Edinburgh, subjected
the women under his care to scientific scrutiny; and he seems to have
become both scandalized and fascinated by the lesbian culture among
them. In some ways, Kay Daniels comments, he anticipates such later
sexual theorists as Havelock Ellis. He divided the lesbian women in the
Factory into two groups. The first group could not be distinguished
from other women except by the fact that they had a far greater liking
for a woman taking the male part 'than for the veritable male himself'.
The second class he called the 'pseudo-male', or 'man-woman'. These
had, he observed, 'a masculine appearance', with 'a lower voice, and the
development of a pair of imperfect moustaches'. He also believed that
these women had 'a preternatural development of the clitoris', which

enabled them to assume the male function in intercourse. These pseudo-males, he went on, were showered with presents by their lovers, and were the subjects of jealous feuds. The young and comparatively innocent class of female convicts, Irvine said, appeared to be those on whom the attention of the pseudo-male was fixed – and were, 'to use the words of one informant, by these means, ruined'.

The women at Ross – as at the colony's other two factories – were very difficult to control: so difficult that nine-foot fences had been erected to separate the different classes. Serious riots took place there. In one of the worst, a constable taking a woman to the solitary cells had been attacked by most of the crime-class women in a body; order could only be restored by using batons. The ringleaders were not dealt with, for fear that the inmates would get entirely out of control. Such ring-leaders – the 'flash characters' who dominated the Flash Mob – were those most respected by large numbers of the women prisoners. It seems likely that my great-great-grandmother had come to respect them too. More: that she had now joined them. I draw this conclusion because her conduct record at the Ross factory – which extends over the next year – becomes filled with charges of insolence and insubordina-tion. She is clearly in rebellion against the authorities, and perhaps against her fate.

On the 16th of September, 1851, she is charged with 'causing a disturbance in the yard': a charge which very likely means that she was one of a group of women who were rioting. For this, she is given seven days in the isolation cells. On January 2nd, 1852, she is charged with 'neglect of duty' – for which she is given two months' hard labour. Then, on January 16th, she is delivered of a son. John Nadin's child was named James Meara, and the birth certificate describes his mother as 'Margaret Meara, single.' Following the birth, however, her rebellious conduct does not stop. On March 10th, she is charged with 'neglecting a child committed to her care' and given six months' hard labour. Whether it was her own child, or that of another prisoner, is not stated.

On March 13th, when her baby is two months old, she is charged with insubordination, and given thirty days in the cells. Then, four days afterwards, on March 17th, the conduct sheet announces that her baby is dead. The death certificate, recording James as a 'convict's child', gives the cause as 'convulsions.' It happened, presumably, when Margaret was not with him, being locked in her isolation cell.

After this, except for a charge of 'insolence' in June, the conduct record becomes silent. It ends with a single terse statement, a little over a year later: 'Certificate of Freedom, 25th May, 1853'. At the same time, Margaret O'Meara is listed in a Convict Department notice in the press, stating that 'the under-mentioned persons' have served their periods of transportation, and are granted their certificates.

She was free; and what she did now was surprising. She went back to Joseph Smith, now sixty-seven years of age, and resumed her marriage.

What had happened? Did she believe when she was consigned to the Factory that John Nadin would wait for her? Did he promise to do so, and then disappear? Or did the loss of his child shatter her spirit, making her long for those sons she already had? Certainly she had reason for grief and anxiety about the eldest, John: two months after she ran off with John Nadin, Joseph had consigned their eldest boy to the Queen's Orphan Asylum in Hobart. John was now returned to them in Launceston; but just at this time, the younger son Joseph died of croup.

From this point onwards, Margaret's life seems to have taken an even course. My great-great-grandfather must have been a man of some forbearance; and certainly the aged Joseph continued to be vigorous, since Margaret bore him two daughters in the years that followed. The youngest, Julia, was my great-grandmother, born in 1856. She and her sister Elizabeth were baptised Catholics.

But the years of stability were brief; the girls would not have their mother for long. In 1859, when Julia was three years old, Margaret died. The cause is given as 'inflammation of the lungs'. She was thirty-four.

Old Joseph survived her by only a few months. He died in the following year; and the two little girls became orphans.

III

There are two different profiles that can be drawn of Margaret O'Meara – this reckless Irish convict girl from Tipperary who is my ancestor, and who will not stop haunting my mind.

The first is the obvious one. She created her own misfortunes. She was a confirmed thief, a reckless drinker, and a promiscuous, turbulent young woman who got into trouble with men as soon as she had the opportunity to do so. Having been given her probation pass, and an opportunity to make good as a domestic servant in a private household, she ran away into the stews and taverns of Launceston. She got herself pregnant there. Then, having married the father of her child, and having been given her ticket-of-leave, she soon deserted him for a younger man, leaving both her children behind. And finally, her record in the Factory shows her to be wild and rebellious.

The second profile is more blurred; but it's one that I see as more likely to be true. Or at least, it raises questions that enable me to feel a tentative compassion.

This profile does not present Margaret O'Meara simply as a virtuous martyr to the system. I'm not a believer in the simple myth of the innocent convict – that victim of nineteenth century hardship who merely stole a loaf of bread to ward off starvation. That is a self-justifying myth which was begun by the old ticket-of-leave men and women themselves – either by reciting it to their children, or through telling their sanitized stories to the newspapers of the day – and it has been thoroughly embedded in the Australian consciousness. Those with convict ancestry have a deep and understandable desire for it to be true; but the documentary sources show overwhelmingly that most convicts – or certainly most English convicts, like my great-great-grandfather Joseph Smith, who was clearly a professional receiver – were criminals who had run up a long list of offences before being transported; that a convict was hardly ever transported for a first offence; and that they often found a life in Australia that proved to be their salvation.

The Irish convicts were sometimes another matter – particularly during the Famine. True, there were habitual thieves from both the towns and the countryside among them, whose cases are the same as those of their English counterparts; but some appear to have been peasants in genuine and desperate need, forced off their land to starve when the potato crop failed and ruthless landlords evicted them. They also included violent political rebels such as the Ribbonmen, who burned farms and stock as a protest against such landlords, and the British rule they hated. So judging these ancestors – if judgement is your pleasure – is a complex and difficult exercise. And once one begins to dig down into the life that spawned the convicts, and to pore over the musty, tall, doom-laden pages of the Convict Department registers, and the contemporary Committees of Enquiry, the picture often becomes more grim than one imagined, but sometimes more light-hearted, more poignant, and more touching. The judgement you then pass on one or more of these shabby and stoical figures from the past – whose sour odours you would probably recoil from, and whose cheerful endurance of endless physical discomfort, fatigue and pain would very likely awe you – will vary according to your personal values and prejudices.

The case of Margaret O'Meara, if one tries to be dispassionate, presents most of these features and difficulties. I do not see her purely as a victim. That she was a thief can't be denied. She stole clothes. Why? If she was a town thief, she had almost certainly given herself to a life of petty crime. The question is, however, where, and under what circumstances did she steal? Since her record shows her to be a country servant, it's more likely that she was working in one of the 'Big Houses' of the gentry, in the country – in which case, she either stole from her employers, or from someone nearby. What is also possible, however, is that she was unemployed, and had fallen into bad company – as the charge of drunkenness makes likely. This at a time of deep poverty for the Irish people generally, with the Famine closing in. It may well have been the case that her father, Matthew O'Meara, had been forced off the usual tiny plot of land, and that he and his two daughters had lost their home and were living from hand to mouth – like so many others. I can never know.

All I can know about Margaret's background is that she was a girl who had lost her mother – either through death, or because her parents had separated. And at twenty, when she boarded the *Tasmania*, she lost her father and her sister for ever. A peasant girl, probably with little of the cunning or street knowledge displayed by the London thieves and prostitutes among whom she would eventually find herself – ignorant, in fact, of anything but the small world of her people in County Tipperary – she landed in unknown Van Diemen's Land; and horror stories of what she could expect were maliciously whispered in her ear on the *Anson*. She was utterly alone, bewildered by the ill-famed penal colony in which she found herself, and probably very frightened of what lay in store. Then she was summoned to the Mills household at the other end of the island, rather like a slave being casually bought and paid for in Virginia.

Here is where many possibilities open up.

For convict servants who were probation pass-holders, the nature of the future depended entirely on the nature of their employers. A kindly and just employer meant a life of reasonable security and peace. A bad employer was another matter – especially for the female convicts. The proportion of females to males in Van Diemen's Land was very low indeed, which made the situation of a young female prisoner doubly difficult. Many of the military and public officials, who would eventually go home to England, took temporary convict mistresses; and in the household she was taken to, a young convict woman would often find herself subject to sexual demands by her master, while the mistress turned a blind eye. Should she refuse, she would be charged with insubordination, and sent back to the female factory.

The era when Margaret O'Meara arrived in the colony was an era of reform in Britain, and in its colonies as well – and some years before, the Molesworth Parliamentary Committee had been set up to investigate the convict system. It had reported, among other things, on the situation of convict women in Van Diemen's Land; and the report is extremely damning. While claiming that most convict women were 'excessively ferocious' and 'profligate', the Molesworth Report flatly declared that even had any of them wished to be 'well-conducted', the scarcity of women in the colony meant that they were 'exposed to irresistible temptations':

> For instance, in a private family . . . a convict woman, frequently the only one in service, perhaps in the neighbourhood, is surrounded by a number of depraved characters, to whom she becomes an object of constant pursuit and solicitation; she is generally obliged to select one of them as a paramour, to defend her from the importunities of the rest; she seldom remains long in the same place; she either commits some offence, for which she is returned to the Government; or she becomes pregnant, in which case she is sent to the factory.

And the passage concludes by saying that many respectable settlers refused to accept female convicts – with the result that they went to 'the lowest description of settlers, by whom, it is notorious, they are not uncommonly employed as public prostitutes'. Here, then, is a glimpse of the reality that lay behind the worthy intentions of the system. It would almost certainly have been the reality that closed around Margaret O'Meara when she went to the Mills household in Launceston.

On the basis of that glimpse, together with the few bare facts at my disposal, I believe I can make some educated guesses concerning what really happened to my great-great-grandmother. Guesses are all that they are, of course, and all that they ever can be: but doesn't that often take place in the writing of more important histories?

To begin with, I believe that when she first became pregnant, the child was not Joseph Smith's. I think it highly likely that she was already pregnant when she ran away from the Mills household – and in fact, that this was *why* she ran away. What probably drove her to flight was that she had been sexually coerced or even raped by Mr Mills – or else had been pressured into sexual relations with one of the 'depraved characters' the Molesworth Report speaks of: in other words, one of those male convict servants who preyed on young female pass-holders. Where was she to turn? Nowhere in that household, presumably: there was no protector. Pregnant – itself an offence under the system – she ran. Where she ran to, in the town of Launceston, or perhaps in the countryside beyond, and what she did in that period, can never be known. But at this time – before being caught, and sent to the Factory – she must have met Joseph Smith and grown close to him.

Why did she steal, in the second household she was taken to? Perhaps she was just light-fingered – but I think she may have wanted to be sent back to the Factory, where at least she would not be harassed by men, and where she could have her baby in peace. Her marriage, and her early ticket-of-leave, were matters that would have been arranged by Smith while she was still in the Factory, through a petition to the Comptroller of Convicts. And the price the old man was paying for his young bride was to take on responsibility for another man's child.

Why do I assume all this? Because when Margaret deserted Joseph Smith for John Nadin, Smith put the elder boy, John, into the Orphan Asylum, and not the younger boy, Joseph junior – who was certainly his own. The old man was to prove long-suffering, but I imagine his thinking was this: why should he keep another man's illegitimate child when its mother had deserted him? It seems proof of a generous heart that when Margaret returned to him, Smith brought John back to her from the orphanage.

Some young women, adrift in a dangerous world, seek a father figure as protector. What Margaret had found was a grandfather figure: a man who was almost forty years her senior. No doubt Smith lied to her about his age, as he did to the authorities; but she must have known he was quite an old man. What Margaret was primarily seeking, I believe, was not good times, but escape from the situation in which she found herself: as possible prey for the master of the house, and as a sort of unpaid prostitute for the male convict servants. Somewhere in the taverns or back streets of Launceston, she found her protector in Smith – who offered to marry her, knowing her to be pregnant. It's possibly a measure of her desperation that she accepted. Even though he was an old man, he was free, and could give her a home – if only she could gain her own freedom. And he was probably kindly and strong. So she struck a bargain with him. She may even have felt genuinely fond of him.

What sort of a man was Smith? An extremely tough one, to begin with.

At sixty-two, having been transported in his middle age, and having lost his original family in England for ever, this great-great-grandfather of mine had taken everything the convict system could throw at him, and had survived to earn his freedom. Having been a fence, he was probably reasonably shrewd. He'd been sensible enough to serve his fourteen years without getting into serious trouble, or being sent to Port Arthur. He was reprimanded for drunkenness occasionally; but drink didn't lead him to destruction. He was able to control other men, and was seen as trustworthy by the authorities: hence his being made a supervisor, and a Javelin Man. But his first loyalty was not to those authorities: he turned a blind eye to let a mate try and escape Port Arthur. I see him as kindly, charitable, cunning, and unbreakable.

Looking at his motives for marrying Margaret O'Meara, it's easy to be cynical. A man of sixty-two, clearly still virile, he was taking into his bed a young woman of twenty-four – and probably a pretty one, at that. A man of his age could put up with a good deal, in gaining such a prize. Nevertheless, his taking her back after she ran away with John Nadin is really rather extraordinary. This is the sort of action that may be seen either as fond foolishness, or else as real love. I have formed my own conclusion; readers will form theirs.

Why did Margaret run away from him? And more interestingly, why did she go back? Looking at the pattern of her short and driven life, I'm able to hazard some guesses.

Her record, which at first might make one see her as flighty and promiscuous, shows her to be less easy to label once the detail mounts up. She had come to Van Diemen's Land to find herself defenceless in the hands of private householders who were almost certainly prepared to see her sexually abused – and one of whom had very likely got her pregnant. She had lost her country; her family; her own father. She sought refuge with a hard and kindly old villain who would shelter her from men who were much worse – and through marriage, persuade the authorities to give her early release. And for a time, all was well: she bore the child, which he adopted, and then gave him a son of his own. But then, somewhere, somehow, she met John Nadin – a young, attractive man of her own age – and fell wildly in love: so much in love that she was prepared to give up everything for him: her safety with the ancient man she'd married; her children; even her new-won freedom.

With Irish impulsiveness, and without thought of the consequences, she ran away with Nadin – breaking the conditions of her ticket-of-leave, as well as deserting her marriage. It was the one attempt in her life – or at least, in her life in Van Diemen's Land – to find true love. And it all went wrong. Nadin deserted her, and she must now serve out her sentence in the Factory in payment for a romance that had dissolved like a dream. As well, she must soon endure the pain of losing the infant that was Nadin's legacy: an infant which died – possibly through another woman's neglect – at a time when she had been forcibly separated from it; consigned to an isolation cell as punishment for some expression of defiance. Is it any wonder she became even more insubordinate? She was finally expressing her anger at a system which had tormented and entrapped her at every turn – and there were others to join her in her rage. The factory at Ross may have been well run, and Colonel Mundy may have found the women 'quiet' when he went there; but dozens of women do not explode into the most savage violence, as these women did, unless they are driven by what they see as acts of persecution. How the Ross Factory was really run, and in what ways these women were goaded, we will never discover; but guesses aren't hard to make. Small, mean tyrannies; small humiliations: these are the things that often do more to create revolt than the larger injustices.

That Margaret O'Meara was not the loose-living woman she might at first appear to be is proved, I believe, by what she did next, in going back to Joseph Smith. This time, Joseph was not helping her to gain her freedom, or offering her protection. She had already been given her freedom; she had served her time. Had she been promiscuous and pleasure-loving, like so many ticket-holding female convicts, she had her opportunity to show it now. She could go where she pleased; do what she pleased. She was still young, and women were desperately sought after, in this predominantly male colony. She could have plunged now into the taverns of Launceston; picked up another man; looked for any kind of adventure. But she did not; she went back to old Joseph, and her two young sons – and presumably she humbled herself, and asked him to forgive her. When he did so, she stayed with him for the rest of her short life, and gave him two daughters. After she died, Joseph lived on for only a few months more, dying in 1860.

Perhaps theirs is the true love story, ill-matched though they were.

TWO

The Gully

I

EIGHTY-THREE YEARS after Margaret O'Meara's death, I sat in a country bus with her granddaughter: the grandmother I called Nana Hurburgh. It was near the end of January, 1942, and I was ten years old.

We were going from Hobart to Swansea, on Tasmania's east coast, where we'd spend our annual summer holiday. The engine of Connolly's blue and red bus whined and whined on the long, steep hills, its rhythmic, falsetto ululation promising us the place we both loved, eighty or so miles to the north, and filling me with joy. The driver changed gears, the hills overcome, and the bus coasted down towards the village of Buckland, running above gullies of tall, glinting gums, clouds of pale dust and blue exhaust smoke billowing out behind. Soon, the sea would appear, glittering and amazing between the heads of the trees.

For me, sitting beside my grandmother, this was a blissful platform in time. For Australia, in that year, it was the most perilous and fateful week in the nation's history.

A few days before, on January 23rd, much farther north of us than Swansea, a contingent of the Japanese invasion force that was sweeping through South East Asia had seized the key harbour of Rabaul, on the tropical island of New Britain. A garrison of Australian troops, out-numbered twenty to one, had fought them until all hope was lost, and had then retreated west through the jungle. The battle for Australia had begun.

Everyone on the bus seemed to know this, I remember. All of them were talking about the Japanese, and whether they would actually reach us; and the words *Rabaul* and *the Japs* sounded many times. That the Japanese intended to take Australia nobody doubted. I didn't understand all that was being said; but I was able, as children often are, to sniff out the feeling underneath the talk. The people on the bus were cheerful and jolly, as always; but when the talk dwelt on the topic of the Japanese their mood briefly altered. It was one of quiet and sober apprehension; and perhaps of something more. I had never encountered a mood like it; but whether it perturbed me or not I can't truthfully say; memory doesn't relay this back to me. I'm inclined to think not, on the whole. I had grown up in a world that was always entirely safe, and I doubt that the threat which hung over us all could even have been made real to me.

Tasmanian country buses in those days had yet to introduce the torment of piped music, and passengers carried on a running con-versation with each other. Those at the back whose remarks could not be heard properly had them relayed forward. The driver, in his grey dustcoat and peaked cap, offered contributions over his shoulder. We were like a large family setting out on an excursion; and the bus made many stops. When the fishing village of Triabunna was reached, there would be the ritual morning tea of scones and cakes in the old hotel, served by ladies well known to my grandmother. The bus also picked up and delivered mail for farms along the way: at their gates, a blue canvas sack hung on a pole, with letters to be posted; the driver would stop to remove it, and replace it with another containing fresh mail. When there was no new mail, he would whip the sack from the pole without stopping: a feat I greatly admired, and which made up part of the enchantment of the journey to Swansea, whose elements were the splendour of speed, the heady smell of exhaust, and the sharp tang of gum leaves from the roadside, coming through the open windows. These stops, and the fact that the East Coast highway was narrow and winding and unsealed, its macadamized surface throwing up pebbles and white dust, meant that our journey took at least four hours, and we would all get to know each other, without exchanging names. My grandmother had as much to say as anybody.

She was a cheerful, confident woman: pink-faced, white-haired, plump, and with a tendency to jowls. She was friendly with everyone, and sure of her opinions, which she delivered in a forthright manner, the handbag on her lap clutched like a defensive weapon. As always when she went abroad in summer, she was clad in a light linen overcoat and light gloves, a straw hat decorated with artificial flowers set squarely on her carefully waved hair. Many of her remarks were addressed to the driver, since we sat only two seats behind him.

'Don't you worry, driver,' she said. 'Those little Japs will never get here. Our boys will stop them in New Guinea – with a bit of help from the Yanks. My own son's on his way there: he's joined the AIF.' She was talking about my Uncle Gordon. 'He and his mates are in camp on the mainland,' she said, 'and it's no secret where they'll be sent next.'

There was general agreement. Our boys would stop them, people said. Then a wizened old man in a grey felt hat turned around and demanded of the bus in general: 'And what are the British doing to help us? That's what I'd like to know. They've got most of our soldiers in the Middle East. What use are they there, if the Japs come?'

'Churchill promised he'd help us,' a voice said.

'Churchill!' My grandmother snorted. 'Churchill will do nothing for us. The British want our men to fight their wars over there. John Curtin knows that.'

She was speaking of the Prime Minister she revered, and gazed challengingly about the bus, firm chin tilted upwards, pink jowl faintly trembling. There were murmurs of doubt, but louder murmurs of agreement.

'Remember Mr Curtin's New Year message,' she went on. 'He told us that we can only look to America to help us now. The British? The British would leave us to be overrun.' And she gave a definite nod, lips compressed in a way I knew well, settling the matter.

Her remarks were somewhat shocking, which is why I remember them. Normally, they might have aroused antagonism, since loyalty to Britain was as general in Australia then as belief in God. Children of the British Empire, most of us on that bus had been taught to believe in 'the ties of blood', and to trust and revere what was still called 'the mother country'. Churchill, too, was revered. So I remember this exchange because my grandmother's remarks, and those of the man in the felt hat, were not rejected, but agreed with – or else heard in acquiescent silence. The full implication of Curtin's New Year message – now seen as a turning point in Australian history – was naturally lost on me, at ten years old; but looking back, I find many meanings in that moment.

The Prime Minister's message, published around the world, had included the following passage: *Without any inhibitions of any kind, I make it quite clear that Australia looks to America, free of any pangs as to our traditional links or kinship with the United Kingdom. We know the problems the United Kingdom faces. But we know too that Australia can go, and Britain still hold on.* This had outraged Churchill, who called it 'insulting'. But what was giving deep concern to Curtin and his government, in those days before the shattering fall of Singapore, was the fact that as the invincible Japanese invasion force swept south – with Australia as its ultimate objective – the country was virtually undefended, its troops deployed elsewhere in defence of the Empire. What was needed was to bring back the 6th and 7th Divisions from the

Middle East to defend mainland Australia; but to this, Churchill would not agree. They were wanted elsewhere, he told Curtin: in India, Malaya and Burma. After the fall of Singapore, however, and after many angry exchanges with Churchill, Curtin finally insisted. The troops came back to defend their own country, in alliance with the Americans; and it was the American victory in the Coral Sea that would decisively end Japan's hopes of conquering the southern continent. But Japan was also held at bay by a thin line of Australian troops (Captain Gordon Hurburgh among them), slogging through the New Guinea jungle, plagued with yaws and malaria. Before the Americans were fully engaged, these men confronted a numerically superior and better-equipped force, sometimes in hand-to-hand combat. Their fate could well have been that of the Spartans at Thermopylae; but in the end they prevailed, and nothing would be quite the same, afterwards. The tie with Britain was irrevocably weakened.

This gave sadness to Anglo-Saxon Australians; but for many Irish Australians – particularly those in the Australian Labor Party, which they dominated – it confirmed a long-held view of perfidious Albion. My grandmother, whose brother was a Labor politician, was such an Irish Australian; and when she spoke on the bus of her hero John Curtin, she was speaking of another Irish Australian, engaged in a struggle with the English: those faceless overlords who still seemed to rule us from London.

How much of this did I realise at the time? Nothing, really: politics are both mysterious and boring, to a child. I only knew that Nana Hurburgh sometimes spoke scornfully of the English. My father, who disapproved of her views, said that this was because she was Irish. I didn't know why she held this antagonism, which only came out at odd times; she was generally lively, humorous and sympathetic, and seldom spoke badly of anyone. Now I see that hatred of the English had come to her from a very close source: she was, after all, Margaret O'Meara's granddaughter.

She never spoke of her grandparents, that I remember. Did she know? Did she know that her own grandmother – dead before she was born – had been a convict? She must have done: her mother must have told her. But she took her secret to the grave, only four years later; and all the questions I would like to ask her now can never be answered.

For every child – or perhaps I should say for every fortunate child – there is one place on his or her inward map that is marked *Paradise*. For me, this place was Coswell, a farm on Tasmania's east coast, a few miles south of Swansea, on Great Oyster Bay. My grandmother had brought me there for our summer holiday every year since I was six years old. Sometimes my younger brother came too; but usually I went with her alone. I think she was as fond of it as I was; and my passion for Coswell, amounting to a religious fervour, must have pleased her. The farm was owned by an old lady called Mrs Parsons, and run by a middle-aged manager – a bachelor called Wally Donne. They kept a few sheep and cows and pigs, and large numbers of roaming hens, but they didn't seem to farm very intensively. Wally had a mail-run to a nearby tourist resort called Coles Bay, on the Freycinet Peninsula, driving there each day in his old blue Buick. Coswell took in a small number of paying guests in the summer, most of whom came from Hobart, as my grandmother and I did. They were all friends of Mrs Parsons; she didn't take in strangers. My grandmother had known her for many years; they were of much the same age, and were close friends. There was a Mr Parsons, but he no longer lived there; my grandmother told me that old Harry Parsons 'liked the bottle', and had turned into a swagman, roaming the bush. He visited once, when I was there: a tall, jolly, talkative old man in spectacles and a battered hat, a sugar bag slung on his back. Mrs Parsons seemed to receive him amiably enough, but soon he disappeared again.

The east coast of Tasmania has rather poor soil, and is the driest part of an island that is deluged in the west by the rain-bearing winds of the Roaring Forties. So the west coast, with its dripping rain-forests, remains almost unsettled, while the mild, open east is a region of villages and Holiday: the best place to go for warmth and ease in an island whose weather is as changeable as that of Ireland, turning cold in any season, and bringing snow to the high country even in mid-summer. The coast's long white beaches and moderate surf are ideal for swimming, and Coswell was set on gently-rising ground a few hundred yards from such a beach, looking out over white-gold paddocks and long, drystone walls to the blue expanse of Great Oyster Bay. The paddocks' open spaces were dotted with a few lone gum trees, and dark little Oyster Bay pines grew in the hollows. The beach was usually deserted, except for Coswell's few guests. A creek flowed into the sea there, with a rickety jetty and diving board; an old wooden dinghy lay near the marram grass on a dune, and had lain there for as long as I could remember. At each end of the beach were great, smooth rocks of pinkish granite; beyond them, to the north, more white beaches could be seen, with a few tiny dots that were people, and occasional beached dinghies. Set with tall towers of spume, these long, far beaches curved off into mauve and white distances whose features grew tiny and illusory, faint as a distant music: a region beyond Swansea and the common world; perhaps beyond the real world altogether.

The sun came and went, on Coswell's beach, and the light was constantly changing: the light of a region whose weather was never the same. It whirled and hugely swayed, like transparent cloths drawn across the air; it dimmed and then brilliantly glittered, while attendant, flaring seagulls mewed and wheeled and cried, and the bracing, ice-touched winds set up a tingling at the back of the nose. On the other side of the bay was the Freycinet Peninsula, from which rose three peaked mountains called the Hazards, composed of the same pinkish granite as the rocks on the beach. Seen from the verandah at Coswell, they were a deep blue, turning pinkish-violet at sunset, and appeared to me not like a place in Tasmania at all, but perhaps like those tropical islands far to Australia's north.

Coswell was a long, low farmhouse with a steeply pitched roof which was iron now, but must once have been shingled. From the front – whose verandah looked over Mrs Parsons' flower garden and a drystone wall and gate to the paddocks and the bay beyond – it appeared single-storeyed; but there were attic windows at the back for rooms under the roof. The tall, multi-paned windows on the verandah were in the Georgian style, like those of so many old buildings in Tasmania. Coswell had been built in the 1830s by a pair of Scottish brothers called Addison, who had come to the colony as builders, and grew wealthy. How it passed into the hands of Mrs Parsons and Wally Donne I have never learned.

It was a house that still lay locked in the nineteenth century. Its small, close rooms, with their dark wainscoting and low ceilings, smelled of that century: a smell that was a mysterious amalgam, composed (so far as I could tell), of dried flower scents, of the tang of old, stained woodwork, pickled in the sun, of ghostly odours of scones and bread that had been baked a hundred years ago, and of other, nameless things belonging to the past: some of them forbidding. I loved that smell; arriving from the bus through the door on the back verandah, while Wally set down our suitcases, I inhaled it with ecstasy. Coswell also smelled of kerosene, since it had no electricity: it still burned kerosene pressure lamps. At evening, Wally would line all the lamps along the rail of the back verandah, lighting them one by one, and then carrying them in to the various rooms, to be hung by special hooks from the ceiling. I would always come out to watch this ceremony, thrilling to the reek of kerosene, and the leap of shadows in the verandah, and the looming, slow-gathering country night, and the hidden hills of bush beyond the farm, where old Harry Parsons roamed. Wally would smile at me, his cheekbones orange with the lamplight. He was a tall, quiet, balding man with pale green eyes, invariably wearing leather gaiters, who resembled the cowboy film star Gary Cooper. He was always serene and kindly, and always good-humoured; yet I sensed a faint sadness about him, expressed by his long upper lip. There was a sixteenth-century clock on the wall in the sitting room that my grandmother said had come out to Tasmania with Wally's family. It was only many years later that I discovered that Wally – who pronounced his name 'Don' – was descended from the poet John Donne.

When the weather was fine, I would sleep in a stretcher bed on the front verandah: the place where the guests sat by day in battered easy chairs, looking out over the bay, and where small, white-haired, cheerful Mrs Parsons served morning tea, helped by a girl who worked in the kitchen, setting the tray on top of an old yellow chest of drawers. The tea was accompanied by hot scones, made in the black, wood-burning stove in the kitchen, and by jam and clotted cream from the dairy. There was also a peculiar snack contrived by Mrs Parsons: fingers of stale toast left over from breakfast, with butter and orange marmalade. These toast fingers had a great specialness for me, like the kerosene lanterns and everything else at Coswell: I saw them as a delicacy that could be found nowhere else. So to sleep alone on the verandah, that place of happiness, which smelled by day of hot tar paper, was a great delight; and when I woke at dawn, it was to see the sun come up over the Hazards, on the other side of the bay, turning their dark blue to violet, and laying a dazzling track towards me across the water. The birds at Coswell were exceedingly tame, being fed by hand; little blue wrens, with their long, flickering tails, would alight on my bed's tartan rug, hopping to within inches of my hand, looking for crumbs.

If the weather was cold and rainy, I slept with my grandmother in one of the bedrooms whose windows looked on to the verandah. At an earlier age, I had slept there every night. Nana Hurburgh had a big double bed in the middle of the room; I had a stretcher under the window. I was deeply fond of my grandmother; but I now preferred the verandah, much though I enjoyed her company. For one thing, this was still an era of china chamber pots under beds; in the middle of the night, in the dark, I would hear her passing water. As well as this, she snored very loudly. The snoring didn't keep me awake for very long, but the sound had a strangeness, a sort of mournful menace that made my grandmother cease to be Nana Hurburgh, and was quite divorced from her. When I was younger, it had a power to frighten me, and this was because I somehow associated it with the place called the Gully. The Gully was at the side of the house, and was not a place to linger in: it was one of the few parts of the farm I avoided: I wasn't sure why. Grown with eucalypts and bracken and grey-haired she-oaks, it was very deep and gloomy, and no-one ever went there; but there wasn't anything particularly alarming about it. Why it wakened fear in me, I wasn't sure; but the first time I came to Coswell, at six years old, the fear was quite strong.

The candle beside Nana's bed was blown out. Here in the dark, in the old, old bedroom with its pink, flowered wallpaper of a hundred years ago, my grandmother slept, lying in a black iron bed with gleaming brass knobs on its posts – propped against many pillows, her white hair and nightdress only just visible in the dark. But I was awake, listening to the sounds of country night. The chief of these sounds was the soft boom and sigh of the waves on the beach; I lay listening as they gathered themselves in, paused and then fell again, hollow on the sand. After a time, another sound began, which was very mysterious to me: a sound of voices, very far off, somewhere down near the sea. They had no words, they merely called: two long notes, high and low, repeated over and over: a sweet, musical plaint, filled with a tragic sorrow I could never understand, but in which I heard high, retreating vistas: far; very far. I thrilled to this sound, despite its solemn sadness; and at six years old, with that curious acceptance of the inscrutable that children have, I decided that it was made by a race of unknown people, who only come out at night. I imagined them as somewhat like fairies, and somehow magical – but of adult size, and clad entirely in white. It was only some years later that I discovered that the sound was made by fairy penguins, down on the rocks.

The bigger sound I listened to was my grandmother's snoring. Deep, ringing and hollow, tremendous in the dark, it seemed to carry me down into the Gully. This fancy was very strong, and persisted through the years. At ten, I was no longer really afraid of the Gully, but the snoring made me see it more vividly than I'd done when I was small; and what I was encountering was an ancient, worrying sadness. I understood now that what I was seeing was the Gully and the bush of a hundred years ago; all the country night of a hundred years ago, and the many sad things that had happened there, and the people who were lost. A child may sense such things, I believe, without having knowledge of the details; without even knowing what the details are. The child senses presences; and what I was hearing, in Nana Hurburgh's snoring, in that old bedroom at Coswell, were presences from the nineteenth century: that century in which Nana and Mrs Parsons had been girls, and in which they'd grown up. The white china jug and basin on the wash stand, where Nana and I washed our hands and faces before we slept, had been used by those presences: people without names, a hundred years ago. Outside in the night was old Van Diemen's Land; and lurking in the night of Van Diemen's Land were the lost Aboriginal people – doomed by the coming of the whites – who had hunted kangaroo in the bush here, and gathered shellfish down on the rocks. Outside too were the old, pass-holding convicts: some of them jaunty, others weighed down with sorrow. Outside were floggings, and bare-knuckle fights, and murder. Outside were the ancestors, their paper-pale faces peering, their clay lips moving with no sound. Their sadness was not far away. It resounded in Nana Hurburgh's snoring; it moved like a mist in the Gully.

Nana Hurburgh, whose first names were Mary Julia, was born in 1879, in a country district called Broadmarsh, in the south of the island – the daughter of Charles and Julia Culley. Julia, before she married, had been Julia Smith: one of the two daughters of Joseph Smith and Margaret O'Meara.

When Joseph died, in 1860, his two orphaned daughters were put into the Queen's Orphan Asylum at New Town, in Hobart, where their brother John had been. (He was now sixteen and 'in service'.) The application for their admission states: 'Parents both dead, left no provision for their children'. Julia, the younger, was only four years old. She emerged from the orphanage at fifteen, and was apprenticed as a servant. Like her mother, she absconded from her situation a number of times, but finally settled down and served out her time until she was eighteen. At twenty, she married James Culley, a shoemaker, who had also been in the Orphan Asylum. They lived in the Midlands village of Campbell Town, a few miles from Ross and its abandoned Female Factory. James Culley was a Protestant – but Julia did what her mother had done, and had Mary Julia and her brother Charles baptised as Catholics. Her husband died young, and she went with her children to live in a cottage in Launceston: strangely enough, in a little street called Middle Street, directly opposite the Factory where Margaret had served her sentences. Here my grandmother grew up, before marrying my grandfather Hurburgh and being carried off south to Hobart.

Grandfather Hurburgh was advertising manager of the Hobart *Mercury,* the island's biggest newspaper, and he and my grandmother were comfortably off. Theirs was a middle class life, and my mother's upbringing had been what used to be called 'sheltered'. But Nana remained incorrigibly working class Irish, in her speech and attitudes; she laughed at gentility, which I think she saw as English. When I remember her, she is nearly always laughing, her wide-set blue eyes narrowed and filled with light. Irish eyes. That her consciousness of being Irish was so strong can only have been because of the influence of her mother, Julia – her father having been an English Protestant. And Julia was surely a transmitter, passing on to her son and daughter the Irishness and suspicion of the English brought to the island by her mother, Margaret O'Meara. Perhaps, as she did so, she pointed out the frowning walls of the Factory that had held her mother captive, just across the road from Middle Street.

My grandmother's Catholicism, too, was Irish: that Catholicism inextricably entwined with Irish nationalism, embodied in the song 'Faith of our Fathers', which we fervently sang at school:

Faith of our fathers, holy faith,
We will be true to thee till death . . .

The women of her family seem to have made a practice of marrying Protestants, and Nana had done the same. But she had also followed their example – as the Church demanded – in bringing up her children, Gordon and Phyllis, as Catholics. Our mother had followed suit with my brother and me, making us Catholics too; but her success had not been complete. Our father gave in only reluctantly, remaining Anglican in his loyalties and convictions, and we were not at first sent to a Catholic school. He sent us to his old school, Clemes College – which was nominally Quaker, but which seemed very Anglican in its style, being staffed almost entirely by English teachers, loyal to the Empire and the Mother Country. This became the cause of a constant, mostly subterranean struggle between my father and Nana Hurburgh, who was determined that we should go to the Christian Brothers, as Uncle Gordon had done. In the end, when I was nine and my brother seven, my grandmother had won: we were sent to St Virgil's College.

At Coswell – and at home, when she came visiting – in the years before this victory, my grandmother added her own Catholic instruction to that of the nuns who taught my brother and me at Sunday school – always hearing our prayers at night, and giving us what were called 'holy medals', stamped with the Virgin and St Christopher, to wear around our necks. In the background, my father sniffed and muttered:

Catholic superstition, he said. My grandmother's faith, recalled now, gives off the ancient fragrance of a lost and supplanted culture: the Catholicism that has vanished since Vatican Two. It was the old Catholicism of Rosary beads, the Stations of the Cross, fish on Fridays, frequent Confession, profound, unquestioning awe of God and of the hierarchical Church, and of attendance at Mass every Sunday, 'on pain of mortal sin'. I can still smell its scent: the perfume that came from the pages of my grandmother's missal, which she always kept in her handbag, and which I inherited and took to Mass after she died. Described, this faith of hers will seem a caricature; a faith based on what today's crypto-rationalists would call superstition, as my father did – and peasant superstition at that. But I do not see it in this way, even now. My grandmother's belief was absolute, and her faith in Christ, the Blessed Virgin and the saints was unshakeable, filling her life with a quiet, unostentatious joy: a joy she had no compulsion to share with others – except, of course, with her grandchildren. And if what Catholics used to call 'a good death' is proof of the quality of faith, then hers stood the test; dying in hospital, she received us at her bedside with glad, faded smiles, certain of where she was going.

At Coswell, she heard my prayers as she did at home, making me kneel beside the stretcher bed while she sat next to me. When I had said the Our Father and enough Hail Marys, and had blessed everyone I knew, I would get into bed and she would tuck me in and kiss me, uttering a changeless litany of her own which seemed to cause her voice to take on stronger traces of the Irish accent that always hovered there – Margaret O'Meara's accent, passed on though Julia Culley. *'May the Guardian Angel watch over you while you sleep, my darlin', and protect you against the snares of the Devil.'* The Guardian Angel, she explained, stood behind my bed while I slept, and by day was generally floating behind my right shoulder; each of us had such an angel, vigilant against the Adversary who waited always to tempt and destroy us. I never doubted her, so strong was the force of her conviction. This was no game; no fancy employed to amuse or instruct a child: this was the belief that steered and governed her life. And however simple or hack-neyed the symbolism she used might be, my grandmother had a Celtic awareness of that other world which lies behind appearances, separated from us by a very thin film. She did not need to explain or justify this to me: the same sense had been there in me since infancy, humming in my unconscious. That not everybody had it was something I would take a while to learn.

II

The culture of the Christian Brothers of my boyhood is gone now, as are most of the Christian Brothers themselves – like the old Irish Catholic Church that produced them, and the Jansenism which lay at the heart of their beliefs. It was a culture that contained a good deal of fear.

When my grandmother finally had her way, and my brother and I entered St Virgil's College, high on a hill above South Hobart, we found ourselves in a place that in many ways resembled a concentration camp: a camp patrolled by the Brothers, in their sinister black soutanes and white, reversed collars. Their instrument of discipline was a black, snake-like strap, carried in an inner pocket of their soutanes, which they referred to as 'Doctor Black'. They wielded the Doctor for the most minor infringements, leaving our hands constantly bruised and swollen.

This took some getting used to, as did the fact that we had entered an enclosed world, on that hill: a world that was almost purely Irish. The Brothers were either Irish, or Irish-Australian. Nearly every boy in the school was Irish-Australian. When the roll was called, and we sat in our desks calling 'present', in our buttoned-up grey suits and St Virgil's neckties, the Irish names resounded – *Sullivan, Kennedy, Fahey,*

Paterson, Kinsella — until, like a jarring note, mine was called, to spoil the harmony. I was that most wretched of all creatures, in the era I'm summoning back: a half-and-half. Not only was I half Anglo-Celtic and half German (and this at a time when we were at war with Germany) — I was half Catholic and half Protestant. Clemes College — an outpost of all that was British and imperial — had my brother and me during our earliest and most formative years, and it had left its mark. Even our accents sounded English — a thing we now set about remedying, as a matter of survival — and we found ourselves in a milieu that was familiar yet foreign. Anglican hymns, such as 'Who would true valour see', and 'Hark! the herald angels sing', were replaced by *'Panis Angelicus'* and 'Faith of our Fathers'. Were these *my* fathers we were singing about? I wasn't really sure; I didn't seem to fit. I did not say 'haitch', as the Brothers and my classmates did; I said 'aitch'. And when the Brothers warned us that Protestants would be fortunate to get into Heaven, and that Protestant examiners would mark us down in our external exams if ever we had to write our names, not numbers, I felt uneasy. My father was a Protestant, after all. His paternal great-grandfather had been one of a group of Prussian Lutheran Dissenters who had migrated in a body to South Australia in the 1840s; and his mother's people were Anglicans.

The fact was that I felt almost as much a Protestant as I did a Catholic. And what had Irishness to do with me? I had been made aware of it only through Nana Hurburgh, and its outlines were vague. The only thing I really knew of that was Irish was a song called 'Danny Boy', which my grandmother loved. I had grown up revering England. England was the home of all that was decent, true and kindly. A.A. Milne, Beatrix Potter, Kenneth Grahame, Charles Kingsley and Rudyard Kipling had been read to my brother and me almost as soon as we could speak; the Sherlock Holmes stories and Richmal Crompton's *William* books and P.G. Wodehouses's Bertie Wooster stories were now my most cherished places of imaginative refuge; and the Royal Navy of Nelson's day, in which my Hurburgh ancestor had served, woke a special tingling in my blood: I read stories of naval warfare and pirates, and wanted to join the Navy. At Clemes, in the infant school, we had taken a deep interest in the British royal family and in 'the little princesses', Margaret and Elizabeth – cutting out their pictures and pasting them in our scrap albums, as our teachers told us to. Now, at St Virgil's, we must cut out and paste holy pictures from Catholic calendars. There were new icons here, it seemed, and a concentration on Christ and the Virgin Mary every day, instead of just on Sundays.

Not all of this was unappealing. St Virgil's was profoundly steeped in Catholic belief: the passionate, mystical belief of the old Church. There were Brothers who transmitted this; Brothers whose smiles were open, and used the strap less than others; Brothers who seemed to wish to dispense the Faith to us like a balm. More; they made us understand the most essential fact about divine mystery: that it can never be comprehended through the intellect. I would learn later that the world is divided between those who understand this truth and those who do not. St Virgil's, despite its cruelties, made me a Catholic. My spirit responded to the rhythms and panoply of the Faith: to the Angelus, when the bell tolled at noon, its sound going out above the town while we stood to intone the great liturgy to Mary; to Benediction in the Chapel, where the mysterious red sacristy lamp glowed in its niche, and a blue-eyed, Nordic Virgin Mary smiled down on us with a sweetly ineffectual compassion. In Scripture lessons, youthful and handsome Brother Keltie talked to us about Christ with an affectionate, matter-of-fact reverence that bore little resemblance to today's squalid efforts to make the Redeemer into a buddy, and which probably resembled the respect with which a rank-and-file member of Sinn Fein would have spoken of Michael Collins. Our Lord – as the Brothers usually spoke of him – was ours in a special way; Brother Keltie left us in no doubt of that. And no-one knew better than an Irishman how to explain his betrayal. His brogue deepening, Brother Keltie told us how Jesus had been denied 'even by poor old Peter', and how most human beings will betray what they love if only they are made fearful enough. We listened with a mournful comprehension; we now knew Peter intimately, and pitied him, and understood his fear.

St Virgil's, with its culture of violence, also taught me how to fight. At Clemes College I had been a timid boy who was bullied, and something of a cissy; but it simply wasn't possible to remain a cissy under the iron rule of the Brothers. Not only was fighting in the playground not forbidden; it was actively encouraged, especially in the Junior school. (The Seniors, who could do each other more damage, were required to put on gloves in the gym.) If a serious fight broke out between a pair of Juniors, anywhere in the extensive grounds, the Brother on duty would stroll up, order the spectators into a circle, and supervise, enjoying the entertainment as much as everyone else. Queensberry Rules were adhered to: no hitting below the belt; no gouging or butting. If a boy began to bleed too much, the fight was stopped; not otherwise. It was a Celtic culture of battle: of the joy of battle for its own sake, in an all-male world.

I lost most of my fights at first, even though I was never foolish enough to fight someone above my weight; I was a clumsy boxer. But I began to improve, and there came the unforgettable day when I had a win. Red-haired Mick Fahey and I, evenly matched, fought a deadly battle on the old tennis court, a large, shouting circle around us, Brother Keltie supervising. Mick and I had nothing against each other as a rule; but some now-forgotten insults had been exchanged, and the fight was a serious one. We hammered each other for what seemed most of the lunch hour; I grew tired, I had a cut lip Mick was working on, and thought I was losing; but all of a sudden Mick dropped his hands, and said: 'All right Koch, I know you can beat me.' This was a glorious and startling moment; I had ceased to be a cissy. I had also discovered in myself the Celtic lust for battle, and a happy enjoyment in fighting. I didn't exploit this when I grew up, and lost the taste for it; but it did serve me in good stead in some encounters outside dance halls in my teens.

In that year when I was ten years old, on March 1st – some five weeks after the Japanese attack on Rabaul – an unidentified aeroplane was sighted over Hobart, and the braying of air raid sirens began. It was a Japanese sea-plane, launched from a submarine to assess the concentration of allied shipping in the port. Hobart now knew that it could be bombed at any time, and hasty digging of air raid shelters began, in public places and suburban back yards. At St Virgil's, extensive shelters and trenches were dug on the spacious hillside behind the school buildings – the site of an old Catholic cemetery. This made possible a new level of playground violence.

Trench warfare began; we hurled rocks across no-man's-land. Teeth were knocked out, and more serious injuries sustained, and the Brothers ceased to be amused. Our wars, and our use of the shelters, were strictly forbidden. But this edict was defied by an extraordinary figure called Ginger Donovan, a Senior who organized a gang and went underground, setting up headquarters in one of the more remote shelters. He was probably deranged: a boy psychopath. Certainly he was terrifying, with a dead-white face, ginger hair and wide, staring eyes. He was greatly feared, not only by the peaceable citizens his gang attacked, but by the gang members he commanded. He was a tyrant, ruling through fear, with trusted henchmen and lieutenants around him, and large numbers of troops. Often, like a true tyrant, Donovan himself did not appear, but remained in his underground kingdom, sending out troops and raiding parties to put his orders into effect – which meant savagely beating anyone who opposed him. The school was in fear of him; almost everyone joined his gang for fear of recriminations; the pathetic groups who had opposed him dissolved, and the rest of us chose cowardly neutrality. A few brave individuals joined his organization as spies, going down into the shelters and coming back with extraordinary reports. He had brought in furniture and carpets;

he was almost able to live there. And most frightening of all, he had set up a torture chamber. Details of the tortures were vague; but one which he favoured was to put a board across a boy's chest, and his torturers would jump on each end of it. Boys subjected to these procedures now began to report to the Matron with broken arms and other injuries; and this was Donovan's undoing. The Brothers investigated, the head-quarters were penetrated, and Ginger Donovan was expelled. There was general relief at this; but he had certainly been interesting. He had gone beyond violence; he had shown us what evil was about, in a world then locked in a struggle over evil.

Joy in battle was not the only Celtic tradition to which St Virgil's introduced me. It was there that I also discovered the pleasure of oral story-telling – not from the Brothers, but from my school-fellows. In that pre-television age, the comic strip reigned supreme as escapist entertainment for little boys, and its heroes – mostly American – had a weird glamour for us: Buck Rogers; the Phantom; Flash Gordon; Tarzan. As the war advanced, and paper became scarce, and fewer and fewer convoys reached Australia across the Pacific, the flow of comic books dwindled and became precious. We hoarded and swapped them; and in the lunch hours, sitting in the grass on the hillside with our sand-wiches, the town and the wide blue estuary of the Derwent spread out below us, we told each other stories from the comic books we kept at home. I recited the plots of various Phantom and Buck Rogers books; but my favourite was Felix the Cat. I had a mystical devotion to Felix, and my passion for him must have communicated itself. My audience grew larger and larger: from half a dozen friends it grew to a score; to thirty. Soon, few others told stories at all; an expectant circle would gather around me each lunch hour, and someone would say: 'Come on, Kochie – tell us a Felix story.'

But eventually a day came when there were no adventures left to recite: I had used up all of the stockpile in the box of Felix books that sat under my bed at home. I confessed this to my audience, and for a moment there was silence; disappointed faces looked at me. Then sandy-haired Dan Sexton, one of the toughest boys in my class, leaned close to me and grinned. It was an odd grin, encouraging and conspiratorial, seeming to urge me to something illicit.

'Make one up,' he said.

I was startled. Boys didn't make up stories; such an idea would normally have been treated with the scorn reserved for activities that were in some way unmanly, or peculiar. Yet the invitation had been made, and made by Dan Sexton; so I complied. I made up a Felix story which seemed to satisfy my listeners, and followed it with another. And the next day and the next the circle on the grass was waiting, ready to hear whatever Felix adventures I chose to devise.

Come on, Kochie – tell us a Felix story. A line had been crossed. I was not a boy who shone, or who was looked up to. I was hopeless at football, a mediocre fighter, and a dunce at most things in class except English. But I knew how to tell a story, in a way that the others did not, it seemed. My warrior companions had discovered a use for me, and the fate of the bard was mine: I was one of those ambiguous creatures destined to weave fictions, for the diversion of more serious people.

III

At the end of the War, and a year after Nana Hurburgh's death, I escaped from St Virgil's and entered the secular world of the Hobart State High School. I now thought little more about things Irish; but in my second year at university, at an age when reading experiences are as intense as reality, I discovered through my reading an extraordinary set of Irish gentlemen: the Young Irelanders.

These rebel patriots of the mid-nineteenth century had been brought to Tasmania as political prisoners. In the excitement of 1848, when many new nations were claiming their independence in Europe, they had called in their newspapers and speeches for an end to British rule in Ireland; and finally, they had led an abortive peasant rising. Convicted of sedition, they had found themselves transported to what was then Van Diemen's Land, for terms of fourteen years. Since most of them were from the Protestant or Catholic gentry, and were celebrated in Europe and America, the British Government treated them with care. They were not imprisoned with other convicts, but instead were treated like prisoners of war. Granted tickets-of-leave which meant comparative freedom within the colony – they were allowed to bring out their families, to mingle in the colony's more genteel circles, and even to take up land, if they wished. But a ticket was given to each man only when he had written a special letter to the Governor, giving his word as a gentleman not to attempt to escape.

Despite this, some of them had refused to be pent up for more than a few years – most notably, John Mitchel and Thomas Meagher. These admired and youthful leaders of the cause of Irish freedom successfully fled the island, eluding British retribution by secretly boarding ships bound for the United States, where they were received in triumph by the New York Irish who had funded their escape, and were greeted with nation-wide support, both popular and in the highest circles of government. In each case, to preserve his honour, the absconding patriot withdrew his parole by writing to inform the Governor of Van Diemen's Land, and then – hunted by the police – was taken on board an American ship whose captain had been paid to transport him. But however short their stay, these Irish exiles had actually been here in Tasmania, moving through scenes that I knew – and I began to find this extraordinary.

I lived in an island on the bottom of the globe, where little of importance in the eyes of the outside world seemed ever to have happened. The Young Irelanders William Smith O'Brien, Thomas Meagher, John Mitchel, John Martin, Patrick O'Donohoe and the rest – had descended here like leading actors from the stage of history, materializing in the

Antipodes. And they had left their traces. John Mitchel had leased a farm in the highlands, at Bothwell. Nant Cottage – a plain stone house where he had lived with his family and his bachelor comrade John Martin – was still there, in those quiet, tawny river-flats below the Western Tiers. Thomas Meagher had married a local girl, Catherine Bennett, who bore him a child that died at only four months: I had often passed its grave in the little village of Richmond, in the Catholic churchyard there. William Smith O'Brien – unlike his comrades – had at first stubbornly refused to give his promise not to escape; until he finally did so, he was confined in a cottage on the penal settlement at Port Arthur.

Like so many other Tasmanians, I had often made the pilgrimage to the ruins of that once-dreaded penal station on its pretty little bay, backed by sombre, bush-covered ranges: the seat of Tasmania's ancestral shame, whose atmosphere was so strangely heavy and silent that no amount of laughter or skylarking could seem to break it, or dispel the odour of hundred-year-old sorrow that hung in that air. Inspecting the place's sandstone skeletons – penitentiary; church; hospital; guard tower – I had wandered into a hinterland of that old, menacing century of which we were all half afraid: the century of the ancestors. Oddly mixed feelings would rise in me: curiosity; pity; unease. And I would stand in the tiny, shingle-roofed cottage where they had kept Smith O'Brien and feel sorry for him – vaguely imagining him to be a poor working man; having no notion then that he was an Irish aristocrat who had sat in the House of Commons.

Throughout my childhood, in fact, these famous political exiles had merely been names; I knew little or nothing about them. To be sure, there was a book about them on my parents' bookshelves, belonging to my mother – *Young Ireland in Exile* – but I had never read it, always passing it over when I hunted for something to read. Now, at nineteen, I finally picked it up, and read with growing fascination. Although it had been published in Dublin, it was written by a local identity: Monsignor James Cullen. Father Cullen was Irish, but had lived in

Hobart for many years. He had baptised me, and was a friend of my grandmother's, and she had always spoken of him with sentimental reverence. ('Father Cullen is a very good man, and a scholar. There isn't a more learned man in the Church.') Like my grandmother, Monsignor Cullen had now been dead for many years; but I remembered meeting him as a child. In his case, Nana's judgement seemed accurate: ruddy, with a shock of white hair, he had smiled down at me benevolently, and had refrained from asking the awkward questions so many priests did.

Father Cullen's account of the exiles was fairly prosaic; but he quoted extensively from the letters the Young Irelanders had written, and the journals they had kept – and these quotations leaped out at me. The passages by John Mitchel and Thomas Meagher in particular were full of imagination, humour and vitality, and their responses to the landscapes of my native island – which they found very beautiful, despite their exile – were like nothing else written about Tasmania, either in the last century or this one. It was as though the young Byron and Shelley had wandered through the Tasmanian bush, and on the streets of its little towns; or as though (in Thomas Meagher's case), Charles Dickens had come here as a tourist, his caustic eye taking in the island's humble and familiar scenes.

Meagher, on his arrival in the colony in October 1849, was sent to the police district of Campbell Town to take up residence, and settled in the village of Ross – where Margaret O'Meara would be imprisoned less than two years later, in the Factory. 'Meagher of the Sword', as he was known, was the privileged son of the Mayor of Waterford, and had been educated by the Jesuits in England. He was perhaps the most charismatic of all the exiles: a mercurial, good-looking dandy, and a born orator, whose pale eyes could produce unease. His literary gift was one he used all too briefly; he combined an imaginative nature with that of a born warrior. Following his spectacular escape to America, he would join the Union army in the Civil War, distinguishing himself in battle and rising to the rank of brigadier-general. He would help to raise the famous New York Irish Brigade, commanding his own company of Irish Zouaves, and becoming a national hero. After the war, he would become Governor of Montana – where his statue on horseback, in the uniform of the Union, still stands outside the State Capitol. This was the man who walked the streets of Ross – 'a little apology of a town', as he called it – where he was forced to find lodgings. I found this piquant; and swaggering Tom Meagher began to be as alive to me as though he had walked into my cluttered student bedroom.

High spirits and a wild sense of humour seldom deserted Meagher; even when he was initially sentenced to death, he gave a party for his friends in his cell in Kilmainham gaol. And his humour didn't desert him now, as he surveyed this tiny colonial town at the end of the world. He had rented rooms in a cottage in Ross which still stands:

> *Just fancy a little lodge, built from head to foot with bright red bricks; two flower beds, and a neat railing in front . . . and then, four rooms inside, each fourteen by twelve, and an oven in the kitchen; just fancy all this, and you will have a pretty correct picture of the establishment in which, with a domestic servant of all work, and a legion of flies, I now have the happiness to reside.*
>
> *My landlady is a devout Wesleyan, an amiable female of stupendous proportions, and proportionate loquacity – her husband is a Wesleyan too, a shoemaker by trade, and a spectre in appearance . . . Upon coming to terms with them in the first instance . . . an agreeable dialogue took place, of which the following may be considered a fair report :*
>
> *'Sir,' said Mrs Anderson, sticking a pin into the sleeve of her gown, and spreading down her apron before her.*
>
> *'Well, ma'am,' said I.*
>
> *'Why, sir,' says she. 'You see as how it is, me and my husband be Wesleyans, and we don't like a-cooking on Sundays, and so if it don't matter to you, sir, we'd a soon not dress you any meat a that day . . .'*
>
> *'As to that,' I replied, 'I don't much mind having a cold dinner upon*

Sundays, but then, there are the potatoes! Potatoes, you know,
Mrs Anderson, are very insipid when cold.'

    This was a difficulty of great magnitude. Mrs Anderson paused, and
swelled up immensely. When the swelling subsided a little, she cast an
inquiring glance at her husband, as if to implore him for a text, a note
or a comment . . .

And here, in Father Cullen's little book, was a letter from Meagher's comrade John Mitchel – that remorseless foe of England and most formidable of Young Ireland leaders, who had called for the taking up of arms to free his country, and whose thinking anticipates that of Sinn Fein. Mitchel was a man of contradictions. Like Meagher, he was a handsome man, in this period of his youthful prime, his face combining an artist's sensitivity with the hard, wilful stubbornness of his Scottish ancestors. The son of a Presbyterian minister in Northern Ireland, a Trinity College graduate, briefly a solicitor, and the editor of a patriotic newspaper, *The United Irishman*, he wrote essays that still live as literature – in particular his searing pieces on the Famine, for the *Nation*. Mitchel was described by all who knew him as gentle and charming; yet his hatred of English rule was fanatical, and his lack of tact when ideas were at stake earned him many enemies. Brilliant, but sometimes wrong-headed and majestically intolerant, he never understood compromise, and feared no-one. When he escaped to America he would tragically join the South, in the Civil War, and champion the cause of the Confederacy.

Mitchel's letter was written to a friend in Ireland, and describes the wild Tasmanian highlands – that empty roof of the island which is empty still: a country of lakes and stones and snow-covered mountains and tall stringybark gums, where the clear, biting air is like that of a purer planet. He and his fellow-exile, the entirely gentle John Martin, would ride up there from Bothwell to meet their comrades in secret, since such meetings were forbidden by the island's penal Government. Meagher, who was never short of money, had built a cottage on Lake Sorell, sailing his own boat there, and flying the French and American flags. Describing all this, Mitchel sounds not like a terrorist, but a poet:

Imagine Martin and me, after a glorious ride of twenty miles through noble old woods, lying on the bank of a fine lake, deep in the central mountains. It is noon-day, and so calm, the water is hardly rippling on the pebbles; and the wooded banks and promontories, and the endless wilderness of bush, stretching away through the smoky district to blue peaks of the north-west, are all sleeping in the sun, and bathing and beaming in an atmosphere of gold and purple. A boat nears us slowly, by help of both sail and oars; a sunburnt man in a sailor's jacket stands in the stern-sheets, holding the tiller; by his side, on crimson cushions, sits a fair and graceful girl. The sun-burnt fellow is O'Meagher, and that lady is . . . Mrs O'Meagher . . .

We are . . . welcomed into our friend's newly-built house by his newly-wedded wife. They have elegant little rooms, books, horses, boats – why, it is almost like living. I usually feel our condition here to be a sort of syncope or trance, our movements to be somnambulatory, and our apparent doings and sayings to be sick men's dreams; but this is absolutely a sort of quasi life.

Eventually, many years later, I would discover in an antiquarian bookshop a copy of John Mitchel's famous *Jail Journal* – never published in Australia – and read the story of his long and stubborn defiance of his captors, and encounter many more fine passages describing the scenes of my native place. True, they were a little flowery, in the Victorian manner, but they were superbly vivid and alive: the work of a man whose spirit was as highly charged as that of a creative artist, displaying a flair for detail and poetic feeling which compares not unfavourably with the writing of such contemporaries as Chateaubriand and Thoreau. Yes: Mitchel, the fearless and unbreakable political activist, had the soul of a poet; and he was, as he once admitted in the *Journal*, a man who 'went double'. Perhaps this was why his spirit would never find rest, and why he was so full of contradictions: responsive to much that was good and beautiful, yet full of an inward anger that would take him in wrong directions, and see him, at the end of the Civil War, imprisoned in the same fortress as his friend Jefferson Davis, President of the Confederacy.

After he escaped to America, he would look back to his time in Van Diemen's Land and his peaceful farm at Bothwell with some nostalgia; and he kept up a correspondence with some of the landed gentry who had befriended him there. He would not find such peace again, in his troubled and embattled life – and perhaps he had a presentiment of this. As he took his last look at the island – watching its night-shrouded coast from the ship that was taking him to freedom – he did so with a mixture of elation and regret:

The last of my island prison visible to me is a line of broken peaks over the Bay of Fires. Adieu, then, beauteous island – island of fragrant forests, and bright rivers, and fair women! Behind those far blue peaks, in many a green valley known to me, dwell some of the best and warmest-hearted of all God's creatures . . .

That Mitchel had lived and moved in scenes that I knew was wonderful to me; and I was moved by the fact that he had half come to love them – even though he never ceased to yearn for his country, and the cause that so consumed him. As I read, his spirit seemed to hover at my shoulder, and I understood his divisions all too well. My ancestors had uprooted themselves from their native hemisphere, and this southern zone that was alien to Mitchel was that of my birth and upbringing. But I have found over a lifetime that the other, ancestral hemisphere will never cease to tug at my spirit.

THREE

Dublin Past, Dublin Present

I

IN JULY 2000, the last year of the dying century, my friend Brian Mooney and I set out on a journey to Ireland.

We had talked of this Irish expedition for some time. For him, it would be a return to the country where he'd spent a good deal of his life, before settling down in Australia. For me, it would be a venture into a country I scarcely knew. I would go to Tipperary, and see if any traces of Margaret O'Meara were to be found. I'd seek out Sixmile-bridge in County Clare, and see if 'Deerpark' was still standing. And we would both go anywhere that Irish music was to be heard.

I'd been to Ireland only once, for a week, when I was twenty-three; and all I'd seen was Dublin. That was in 1956. Another age; another world.

Like so many young Australians of my generation, I'd gone to England as soon as I could save the fare, and had lived and worked in London for nearly two years. I was currently between jobs. I'd been working as a waiter; now I'd found a more elevated position as a clerk. With a week to spare before I started in the new job, I decided to see something of Ireland.

I had just enough money to spend about six days there. Travelling young Australians lived very frugally, in that post-war England of the fifties where the wages in most jobs were barely enough to enable us to survive. But my new clerical position made me feel affluent enough to travel to Dublin by air. On the plane, which flew from London Airport in the late afternoon, I found myself sitting with two middle-aged Irishmen: well-dressed, in tweed suits, collars and ties, with somewhat rubicund faces. They were brothers, they told me, and the eldest brother in their family had just died: they were on their way home to County Clare to see him buried. The death didn't seem to depress them; on the contrary, they seemed to be in high spirits. This may have been because they were drinking Irish whiskey; and I had the impression they'd been drinking with some dedication before they got on the plane. I ordered a Jameson's for myself.

Unlike many of the English I'd so far met, who took a bit of getting to know, these Irish brothers were immediately friendly. When they discovered that I was Australian, they seemed to warm to me, telling me that some of their relatives had gone out there. They were impressed that a 'young fella' of twenty-three had come right across the world, and asked me why I was going to Dublin. I said that I had Irish ancestors, and felt that I should see the country they had come from. Now the two Irishmen warmed to me still further, and more whiskeys were ordered from the air hostess.

'Sure, Australians and Irish are like one people,' one of the brothers said. 'You lot have all got Irish blood – isn't that right, now?'

We toasted Ireland and toasted Australia; more whiskeys arrived, and the brothers became very enthusiastic indeed about my journey. I must see more of Ireland than Dublin, they told me: I must come to

County Clare with them, to their native town of Crusheen, and attend
the funeral. There would be a fine party afterwards; and I could stay in
their house. Exhilarated by the whiskeys I'd drunk on an empty
stomach, I agreed without hesitation. We shook hands on it affection-
ately; we told each other jokes. A fine adventure was beginning; we
were all laughing immoderately, causing the air hostess to frown at us
as she swayed up the aisle. We were all, in fact, half smashed.

This may account for the fact that soon after our arrival in Dublin,
the brothers were lost to me. How I lost them is no longer certain, since
things now took on an hallucinatory quality, and come back to me in
flashes, with puzzling gaps between.

The first of these flashes finds me with the brothers in a pub in
O'Connell Street, to which we went immediately we came off the
airways bus. We are drinking pints of Guinness stout, and have made
friends with others at the bar; lamps glow on the polished wood, and
there's an atmosphere of great cosiness and conviviality. An old man
sings 'I'll Take You Home Again, Kathleen', and when it's discovered
I'm Australian, I'm asked by our new friends to sing 'The Wild
Colonial Boy' – that song about an Irish bushranger which is part of the
folk tradition of both countries. Fortunately, I know the words, and
oblige. This is well received; the brothers are proud of me, I'm clapped
on the back, and urged to drink more Guinness. The tall black glasses
multiply on the bar; I keep pace with the brothers and our new-found
friends. But I've not drunk Guinness before, and underestimate its
strength. Very soon, and without quite knowing it, I'm seriously
drunk; but drunk in a profound, happy and dreamlike way that moves
me onto a plane beyond reality.

It's in this dimension that I lose the brothers from County Clare.
How it happens is mysterious. They seem to disappear from the bar,
perhaps when I'm out in the urinal. Perhaps they lose me deliberately,
regretting their rash offer to take me to Crusheen and the funeral.
Impossible to say; but the next flash finds me out in O'Connell Street,

not quite sure why I'm there, clutching the overnight bag which is my only luggage. I'm sorry to have lost the brothers, but only in a vague and childlike way, and I find myself chuckling. It's April, and quite cold; there's just been a shower of rain, the crowded pavements gleam, and I turn up the collar of my secondhand Royal Australian Navy overcoat. It's not yet dark, but a monochrome evening is closing in: an evening I ought to find forbidding, but instead find obscurely exciting. I decide now, in a muddled way, that the best thing I can do is to find a place to stay.

The hotel I've emerged from is almost opposite the tall grey pillars of the General Post Office, and I'm looking up at Lord Nelson on his monument: imperial relic, doomed to be blown up in ten years' time by the IRA. As I begin to walk, looking about me at the immensely wide spaces of O'Connell Street, with its central trees and statues, I'm seeing Dublin properly for the first time; and Dublin is very strange. Despite O'Connell Street's handsome vistas, there's a look of grim hardship here. I wander down a side street of merciless, dripping brick buildings; and now I find a poverty more extreme than any I've seen in London. The city is apparently little changed since James Joyce's day. In the deep and menacing lanes, I pass people who are shabby, threadbare and dirty; and I'm accosted by little beggar boys, barefoot despite the cold. They are clad in the dress of 1904: baggy trousers held up by braces; ragged, filthy shirts; hand-me-down jackets that are many sizes too big for them. They know instantly that I'm a tourist: probably it's the overnight bag.

'Give us a penny, Mister! Give us a penny!'

I press pennies into their hands, and walk on. But they follow, dancing and laughing.

'You English, Mister? You from London? What *are* yez, then? Come on, give us a penny!'

A little old man moves out of a doorway, driving the swarm away with a few vigorous shouts. Then he blocks my way, smiling up at me.

He's thin and gnome-like, with a mane of tangled grey hair, a sharp face, and humorous blue eyes. He seems to have been expecting me.

'Me name's Mick Rooney,' he says. 'You're from London – am I right?'

I tell him yes, and he shakes my hand with a joyful air, asking my name.

'You'll be looking for a place to stay, Chris. Somewhere reasonable – isn't that so?'

Yes, I say, that's so.

'And I've just the place for ye,' he says. 'Follow me.'

I follow, and he leads me through a confusing maze of streets, to beckon me eventually up the steps of a tall Georgian building whose door has a broken fanlight. We climb narrow, dark stairs, Mick in front. Occasionally he turns to smile at me over his shoulder, beckoning and murmuring encouragement, like a goblin leading me into his kingdom. This all seems very natural. But what follows ceases to be natural at all.

Mick gestures, urging me through a door. I obey and come to a halt, holding my overnight bag, blinking after the dark of the stairs, my senses winking in and out. I find myself in a long, incredibly cluttered room of mysterious and unfathomable extent, with pink floral wallpaper and ornate Victorian furniture, lit by many shaded lamps. Huge, luxuriant indoor plants add to the density of things, making the place resemble a conservatory. A number of old ladies are sitting about, in bamboo chairs and on sofas, fussily dressed in the Victorian manner, with high collars, brooches and shawls. Just how many old ladies are actually here is uncertain, since the place is too large and confused for me to be sure – and since the Guinness has affected me so powerfully that I can no longer trust anything I see. As well as the old ladies, there are many parrots and brightly coloured tropical birds here, roosting in cages and on perches. The exact number of these is also uncertain, but they add the final touch to my bemusement; I find their presence not only bizarre but sinister. Am I being asked to believe that this a *rooming house*? The very idea is preposterous. Clearly I've invaded a private, eccentric salon whose purposes are obscure, presided over by these old ladies. I'm easily embarrassed, at twenty-three, and my embarrassment now is intense, despite my drunkenness; I turn to Mick for an explanation. But Mick has vanished.

Even in memory, the reality of that room seems dubious. One of the things that makes its materiality suspect is the fact that it's entirely static – and that there is absolutely no sound. I might have stepped into a picture. Nearest to me in the picture two old ladies sit at a table, frozen in the act of drinking tea. One of them wears a frilled white blouse and a hat trimmed with flowers; thin and elegant, teacup suspended, she looks at me and smiles as though she knows everything about me; but she neither speaks nor moves, and neither does her friend. Still no sound; it's as though everything is muffled in cotton wool. This, more than anything else, is what causes me to panic. I run from the room, and thunder down the stairs.

Coming out into the street I find Mick waiting. He purses his lips sympathetically.

'Did that not suit yez, then? Too expensive, maybe, for a young fella like yourself. I'll tell you the best place for ye: Mrs Donnelly's boarding house, out at Glasnevin – in Finglas Road, by the Cemetery. It's clean and cheap, and she's a nice woman. Have ye got a piece of paper? I'll write it down for ye, and tell yez where to get the bus.'

I give Mick two shillings, with which he seems pleased, and stagger away into the rain. That I find the bus stop, and travel successfully out to Glasnevin, seems remarkable; but I am operating on that automatic pilot which sometimes takes care of the very drunk. I have still eaten nothing since breakfast, and have no desire to do so; what I want now is a bed, before I fall into oblivion.

I'll find it at Mrs Donnelly's; but this won't end my troubles.

Glasnevin is like one of those complex, tedious dreams one urgently seeks to escape, and can't. Rows of tall, frowning houses run into blue-lit infinities; the world is grey as steel, and the softly falling rain goes on, plastering my hair to my forehead. Why am I here? There are places in Melbourne and Sydney like Glasnevin – places I avoid – but they are less intimidating. What they lack is the ultimate, threatening grimness and the old, historic threat which are native to the northern hemisphere: a threat that I remember in my blood. In Finglas Road, near Glasnevin Cemetery, I knock on the door of a two-storeyed house with bay windows which belongs to the turn of the century. I'm admitted by Mrs Donnelly: a tall, cheerful woman with her hair drawn back in a bun.

'Well, ye *do* look wet,' she says. 'I hate to turn yez away – but the only room I can give ye is a shared one. You'd be sharing with Mr O'Malley. But it's a good big room, and he's usually home quite late. Will that be all right, now?'

I say that it will be. I've no wish to go out into the rain again, and I have to concentrate hard to speak with any coherence. If Mrs Donnelly notices this, she makes no sign; instead she shows me into a big, gloomy, featureless bedroom which could be that of any cheap boarding house in Australia, except for a print on the wall of the Sacred Heart: the same print which was on the wall of our classroom at St Virgil's. Things are strangely and worryingly familiar; I seem to be re-entering a life I've lived in before: a life that will lead to no good.

There are two beds in the room: a double bed by the door and a single one by the window. Mrs Donnelly points to them.

'Yours is the single bed – Mr O'Malley has the double bed. Breakfast starts at half-seven.'

Soon unpacked and undressed, I turn out the light and collapse into the single bed – which is very narrow and uncomfortable, with a lumpy mattress. For a time the room revolves like a wheel, and I know from experience that it's important to sleep before nausea overtakes me. This is soon achieved; but somewhere in the middle of the night I wake up.

Is O'Malley here? No. Light through the window shows me that his bed is empty.

And now a perverse notion seizes me: a derangement that can only be accounted for by the continuing backwash of the Guinness. If O'Malley isn't here at this late hour, he's presumably not coming, I say. Why, then, shouldn't I take advantage of his bigger bed? Mine is detestably uncomfortable.

In a moment, I'm settled in the larger bed. But not for long. Just as I'm sinking into sleep, I hear heavy boots tramping down the passage. O'Malley! I leap from his bed, dart across the room, and dive into the single bed again. But the boots go on down the passage, and O'Malley doesn't appear.

For a time, I lie quiet; but my derangement will not let me rest. I toss and turn in my narrow bed, O'Malley doesn't manifest himself, and the stubborn desire to take possession of his bed grips me once again. O'Malley will never come, I say; and I return to the spacious comfort of his bed. Before I can sleep, however, boots are heard in the passage again, and I dive for my single bed. Once again the boots go on by – and my derangement continues. Mindlessly, stubbornly, for much of the night, somewhere between sleep and a befuddled waking, repeatedly woken by feet that never enter the room, I leap from bed to bed, driven as a laboratory rat. At last, defeated, with O'Malley still not here, I sink into sleep in my hateful little cot.

In the morning, I find the big bed still empty. O'Malley has never come; and I'm destined never to meet him. I leave Mrs Donnelly's soon after breakfast.

For the rest of that week in Dublin, the driving Spring rain scarcely stopped. The pavements gleamed hopelessly; the gutters gurgled. Everything and everyone smelled of old damp. I'd now found a cheap boarding house in the city: one that gave me a room to myself. This was in Gardiner Street, on the grim, poverty-sunk North Side: just around the corner from 7 Eccles Street, the home of Leopold Bloom – still there, but doomed to be demolished some twenty years later.

Bloom was often in my mind as I trudged about the city in the rain, in my Navy overcoat. My lone wanderings began to seem as sad as his. Poor though I was, I'd seldom been cast down in London, where I'd made a few friends, and where the last, austere, imperial glamour of the fifties continued to impress young colonials like me. But I began to be very cast down in Dublin, over which an ancient, almost supernatural sadness seemed to hang, seeping into its brick and pale grey granite; moving like a fog down the Liffey. I discovered that I must cross the Liffey to the South Side to find the affluent face of Georgian Dublin; but even here the sadness continued, hanging over Fitzwilliam and Merrion Squares, infecting St Stephen's Green and Temple Bar. It was a sadness which seemed to contain a faint touch of menace. Dublin was then in a pit of economic stagnation, though I knew nothing of that. I also knew less of Irish history then than I do now, or some sources of the menace might have been possible to guess at. The shades of Michael Collins and his men lurked in the streets of the North Side, and in certain bars off Grafton Street; and the shades of the starving hung in the back streets everywhere.

I could have escaped, of course, by taking a train to one of the other counties; and I told myself I was foolish not to do so. And yet I couldn't bring myself to leave.

To account for this is difficult. The very sadness of Dublin seemed to hold me, making some obscure demand; I wanted to fathom its mystery. It was a sadness I remembered from some other life – or from memories not my own, yet personal. It somehow concerned me; and its very wish to claim me both threatened and invited me. I walked, a shabby young man with no money, and sad, shabby Dublin was familiar to the point of tedium. Dublin – whose name in Gaelic, I discovered, meant Dark Pool – seemed depressing and unrewarding;

yet at times, as I walked, its melancholy excited me, like remembered danger. It possessed me, as though someone once loved and now dead was demanding my attention and my grief; as though a whole lost life was speaking to me in whispers, saying: *Here. Here. Here. Remember?*

The places that were shabbiest in Dublin were those that seemed to want most to claim me. I had no business in Merrion Square, or in the lounge of the Shelbourne. I sought out those places where the sadness and menace were strongest: mostly on the quays along the Liffey, where I sat over whiskeys in dingy pubs, or drank tea in echoing side streets. Wellington Quay; Ormond Quay; Custom House Quay: I walked them all, crossing and re-crossing the Liffey's line of bridges, in rain and fleeting sunshine. The beggar boys found me, and followed me. *'Give us a penny, Mister! Give us a penny!'* On a corner, an old man stood singing, clad in a torn and filthy tweed overcoat, holding out his cap for coins, his face entirely cheerful.

'That flower I found in O'Connell Street,
In Dublin's fair city . . .'

The rain would not stop. It pockmarked the Liffey's brown surface, while seagulls wheeled and made cries of protest, and ships hooted mournfully beyond the Quays. It streamed on iron railings, and gleamed on the webbing of cranes, reared high against the pale northern sky. Somewhere, in one of the pubs on the quays, or up one of the lanes, the man called Eddy would be waiting.

Eddy had only one name, and had come to me in dreams when I was a child: dreams that were constantly repeated, as childhood's dreams often are. I had never understood who he was: only that he was infinitely daring and remarkable, and everything that I wanted to be. He had thick yellow hair, wide and excited blue eyes, and a jutting jaw; when he smiled, his teeth were white and prominent. His smile was thrilling: it promised joy; elation; danger. He always came at night, and I had the sense that he was on the run from something, and that danger was his life. He would wait for me in night-time lanes like those here in Dublin; he would hurry away (he was always hurrying away, probably on perilous business), and I would follow for a time, and then lose him.

I realized now that Eddy had been Irish. Faces like his passed me in O'Connell Street; and once I found myself looking at his double, across a bar-room on Wellington Quay.

On my third day in Dublin, it was still raining. I retreated from the streets to spend the afternoon in the domed Reading Room of the National Library, reading by the light of a green-shaded lamp. High above, on the rain-swept glass dome, seagulls from the Liffey were perched: spirits of the city, their feet like dark stars on the glass. I began to think seriously of leaving. But that evening, I met a girl.

She sat next to me in a cinema in O'Connell Street. After a time, she spoke to me in the darkness, murmuring something about the film. I managed a reply, and we went on watching in silence for a time. Then we whispered further observations, always about the film, our faces tilted to the screen, but taking each other in with sideways glances. I was able to make out in the dimness that she was rather small, about my own age or younger, and had curly, dark brown hair. Whether she was pretty or plain it wasn't possible to tell.

Soon I became aware that her leg was lightly pressed against mine. Tentatively, I returned the pressure. She affected not to notice, her face upturned to the screen; and she didn't remove her thigh. I was encouraged and amazed. In Australia in that era, such things didn't happen; a young woman would never have spoken to a man first – and certainly wouldn't have done what this girl was doing now. Did the women pick up the men in Ireland, instead of the other way round? There could be little doubt of her interest, and I seized my opportunity when the lights went up, inviting her for a drink.

We went to a pub in O'Connell Street, where we sat at a table in muted, rosy light, drinking Guinness. Her name was Nora Devlin, she told me. She proved to be neither pretty nor plain, but somewhere in between. The brown curly hair framed a broad face with a firm chin and a short nose. Her eyes were her best feature: sky-blue, and lit by humour. No more than twenty, she was short, with a full, somewhat matronly figure, and wore a white, high-buttoned, matronly blouse, plaid skirt, and brown woollen overcoat: clothes that my mother or grandmother might have worn. In no way did she look what was then called 'loose': indeed, she seemed very respectable; almost old-fashioned. She smiled at me in an interested manner, and was very friendly; but oddly, she asked no personal questions – not even where I was from. Nor did she volunteer much information about herself, except that she lived at a place called Dunleary. If she told me her occupation, I've forgotten it. I quickly realised that she hadn't much education, and kept the conversation very simple. Her thick Dublin accent was sometimes hard to understand, and what we talked about is lost.

When we left the pub we walked down O'Connell Street and turned on to Eden Quay, beside the Liffey. It was now near midnight, and there were few pedestrians; it had stopped raining, but was very cold. The tide was out in the river, and we looked over the sloping stone wall at exposed, foul-smelling mud-flats where seagulls squabbled. The dome of the Custom House, in the distance, was like a building in some more noble, unreal city. We drifted on, hand in hand, and turned into a lane where urchins in flimsy shirts and trousers, their faces and hands blue with cold, ran up to us with outstretched palms, their shouts rebounding off the tall brick walls. *'Give us a penny! A penny!'* There were gaping vacant lots here like the bomb-sites in London; we wandered into one of these, and stood in the dark against a brick wall.

As we kissed, Nora whispered fervently in my ear, the phrases she used taken from the paperback romantic fiction of the day: she seemed to be quoting whole passages, for which I merely happened to be the audience. She pressed close, her whispering mingling with the shouts of the urchins; we grappled, standing in the rubble, and then she drew away, lips pursed in reproof, buttoning her woollen overcoat.

'I can tell ye're fast,' she said; but her eyes shone with matronly archness. 'I must go. I have to catch me bus. Will I see you again?'

I asked if I could meet her tomorrow.

'Tomorrow night,' she said. 'Will ye come to Dunleary?'

I said I would, and asked where Dunleary was. She drew a piece of paper from her handbag, wrote on it, and thrust it into my hand. It read:

Go to Dun Laoire, get No. 8 bus. Ask to get off at St Michael's Church, and wait for me there at 7.30.

Love, Nora

Later, when I examined the scrap of paper, I would find that she had written on the back of part of a letter from a friend. It read:

We had a lovely time in Galway and the weather could not have been better, but I would still prefer dear old Wicklow. I often remember the chats we used to have when we should have been asleep. Well Nora I will close now. Hope you are not working too hard like myself.

God bless. Love,

Myra

Dunleary, on Dublin Bay, is Dun Laoghaire, in Irish. Once it was Kingstown: the fashionable resort of Victorian days.

Travelling there on the night-time bus, I studied my tattered guide to the city. Dunleary harbour, I found, enclosed by its two long piers, was where the passenger steamers known as Mail Boats left from, crossing to Holyhead in Wales, and connecting with the Irish Mail service on British Railways. And just to the south down the sea road was Sandycove, where Stephen Dedalus and stately, plump Buck Mulligan had stood above the bay on their Martello tower, while Mulligan blessed the country and the awakening mountains. Dunleary was also the harbour where the nineteenth century convict ships lay. From here (although I was ignorant of this fact, on that night in 1956), the *Tasmania* had sailed, carrying my great-great-grandmother away to Van Diemen's Land.

In freezing cold, Nora Devlin and I walked the long promenade on the East Pier, our arms about each other. Only a few other people were foolish enough to be promenading. Clouds hid the moon, and there was a wild, gusty wind; the night was too dark to see very much, and was filled with the sound of waves. So little of Dunleary could be seen that I scarcely knew where I was; I moved through a disjointed dream, with this girl whom I scarcely knew either. The East Pier was vast, like something out of antiquity, built of yellowish granite rocks; everything seemed vast here, on the edge of the Irish Sea, under the racing clouds. At the end of the pier, a lighthouse rose; and a second lighthouse sent out its beam from the tip of the West Pier, on the harbour's opposite side. We passed ancient stone shelters and a deserted bandstand, swaying through a darkness that was utterly strange: a darkness that was slotted and pricked and spangled with lights. Lights of the town, burning orange around the bay; lights of the long, long piers; lights of small boats, riding at anchor; lights of the Mail Boat, lying at its terminal, pulsing and portentous. The cold grew piercing. We shivered and laughed, hugging each other for warmth. Nora had still asked me nothing about myself; nor had I volunteered any information. It would not help my plans for seduction, I thought, if she discovered I was briefly here from London. I assumed that she knew I wasn't Irish, and guessed that she'd think I was English. But I'd shortly discover I was wrong.

We wandered off the pier and lay alone on a grassy bank, holding each other and kissing. Nora grew fervent, but resisted my attempts to unbutton her overcoat.

'If we were in a nice warm room now, ye might tempt me.'

But nice warm rooms were hard to find in the fifties, and young men and women, meeting in winter, walked or clung together in freezing streets or vacancies like this, locked off from love. From where we lay, we could see the Mail Boat leaving for Holyhead, moving out into the harbour, lights glowing with the potency of voyage, funnel smoking.

'I love to watch the Mail Boats go,' Nora said. 'I imagine I'm on them.'

At that moment, Dunleary became not only strange but enormously sad to me. I did not understand the feeling that gripped me, which had nothing to do with Nora, or with my doomed attempts at seduction. Perhaps, in some secret compartment in my brain – a compartment of which I consciously knew nothing – another ship moved out into the bay, sails spread, carrying Margaret O'Meara away.

When I turned back to Nora, I found her looking at me, as though trying to work something out.

'You talk rather posh,' she said. 'Ye're not from Dublin – which county are *you* from?'

II

A man past middle age who can still get excited by what life brings him is a man worth travelling with. This is a capacity that Brian Mooney has in abundance.

As the weeks passed by that led to our departure for Dublin, he grew more and more elated. The prospect of seeing Ireland again, and of visiting his grown sons in Galway, caused him almost to dance a jig on the spot.

'By Jesus, Chris, I can hear those big jet engines roaring already!'

I laughed. People might think us peculiar, I said: two men of our age travelling about the country together.

'Sure, the merry-hearted boys make the best of old men,' Brian said. He was quoting from the folk song, 'The Bard of Armagh'. 'And were we not merry-hearted boys, you and I?' he demanded.

We were, I said; we were.

As well as being a talented painter, Brian is a folk singer, and still performs in pubs and at festivals and goes busking for money on the streets of Launceston, where he and his wife Phyllis now live. It was his singing that had caused us to meet, when he and I had just entered our thirties. I was then a radio producer with the ABC in Melbourne, and wanted to record some Irish ballads for use in a programme. This was in the sixties, the era of the folk revival, when the singing group known as the Clancy Brothers and Tommy Makem had spearheaded the rediscovery of the ballad tradition in Ireland, at a time when the old songs of the people had almost disappeared. The Clancys, from Carrick-on-Suir in Tipperary, were a classic case of the Irish success story in America: emigrating there in the 1950s, singing in saloons in Greenwich Village, making their first recording, and then being propelled into fame. Brian had been recommended to me as one of the best local singers in the genre that the Clancys had made popular.

He appeared in the studio with a battered guitar case slung over his back: around six feet three, with an athlete's shoulders and lean build, clad in jeans and a tattered red shirt, his hair a wild mass of brown curls. He had clear blue eyes and one of those frank, engaging faces on which thoughts can easily be read; and his singing delighted me. A good deal of his repertoire was familiar to me from the recordings and concerts of the Clancy Brothers, who'd recently toured Australia. Bouncing on stage in their white Aran sweaters, they'd been a revelation. I'd thought until now that Irish music was typified by a few schmaltzy ballads such as 'Rose of Tralee' and 'Galway Bay'. Now I'd encountered that body of airs and ballads matched only by the Russian folk tradition in their beauty, and whose subject, nearly always, is what Robert Graves has claimed is the only one real poetry is concerned with: 'the single poetic theme of Life and Death . . . the question of what survives of the beloved'.

Brian recorded 'Boulavogue', 'Kelly the Boy from Killane', 'The Croppy Boy', 'The Bard of Armagh' and 'The Parting Glass' – far more than I needed, but I didn't want to stop. Then we went to a pub in Lonsdale Street and spent the evening there. Although Brian had an Irish accent, I discovered that he'd been born in Australia of Irish parents. Their influence must have been strong: he was a fervent Irish nationalist. He had spent his early childhood in Hay, on the banks of the Murrumbidgee, and had briefly studied painting in his twenties. His life after that had been nomadic. Roaming around Australia, from Melbourne to Cape York, he'd supplemented his meagre earnings from singing by working as a jackaroo, rouseabout, cane-cutter and circus hand; at one stage he even did a stint as a boxer, in one of those troupes that went around country shows. I found it easy to believe that he'd been a formidable fighter at the physical level; but he was so innately gentle and good-humoured, I found it hard to picture him working up the necessary boxer's rage.

He and I saw each other quite often after our recording session. But then, in 1965, he travelled for the first time to that country he'd always regarded as his true native land. He didn't return for twenty-one years. He lived first in Dublin and then in Galway; he took out Irish citizenship, and married Phyllis, a native of Galway. In the next few years, he established a reputation as a singer. He sang frequently in O'Donoghue's, the famous old folk pub in Merrion Row in Dublin, where the Dubliners and the Clancys and many other talented groups and soloists were performing – in that unrepeatable moment in time when Irish traditional music was still making its way from pubs like O'Donoghue's to New York and London, and so around the world.

I lost sight of Brian until the 1990s, when I was living in Launceston, and he and Phyllis came to settle there. His tangled curls had turned white, but he was still the same Brian – stooped a little, but still built like an athlete, with the same capacity for unaffected joy, and the same devotion to his music and his painting. Once a week he'd come and visit me, in the evening. Sitting over a bottle of Jameson's, we'd listen to the Chieftains and the Dubliners and the Fureys and the

Clancys on my CD player, and talk of the day when we'd wander through Ireland together. Brian would introduce me to his musician friends from the old days, and lead me to the beauties of the West and Tipperary. He still went back to Galway from time to time, and had many friends there.

Dreams take their time to become reality, and this one was no exception. Five years would go by before we'd fly from Sydney to Dublin.

III

Seven o'clock in the morning in the United Arab Emirates, on the Persian Gulf.

Brian and I sit side by side in a hotel shuttle bus, on our way from the airport to the Al Khaleej Palace – the hotel where we'll stay until tomorrow morning. We're travelling to London on an Arab airline, and are stopping over in Dubai. Beside us on the floor next to our suitcases is Brian's hand luggage, which has been fitted into the space with some difficulty. He's come equipped for pub singing, painting and photography, and this has necessitated carrying (1) his guitar in its case; (2) a concertina in an antique wooden box; (3) a small round case of painting gear; (4) a camera; and (5) a plastic bag containing his collection of tin whistles and a mouth organ.

Antipodeans returning to the zone of their ancestors must cross half the globe to do so, and economy jet travel inflicts an exquisite Purgatory on them: twenty-three hours sitting up, in seats designed for narrow-bodied dwarfs, surrounded by an ersatz and mocking luxury which ceases to convince after the first seven hours, when the toilets begin to stink and the air grows more and more blandly foul. Brian and I have decided to divide Purgatorio into two stages: hence our stopover. We left Sydney last night at eight o'clock, and have now served our first sixteen hours. Some glitch occurred in the plane's piped music system, and it played only one tune for the final five hours: 'Over the Rainbow'.

'I'll tell you what,' Brian says now. 'If they'd played that Over the bloody Rainbow once more, I was about to wreck the cabin.'

He laughs; he can never be truly ill-humoured. We both laugh; freed from our tube of torment, we're in a better mood already. We peer out the window at the outskirts of Dubai: a city built on sand.

A stark, grey and white landscape, sunk in enormous glare. A country almost without colour: weird. White sand; white and grey freeways; some building sites where workmen can be seen. Otherwise, no sign of life. A line of faded, grey-green palms beside the highway is the only hint of nature. In the distance, shining white tower blocks, matching the sand. Dubai: a wealthy oasis in the Arab Emirates, shimmering on the edge of the desert and the Gulf.

The shuttle is air-conditioned, but we've already tasted the heat outside: the vast, burning heat of the desert. The sheikhdom we're entering isn't reputed to welcome wandering infidels with any great enthusiasm, and its white, flat, sterile perspectives seem to shimmer with a mirage-like threat. We've only been allowed to stop over here by obtaining special, 24-hour visas. These were scrutinised long and carefully and with ill-disguised hostility by passport officials in the terminal, and Brian's bardic equipment was glanced at with suspicion in Customs. But finally we passed through those ramparts of high desks and computers that guard today's nations against undesirable wanderers, and entered the world of Islam.

We share a large twin room in the Al Khaleej Palace, which is comfortable and modern enough, with efficient air-conditioning, but can scarcely be called a palace. A ferro-concrete building in what seems to be the middle of town, its decor is rather like that of a middle-range Australian motel. The only exotic touch is a round green sticker fixed to each of our bedside tables: it says HOLY MECCA, and an arrow points in what is presumably the direction for the faithful to face at prayer. It's still only eight in the morning. After showering and reclining briefly on our beds, we decide to look for breakfast, and then go out into Dubai. Brian has changed into a t-shirt, shorts and sandals, and I wonder vaguely if this will turn out to be an offence against Islamic law. More cautious, I settle for a shirt and light cotton trousers.

In the lobby, where appropriate potted palms stand about, and portraits of hawk-faced emirs stare sternly from the walls, we discover that Dubai is served by a cosmopolitan workforce. The clerk on the desk is Malaysian, the young woman in charge of the adjoining coffee shop is a Filipina, and a blond male waiter there appears to be Dutch or German. The aristocracy they serve are the Arabs, who sweep through the lobby in spotless robes and the traditional burnous, and brood and frown in armchairs – waiting, no doubt, on meetings of fateful importance. Confronted with the menu in the coffee shop, we discover what it means to have entered the moneyed oasis of the sheikhs: the price of a cup of coffee and some eggs is of Arabian Nights magnitude.

We venture outside, to where taxis wait by the hotel doors. We ignore these, and walk. We discover that what we thought was the middle of town is solely a district of banks, office buildings, and the headquarters of international companies. There is only a little light traffic: the late-model cars of Europe and America. No shops, no restaurants, few pedestrians, no sign of any unskilled Arab workers except for taxi drivers and the doormen who stare from the lobbies of the office buildings. No sign, in fact, of any traditional or even ordinary life. Everything throbs softly with money. This is an island of international business, set down recently on the desert's verge, and the featureless, high-rise buildings of the late twentieth century cluster here in a dream-like vacuum. I gather from the tourist magazine placed in our room that a very pleasant life is led in Dubai by an international community of Westerners who have business interests here, or who work for multinational firms. Photographs show them at dinners and parties with their Arab colleagues, and a gossip column tells of their doings. But they are all invisible, it seems, except for an occasional pale face going by in a car.

It's very quiet in these avenues between the buildings: peaceful and harmless-looking. The veiled hostility of the officials in the airport terminal has not been encountered here: the clerk at the hotel desk and the woman in the coffee shop have been relatively friendly. Yet Brian and I agree that we feel a kind of ominousness, amorphous yet distinct, humming in the air between the buildings. Perhaps we imagine it; perhaps not. The sheikhdom, after all, adheres to medieval practices in its conduct of civil life.

We walk towards the port, in the shadow of the buildings; we cross a wide road, and now we encounter the heat.

Shimmering, burning, greater in intensity than seems reasonable or possible, it envelops and stuns us, and the concrete boulevards that extend in front of us seem suddenly to recede into infinite distance: a distance that looks intolerable to traverse. We stop, and hold a conference. We agree that we no longer wish to try and reach the port; we want instead to find more signs of life. Where are the shops? Where are the cafes? Where are the people?

We hail a taxi, and put these questions to the Arab driver, who speaks a little English. He frowns, not understanding us at first; then he tells us he will take us to the shopping centre, and speeds off down the freeway.

All is explained, when we get there. The shopping centre is under vast, air-conditioned domes of plexiglass, and Dubai's communal life is conducted inside, as is done more and more in tropical nations. The enclosed suburban shopping malls of the West have evolved and flowered on the equator into whole hermetic citadels: cultures whose life-support is the air-conditioning unit, entirely sealed off from the blazing and exhausting reality outside, anticipating those colonies we are promised on the Moon and Mars.

We enter the machine-chilled hive. In its huge main hall and the many bewildering byways opening off it, dense throngs of people flow by: predominantly Arab, but with a number of Chinese and Southeast-Asians, and a wan sprinkle of Europeans. The hive resounds with voices, and booms with American pop music, piped through loud-speakers: here, as everywhere on earth at this end of the century, the inescapable accompaniment to life in a public space. Escalators move human cargoes up to other levels: gallery after gallery running high above our heads under the dome. Black-bearded Arabs pace by, in their billowing white garments, their expressions lordly. A few paces behind, in accordance with custom, come their wives: elephantine in floor-length grey robes and headdresses, veiled to the eyes, herding their children. Like their contemporary counterparts in the West, many of these Arab children are obese – the boys in particular, in their fashionable Western youth gear of dress-like t-shirts and huge, skirt-like shorts, complete with the reversed baseball cap of the New York streets, and the inevitable white training shoes. They feast on junk food as they go, and paw through displays of video games.

Here, in a sealed society, under this sealed dome, is the new global culture, triumphant in its universal reach: an immensely potent, technically gifted infantilism, accompanied by the jabber of rap music. The crowds wander and shop, laden with packages, tasting international delights. All are available here: Starbucks; McDonald's; British chain stores selling clothing, electrical goods, video games and computer discs; Californian restaurants; Italian pizzerias; French patisseries.

We stand in front of a store and watch a local production for children on television. A plump, smiling, middle-aged Arab in traditional robes, somewhat clownish in his style, leads a group of Arab children through fantasy landscapes, accompanied by merry music: a jigging little Arab tune. He is a Pied Piper, it seems, and at each halt on the way he distributes presents: sweets, and the kinds of goods that teem all around us in the shops. The balloon-like children reach out their little hands for the sweets and video games and clothing and toy guns; then the Pied Piper goes on, leading them to more gifts along the way. Nothing else happens; he goes on, he goes on, and so do the children, and so does the little tune – finally becoming maddening. I wait for some twist in the plot; for some challenge to good fortune. It never comes; and the children seem to do nothing to earn their lavish rewards.

Brian and I go into Starbucks for a coffee. There's nothing else to do, in the new consumer Paradise of the sheikhs.

IV

Dublin again, at ten o'clock in the morning. Cloudy, yet sunny at intervals.

We arrived here from London last night, and are settled into a large and impersonal hotel by the Baggot Street Bridge, in Mespil Road, on the southern side of the Grand Canal. The Canal is the eighteenth century waterway that once carried passengers and cargoes right across the country, its barges moving through the Midlands, south to Waterford, and west to the Shannon. Brian is deeply fond of it, and plans to do some sketches here. As soon as we emerge from the hotel, he leads me across the road to the towpath, carrying his paints and sketchbook.

The big, spreading trees are out in full leaf: a tunnel of green, enclosing the canal and its towpaths, reflected in the moss-green water. And as always when I first arrive in Europe, I'm dazzled by this colour: by the live, singing green of the northern hemisphere. Green of these great summer trees; green of the reeds by the towpath! It's a green never found in our olive and silver native vegetation: a green that's still half yearned for in the Australian spirit – though new generations may soon lose its echo in the memory. It has many shades. The lighter hue, on the uppermost leaves of the trees, is the green of pure exuberance; the celebration of the North's precious summer. The deeper hue of shadow, in each tree's heart, is the green of mystery.

Close by the little Baggot Street Bridge, which spans the canal, a life-size bronze statue of the poet Patrick Kavanagh sits on a bench.

He looks somewhat ill-tempered, as he was in life, apparently; but like Brian, he loved the canal, and wanted his memorial to be here. The Baggot Street area, Brian tells me, was a haunt of musicians and writers in the 1950s – including Kavanagh and Brendan Behan. And he settles down beside the grumpy bronze poet to begin his sketch – donning a pair of spectacles he normally doesn't wear, and whose lenses carry many coloured spots: his painting spectacles. He's had a small setback: the Arab airline has lost his big suitcase, and he's clad only in the t-shirt and shorts and sandals he wore on the plane. He seems philosophical about it, but I feel for him, and have made a number of aggressive phone calls to Heathrow. A search is progressing.

While Brian becomes absorbed in his sketching, I set off on a walk to the nearby centre of the city, crossing the little bridge into Lower Baggot Street.

This district by the long, straight canal was once a preserve of the Protestant Ascendancy. The Anglo-Irish gentry kept townhouses here; and I find myself thinking of those Anglo-Irish ancestors of mine who lived in Dublin in the nineteenth century – some of them in this very street. Of Marcella Devereux, one of my great-great-grandmother Jane's many sisters, who married Andrew Rogers, Esquire, of Lower Baggot Street. (Which number? Alas, I don't know.) Of their uncle, Robert Devereux, barrister, of Ely Place; of his widow, Aunt Averina, who induced Ringrose Devereux to make his fatal disposal of the estates in Clare. Remote and unreal, these time-embalmed figures who so obsessed Great Uncle Walter! The Rector was never to come here, to the source of his lifelong dream.

As I walk, I think too of Elizabeth Bowen. Her father's Dublin residence stood quite close by, on this city side of the canal near the Baggot Street Bridge, in Herbert Place ('that row of smallish, light brown brick Georgian houses with high steps, fronting the canal').

In *Seven Winters*, her exquisite set of memories of childhood in Dublin, she recalls that there was a sawmill on the canal's other side, fed with logs by the barges, filling the air with its humming and the smell of new-planed wood. Her nursery, and the other front rooms, 'all had a watery quality in their lightness from the upcast reflections of the canal'.

Elizabeth Bowen's Dublin, where she walked with her various governesses, had the special geography of privilege: a geography that is now all around me. The world that she and her parents inhabited, she says, was still late Victorian. Their Dublin was witty and sociable, with bright-painted front doors, polished fanlights and brass nameplates. Her earliest walk was up and down the canal, as far as the Leeson Street Bridge, which can be seen from the Baggot Street Bridge, and which Brian is putting in his sketch. She would watch the barges go through the lock there, with mingled joy and terror. The Bowens did their everyday shopping in Upper Baggot Street, on the other side of the canal, whose shops were 'well-to-do'. There the child Elizabeth felt safe. ('Everyone had not only manners but time... kind smiles came over the high counters to me, and almost everyone knew my name.') And there, she tells us, stretched across the roofs of Upper Baggot Street, was 'a timeless white sky... a sky for the favoured.'

Longer walks, when she was older, took her with her governess Miss Baird through 'a tract of Georgian streets and squares' into the affluent Southeast which is Dublin's heart: Leinster House; Trinity College; the Bank of Ireland ('that had been Our Own Parliament once'), and St Stephen's Green, with its groves and its lake. With the insight of a gifted child, and of the writer she'd become, she sensed here at times 'a malign temper', and felt that 'the tyrannical grandness of this quarter existed for itself alone. Perhaps a child smells history without knowing it – I did not *know* I looked at the tomb of fashion'. She and Miss Baird went there by Lower Baggot Street, as I'm now doing; and in following the route this sheltered little girl and her governess took, at the beginning of the century now ending, I'm moving towards the old Georgian Dublin of the Ascendancy, and the centres of power and culture in today's Republic, where the mansion of the Duke of Leinster, leader of fashion in the eighteenth century, is now the home of the Irish Parliament.

For Elizabeth Bowen, child of Anglo-Ireland, that Dublin of the Ascendancy's last years was subtly and mysteriously zoned into the places that could be gone to, and places that could not. She and her governess did not venture to cross the Liffey; 'Sackville Street had something queer at the end', and the poorer North side of the city remained *terra incognita*:

> *No swamp or jungle could hold more threats than the tacitly ruled-out parts of one's own city. Even along the verges of Stephen's Green there were canyon-like streets that could intimidate me ... My fear was not social – not the rich child's dread of the slum. It was a charnel fear, of grave-dust and fungus dust ... Only on familiar pavements did sunshine fall.*

All this I find strangely close to the central experience of my own early childhood, in Hobart of the 1930s – which this district is now summoning up. To liken Edwardian Dublin and Depression Hobart – not to say my childhood and Elizabeth Bowen's – may seem somewhat absurd. But there's a kernel of truth in it – at least, for me. My childhood was hardly a privileged one, as hers was; my father, like most of his Depression generation, had walked a tightrope just above poverty, and was always worried about money. Yet having said that, I'm still walking down a street of half-recovered memories. Here in Lower Baggot Street, the terraces and little shops have a spectral similarity to those of certain lost districts that existed in the Hobart of my youth; and I see, not for the first time, that humble old Hobart had a miniature similarity to grand old Dublin. Both were colonial creations, their buildings from the same imperial mould. Both cities have a melancholy wistfulness: the wistfulness of a child of mixed and ambiguous parentage. Both are

Georgian in their style – though Hobart's first public and residential buildings were erected in the early decades of the nineteenth century, not in the eighteenth. The small, aged shops in the suburb of New Town, where I grew up, were very similar to these shops I'm walking past now. And thanks to the prejudices of those days, and childhood's enigmatic visions, I too lived in a city which was divided in my mind into happy, benign zones and 'bad' ones: districts where one didn't want to go, and which contained a formless menace – some of it transmitted from the past.

I walk on. I cross Fitzwilliam Street, and Pembroke Street; now Lower Baggot Street becomes Merrion Row. The Georgian terraces, which grow more and more elegantly redecorated, house fashionable and expensive restaurants in their ground floors, crowded with tourists: signs of the new, high-living Dublin. I have left the old Dublin behind: the Dublin of the turn of the century, and of 1956. I am passed by young men in well-cut suits, mobile phones held to ears, and by bare-armed, pretty young women in jeans, making the most of summer in brightly coloured tank-tops. There seem to be many young people on the streets: Dublin, I'm told, has the youngest population of any city in Europe – half of it under twenty-five. The Irish faces are strangely familiar. The same faces pass me in Sydney: faces of Australians four and five gener- ations removed from here. And all of these Dubliners walk with a spring in their step, and look prosperous and confident.

Gone, my dark and shabby Dublin of the end of ancient winter. Gone like the long-lost fifties, the grey old Dublin of child beggars and threadbare people in lanes. Here instead is a city of bright colours, freshly painted doors, rejuvenated buildings and clean byways. The people seem constantly to smile, and move with an electric energy. Of course, this shouldn't surprise me; Ireland's time has come, as every newspaper tells us, and these are the citizens of the fastest-growing economy in Western Europe. Yet it does surprise me, profoundly. There's an elation in the air: a buzzing anticipation which comes only rarely in a nation's life, and in some nations not at all. Only in New York have I experienced this particular electricity: a charge that says anything is possible. Does it tell the truth? That's another matter. But to experience it is to feel ten times more alive than usual. Perhaps the modern Irish have taken on the old American sense of endless possibilities.

There are many pubs here, and I pass the legendary O'Donoghue's at number 15, where Brian and the Clancys and the Dubliners once sang. But I don't go in, since Brian and I will go there tonight: a nostalgic visit, for Brian. Instead, not far short of Stephen's Green, I turn into the doorway of a combined pub and restaurant called Foley's. The rain has come back, and I decide to have a coffee until it passes.

The spacious, tastefully decorated parlour somewhat resembles a private club; Foley's is conscious, perhaps, of being close to the national Parliament, and to the centres of government and business. The women in here are fashionably dressed, and the majority of the men are in formal suits and ties. Well-lit by large windows along the street, the parlour has handsome wooden fittings, chintz-covered settees along the walls, and framed pictures of horse-racing scenes. Its long bar is of polished, dark mahogany; above it, hanging low, is a row of little drop lamps with glass shades: art nouveau flowers of green and orange. Waitresses in traditional white blouses and black skirts move behind the counter. A beaker of coffee sits on a hotplate there, and a radio is turned down low.

I approach the counter, and a middle-aged blonde waitress smiles at me.

'Are yez all right, there?'

It's the same phrase that's used in Australia, when asking if someone wants attention. ('Are y' right?') Now I realise where it came from.

I ask her if I can have a coffee.

'Ye can, of course.'

This particular construction is new to me, and charms me. I'll come to hear it everywhere in Ireland, when service is given. Merely a local turn of speech, it nevertheless seems to carry a unique friendliness: a personal warmth that's essentially Irish, and unusual in the metropolitan world. 'Ye can, of course.' 'I will, of course.' It reassures; it tells you to make yourself at home. Here in the capital, entering my first hotel parlour, it's as though I've come into a village.

I carry my coffee to a stool by the windows, and set it down on the counter that runs below them, together with a copy of the *Irish Independent* I bought in Baggot Street. It's still raining outside, and people hurry by in Merrion Row; I'll wait until the sun comes back, and read my newspaper. The blonde waitress is talking to another behind the bar; she laughs, and I hear her say: 'Would ye believe it, now?' A little way along from me, two young men in business suits are poring over the contents of a clipboard; a mobile phone goes off, and one of them answers it. The new Ireland is all around me: the society the press call the Celtic Tiger. After a time, I put aside the paper and take out a street map from my pocket and begin to study it.

A voice from my left suddenly addresses me.

'Can you find your way about? Or do you need some help, now?'

A thin, elderly man in round, old-fashioned, gold-rimmed glasses has sat down on the stool next to me, and is gazing at me with raised, enquiring eyebrows. He's wearing a blue rainproof jacket with a formal collar and tie underneath, and is somewhat scholarly-looking: bald, with a monkish fringe of grey hair above the ears. There are two broad categories of male Irish face, it seems to me – though they come in many variations. The first (and most common), is fleshy, good-humoured, and often a little florid from long and friendly acquaintance with Guinness and whiskey. The second kind is ascetic and even puritanical, with pale, lean cheeks and thin lips: the sort of face that's found in some Catholic priests. The man in the blue jacket is of the second type. He looks, in fact, like Father Darcy, a parish priest in the New Town of my boyhood, who was rather remote and chilling. Such phantom images will keep appearing, over the next few weeks. Father

Darcy's double has a tall black glass of Guinness in front of him; people drink it at all times of the day, and advertisements for it are everywhere, like a second national emblem.

I assure him I'm not lost; just getting to know the city.

'I see. You're a tourist. You sound like an Australian,' he says. 'Am I right?'

I confirm that I am, and he asks me have I been in Dublin before. A very long time ago, I say.

'Ah. You'll see changes,' he says. This is a flat, dry statement, made with no enthusiasm. He sips his Guinness, gazing into the rain on Merrion Row. Then he says: 'Yes, changes. Dear, dirty Dublin is gone.'

I express surprise. From what little I've seen, I say, it looks much the same: just a little cleaner.

'No, no, no,' he says. 'Go a little further, and you'll see – that's if you remember the old town. I've lived here all my life, and I'm telling you: the Dublin I knew has been destroyed. There's a little left – but precious little indeed.'

I ask him how this has come about.

He sighs, still looking out the window. He has a frown-line between his brows, and it deepens. 'Greed,' he says. 'We have greedy politicians, and greedy developers: a terrible combination. You'll have heard of the Irish miracle, and our wonderful, booming economy?' He glances at me, making a sound that parodies a laugh: a contemptuous expulsion of breath. He has a habit of sniffing briefly, wrinkling up his nose. 'That's what it's all about,' he says. 'They'll tear down anything to make money. Even here on the South Side, where some of our loveliest Georgian buildings were: they tore them down, even around Stephen's Green. The buggers pretended they were unsafe.'

His voice now takes on the hushed note of elegy; and his speech has that poetic cadence I've noticed in many Irish people. Perhaps it's in the unconscious; the inheritance of a bardic culture.

'Yes, down they went, the old buildings. All that's been preserved is Merrion Square and Fitzwilliam Square. Most of Lower Mount Street: gone. The Russell Hotel and the Hibernian Hotel: gone. The Theatre Royal on Hawkins Street, open for nearly two hundred years: gone. We got Hawkins House in its place – the most hideous bloody office block you'll ever see.' He drains his Guinness and then looks at me, sniffing twice in rapid succession. 'So you see, our old Dublin's being removed: soon it'll be all glass and concrete. And what's under the surface, in their new, rich Dublin? Muggers and bloody drug addicts. Watch where you walk at night.'

As he says 'our old Dublin', I hear the pain of real bereavement, real lost love. Yet he mourns, I feel sure, not just for Dublin but his youth; he's enthralled by that most terrible of masters, the past. He seems to read my thoughts, and smiles for the first time: thinly, like Father Darcy trying to be affable.

'But this isn't what you want to hear,' he says. 'You'll be wanting to enjoy what you can. There are still a few places left. Go and walk around Merrion Square – or walk along the quays by the Liffey. Ignore the glass boxes they've put up. Then you'll get glimpses of that dear old Dublin of ours – just here and there.'

Literature and revolt are the twin souls of Dublin. Two figures are its guardians, I find: James Joyce and Michael Collins.

Joyce is ubiquitous. Summoned up by the old man in Foley's, he reappears constantly as I walk the handsome streets of the Southeast: Dublin's still-Georgian core. In his broad-brimmed artist's hat and tinted spectacles, he's everywhere: featured in the windows of bookshops, and in displays in front of tourist offices – which offer a *Ulysses* map of Dublin. In the doorway of one bookshop I pass, he stands guard in the form of a life-size cut-out: black-clad and sinister as Count Dracula. On the rough old North Side, I'll later discover, his bronze statue stands in

Earl Street: hat tilted, leaning on his cane, jaunty as an old-fashioned stage-door Johnnie, except for the damaged, tormented eyes.

And I see what's happened. Joyce's posthumous fate, having exiled himself from Dublin in life, is to become a tourist logo; an icon of the city. For a patrician intellectual who loathed his native place, this seems the ultimate degradation. Dublin, on which he poured such scorn, has had the last laugh, embracing him with a vulgar enthusiasm as harrowing as its one-time rejection. I imagine his searing contempt – but perhaps I'm wrong. After all, Joyce was in love with vulgarity, and in love with the city he hated. Who knows, he may be amused and delighted, in whatever dimension of Purgatory he's found himself.

Today, at all events, Dublin glitters. An air of jubilation throbs in every byway – and who could begrudge it that, after the long decades of gloom? Despite the lament of the man in Foley's, the city seems less vandalized by the present than most other capitals in the world, and is certainly less invaded by today's high-rise boxes. I pass the railings of the Shelbourne, on the corner of Kildare Street and Stephen's Green: the 'big red house' where Thackeray stayed in 1842, and whose past, says Elizabeth Bowen, is related to that of Ireland – by which she largely means Ascendancy Ireland. On Easter Monday 1916, when the end of the Ascendancy world was signalled, Dublin society took tea as usual in the drawing room – until the entry of a stray bullet forced them into the writing room at the back. The red brick facade and cream window mouldings seem quite unchanged; the uniformed doorman in his peaked cap stands on the steps, like a flashback to 1910. In Stephen's Green across the road, a fresco of summer trees billows and waves: Edwardian.

The sun is out again. Surrounded by elegant fanlights and wrought-iron balconies, I move up Kildare Street. I pass the gates of Leinster House, and the rotunda of the National Museum. I pass the National Library, where a lonely young man in a Navy overcoat took refuge under the dome, long ago. I go on along Nassau Street and turn into Grafton Street, and so to College Green: past the railings of

Trinity College and the pillared curve of the Bank of Ireland, that was once the Ascendancy Parliament. And the pale grey stone of all these buildings has been so refreshed that they seem recently erected, and the eighteenth century looks new.

But when I go down Dame Street into the busy, commercial Southwest, and wander the mazes of Temple Bar, I begin to see what the old man in Foley's meant. This was once an old-style, disreputable bohemian quarter; now it's an expensive and fashionable pleasure district of restaurants and art galleries and coffee shops, crammed with tourists. This is the new Dublin. White wine is drunk here rather than Guinness, and black-clad advertising copywriters and arts executives and film people in their thirties dine on calamari and seared salmon and North African couscous, rather than Irish stew or mutton chops. Leopold Bloom seems very far away.

He was still truly present in that other, shabby Dublin of 1956, in the rain. Joyce had no memorials here then; his books were still frowned on and almost impossible to obtain, and his face didn't appear on posters, or in bookshop windows. But that other grey Dublin of the fifties was still Joyce's Dublin. Now, although he's everywhere – lurking near the brightly painted doorways and the new, fashionable bars with their plate glass windows and international names (Pravda; Zanzibar; Dakota), he is only a cutout. I doubt that his ghost is even present. And just for a moment, I begin perversely to miss those strange, echoing lanes that ran into the dark nineteenth century, and the urchins in braces and waistcoats, and quiet, mysterious little bars that were like private parlours, where men muttered secrets, and the shade of Eddy might appear.

I go back up to Grafton Street, looking for some lunch.

Grafton Street is now a smart, brick-paved shopping mall, along which flows a river of international tourists and backpackers and locals. The place resounds with street musicians: Irish folk singers, and three unshaven Romanian men with piano accordions, playing gypsy music.

One man is singing Pete St John's 'Dublin in the Rare Ould Times': a lament that might have been written for the man in Foley's:

'Fare thee well my Anna Liffey!
I can no longer stay,
And watch the new glass cages
That rise up along the Quay.
My mind's too full of memories,
Too old to hear new chimes,
I'm a part of what was Dublin
In the rare ould times . . . '

Flags hang from the brightly coloured Victorian buildings; Marks and Spencer is here, and The Body Shop, and many music shops and bookshops. I turn into Duke Street, and discover Davy Byrne's pub, whose sign is freshly painted and huge, so that tourists won't miss it. And they don't. Outside, at tables under umbrellas in the sun, sits the sort of international crowd to be found at sidewalk bistros in Rome, Paris or Milan.

I go in, looking for what's left of the quiet 'moral pub' that Davy Byrne ran, where Leopold Bloom ordered his cheese sandwich and glass of burgundy. It glimmers like a stage set in here, and hums with the life of fashionable Europe. People sit at small round tables, and on blue plush stools along the bar, sunglasses pushed back on their heads. They are served by handsome Irish waiters in uniform white shirts and black waistcoats, with smart navy aprons. The decor is tasteful, in shades of lemon and grey. I sit on an upholstered bench at a polished, rustic wooden table, and order a beer and a sandwich. Next to me, an elderly German in a suede jacket is attempting to enter into conversation with a slim young Italian woman in a sleeveless purple top that fashionably exposes her navel. In the doorway, two Swedish girls greet each other with the elation of Hollywood stars, and kiss. Opposite, at the bar, sit two Irish female executives in black suits, one of them engaged in urgent conversation on a mobile phone: children of the Celtic Tiger, and of the European Union that nurtures it.

Nosey Flynn and Paddy Leonard and Bantam Lyons, where are you? Not here; not here: old Davy Byrne's is gone.

Grafton Street again. I walk in the direction of the Liffey.

Images of Michael Collins, like those of Joyce, are everywhere in Dublin. The handsome, thin-lipped face under the high shock of hair, or shaded by the Irish National Army officer's cap he wore as Commander-in-Chief, is to be seen in bookshops; in the National Museum; in the General Post Office in O'Connell Street where he fought in 1916: where the Republic was born in blood, and bullet holes still pock-mark the pillars of the porch. His giant portrait, like an icon to be prayed to, looks down on the marble hall and the stamp counters, together with the Republic's other heroes, and the great bronze figure of the warrior Cuchulainn: dying, with the raven on his shoulder. But unlike Joyce's shade, that of Michael Collins is not locked in a past that has almost disappeared. That story whose climactic sequences began with the Easter Rising still continues, its last act in the North not yet played out. Its latest development is reported today in my copy of the *Irish Independent*. A final batch of Republican and Loyalist prisoners is soon to be released from the Maze Prison in Armagh – after which the hated Maze will close down.

Collins was often here in Grafton Street, moving about on his secret missions: the man Dublin Castle couldn't catch, or even identify. His is a shade that will not disappear; his glamour lingers over the city. I see him hurrying by in Grafton Street, glancing shrewdly into doorways. How can one not succumb to the Collins charisma, if one has any Irish genes? Cut off in his youth, like most mythical heroes, he's as difficult to resist now as he was to his followers in life. Fearless, honourable and unbreakable, the man who did more than any other to end British rule in Ireland was surely inspired as only a few leaders in history have been inspired. How my Grandmother Hurburgh must have revered him! And how Margaret O'Meara would have adored him! But he invented modern terrorism, his methods involving atrocity; so I'm divided in my mind about Michael Collins. I don't discuss these reservations with Brian, however. Some of his relatives were followers of Collins, and one of them was wounded in the Post Office, fighting beside James Connolly.

I'm almost to the corner of Nassau Street. Near here, according to Collins's biographer Tim Pat Coogan, was the Dublin institution known as Kidd's Back: the notorious bar off Grafton Street behind what is now the Berni Inn. When Kidd's Back was here, Grafton Street must have whirred with an underground tension; with a thin, drawn-out note of danger. This can't be heard any more; not here, among the flower stalls and street entertainers and music stores. Yet only a stone's throw away, in a bar-room that's long gone, the shades from 1920 are gathered: figures from that murderous and crucial year of Collins's struggle. There, in Kidd's Back, British intelligence officers and Dublin Castle spies drank unwittingly with some of the leaders of Collins's secret Republican Army: with Liam Tobin, Frank Thornton, Tom Cullen – and with Collins himself. And there, Coogan says, part of the war Collins was waging against the Castle was fought and won, as a set of extremely dangerous men played cat and mouse with each other.

Collins, I sometimes think, must have resembled some of my classmates at St Virgil's: those entirely Irish boys who were born on the other side of the world. In some of his moods, after all, he was still a rowdy, violent and thoughtlessly cruel boy himself. His habit of letting off steam through rough practical jokes; his way of mercilessly baiting some of his most loyal followers; his mad furniture-smashing and wrestling matches – all this brings back my school-mates. They could warm you with their smiles in one moment – smiles which had that wildly joyous quality I have come to see as peculiarly Irish – and set upon you in ecstatic rage the next. Life among Collins's men in off-hours – holed up in safe houses, meeting in favoured bars on the North Side – must have somewhat resembled life in the grounds of St Virgil's in the days of Ginger Donovan's gang – except that these men of the Irish Republican Army had much more deadly purposes, and carried revolvers. Did Collins perhaps resemble an adult and more intelligent Ginger Donovan? And was Eddy one of his men? The Big Fella seems not far away, as I walk towards the Liffey and the quays.

I once knew a man who had met Michael Collins – or rather, who encountered his *doppelgänger*. This was his earlier biographer, the writer Frank O'Connor, who lived through the struggle in the '20s, and was in the Irish Republican Army – but who never met Collins. In *My Father's Son*, O'Connor writes of a very strange experience he had, twelve years after Collins's death. He and Dr Richard Hayes were interviewing Joe O'Reilly: formerly one of Collins's most faithful soldiers, but one whom Collins had at times driven so mercilessly that he had caused him to break down in tears. When O'Connor and Hayes spoke with him, O'Reilly was President of the Irish Executive Council: in effect, Ireland's Prime Minister.

O'Connor asked him to tell them how Collins behaved when he had to order someone shot. At this, O'Reilly responded in an extraordinary manner. He seemed at first to collapse: 'something had gone wrong with him,' O'Connor says. Then he went into a state that resembled self-hypnosis – in which, it seemed, he actually *became* Michael Collins. He stamped about the room so savagely that it shook the house; threw himself on a sofa and pretended to read a newspaper; tossed it aside. Then he spoke in a coarse country voice:

'Jesus Christ Almighty, how often have I to tell ye . . . ' It was no longer Joe O'Reilly who was in the room. It was Michael Collins, and for close on two hours I had an experience that must be every biographer's dream, of watching someone I had never known as though he were still alive. Every gesture, every intonation was imprinted on O'Reilly's brain as if on tape.

I emerge on to Aston Quay beside the Liffey. As I do so, Frank O'Connor smiles at me quizzically, elbow propped on the table in front of him, supporting his head with his left hand, the fingers of that hand holding a smoking cigarette in a slanted yellow holder.

I knew him over a period of some four months, in 1961, at Stanford University in California. I had just published my first novel, and had won a fellowship to the Stanford Writing Centre. This involved attending a 'writing class' at the university twice a week over an academic year, together with a group of other young men and women who were aspiring novelists and short story writers, and most of whom had already published with some success. The group included Larry McMurtry and Ken Kesey — both of whom, a few years later, would have their novels filmed, and achieve that kind of fame which can only be found in the United States: Larry with *Last Picture Show,* Ken with *One Flew Over the Cuckoo's Nest.*

Few of us in the class believed that writing could be taught — I certainly didn't — but the Fellowship gave us a generous amount of time to write, and we enjoyed airing our work in front of each other. Sitting around a table in the big tutorial room, the Californian sun streaming through the windows, we would read excerpts from work in progress, and then face up to the criticisms of the group and the judgements of our tutor. In the second semester, our tutor was Frank O'Connor.

I knew little of him, then; I had read only one or two of his short stories. But strange things were murmured about him by my fellow-writers: he had been an IRA gunman, they said. Later I learned that he had indeed been a member of the IRA, and had fought on the Republican side in the Irish Civil War. Just as impressive was the fact that he'd been a protégé of W.B. Yeats, and had been a director of the Abbey Theatre. He had lived for many years in America.

He seemed friendly and mild enough, at first; but as we went on, he displayed a fiery and irascible side. He had probably reached a stage in his life where any sort of pretension bored and irritated him; and in the work of young writers in their twenties, pretension is inclined to flower. As well, my American colleagues were discovering and even pioneering the new values of the sixties – Ken Kesey in particular – and these did not enchant O'Connor, who proved to be pretty much of a Victorian in his beliefs.

As I walk along Wellington Quay, the reaches of the Liffey extending on my right, he is suddenly very vivid in my mind, printed there from those sessions that extended over many months, long ago. He sits at the end of the long table, smiling at us all in a somewhat bemused manner, like a man suddenly set down among the inhabitants of an alien planet. He screws a cigarette into the holder: a slightly stooped man with a California tan, sparse white hair swept back from a high forehead, and a blunt military moustache. He is fifty-eight, but looks older. His sports jackets and shirts are quiet and nondescript; his only note of flamboyance is a string tie, secured by the silver head of a Texas longhorn. His eyes, behind their spectacles, are a curious amber colour, and are usually narrowed; though he smiles easily and often, they retain the cold and cautious watchfulness that betrays the writer. He has a habit of propping his arm on the table and cupping his cheek in his hand, leaning a little sideways, his expression quizzical, the cigarette in its yellow holder tilted upwards in the fingers that enclose his cheek. The pose has a hint of the aesthete in it; but in every other respect, he looks anything but an aesthete: a tough, weathered-looking man who could be a retired military officer. It's easy to believe that he was a soldier for the IRA.

As time goes on, the efforts of the short story writers in the class seem particularly to exasperate him. His voice, with its hard Cork accent, is sounding in my head now, as I walk beside the Liffey.

'For God's sake, man, learn to tell a story! That's what it's all about! Where's the story in this thing you've just read? Some fine writing, yes – but what are you trying to *say*? Forget all this bloody symbolism, for Christ's sake. Tell us a *story*!' He snatches the cigarette holder from his mouth and looks from face to face: some of them amused, others resentful. 'Let me tell you what short story writing is all *about.*' He leans forward, grinning a little, his long teeth suddenly noticeable and predatory. 'A fella comes into a pub.' He pauses, making sure of our attention. 'And this fella goes up to a friend and grabs him by the lapels. "Listen!" he says. "I've got something to tell ye!" He can hardly wait to get it out; he's bursting with it; he's got a *story* to tell. And by God, he's got his friend's attention! Well, now: *that's* how it should be when you write a short story. *That's* what the reader should feel: that you've got a story to tell him, that you've grabbed him by the lapels from the first sentence, and you can't wait to get it out! Do you see?'

He looks around the faces. Some are smiling and nodding; others are set hard against him. He sighs, and draws on his cigarette.

O'Connor and I got on well, at first. This was because we two seemed to have more in common than either of us did with my American class mates. An Irishman and an Australian – though of different generations – shared, it seemed, very similar values and associations. Again and again, as literary debate took place, it set us apart from my American fellows in the class – nearly all of whom I'd come to like, all of whom were of my age, and whose company I enjoyed. As they defended the new permissiveness of the sixties, or a rambling and formless writing style deriving from Jack Kerouac, O'Connor's eyes would meet mine, down the table; we would smile at each other in silent agreement, and he'd shake his head. Then he'd say: 'What do *you* think, Chris?'

He could be pretty sure that my views would match his own; but there came a time when they did not.

He had reached a peak of irritation with the short story writers – the novelists didn't trouble him so much – and he came up with a plan. They should submit proposed plots to him; only when he found these satisfactory would they then go ahead and write their stories. And if they were not satisfactory, he would suggest plots they could work on. In this way, he would teach them to master their craft.

But this proposal caused open revolt – in which I joined. Having discussed it heatedly at a number of late-night parties, over our flagons of Californian wine, we decided that Frank must be told he'd gone too far: he could not tell a writer what to write; he could not make him work on a plot that was not of his own devising. We were all agreed, the novelists included – and the revolt took place at the next session, with Larry McMurtry stating our case, in his soothing Texas drawl.

It was 'pernicious', he told Frank, to ask writers to write to a prescription. We all respected him, Larry said; but nevertheless, we objected to such a method.

Frank was clearly shaken. Staring from one to the other of us, his expression one of outrage, he defended his position. He had been invited here to teach us the craft of writing – a craft at which he was acknowledged to be a master – and this was what he was trying to do. What possible objection could there be to that? One by one, the members of the class answered him, giving their objections. Finally, he looked at me.

'And what's your view, Chris?'

Reluctantly, but with the unthinking arrogance of my twenties, I gave my answer. I agreed with the others, I said. More: I didn't even believe that the craft of writing could be taught. It could only be won by private struggle.

He stared at me down the table as though at a betrayer, the cigarette holder poised in his fingers, like a dart he was reluctant to throw. The hurt in his eyes has often come back to me, over the years. Later, we apologised in a body; but he was not the same after that: he became subdued. And his fellow-feeling with me would not return. At the end of that year at Stanford he had a stroke, and returned here to Dublin. Five years later, he died.

I pause on Wellington Quay, and lean on the stone parapet. I stare up the river, looking towards the arches of the Capel Street Bridge, with its lacy iron railings. The lines of old buildings recede into the distance on each side of the Liffey; small on the horizon is the green copper dome of the Four Courts. The sun has been withdrawn again: the sky has gone white, and the Liffey is gunmetal silver. The tide is out; black flats of mud extend below the wall, and the seagulls wheel and squabble there as they did when I walked beside this parapet with Nora Devlin: birds that seem always the same birds; birds that exist outside Time. The man in Foley's was exaggerating: Dublin is little changed, at least along the Liffey. Its true, metallic colours have returned, with the hiding of the sun: colours of mournfulness, and of a cold and sourceless excitement which would give me no rest, if I lived here; which perhaps gives no rest to any of its children, and whispers always of escape.

I make my way back to O'Connell Bridge. I cross the river into O'Connell Street, and take a bus into the North Side. I'm bound for the Dublin Writers' Museum, which Brian has urged me to visit. It's at 18 Parnell Square: an eighteenth century townhouse with an imposing entrance hall and pale, decorative plasterwork in the Adam style. I move through peaceful, near-empty rooms, among glass cases of literary remains: those of Wilde; Shaw; Liam O'Flaherty. Here are relics of Yeats, and the manuscript of a poem he wrote at Coole. And here, without warning, are relics of Frank O'Connor, lying under the glass like laboratory specimens.

So here is what's left, besides his published work. Here are his spectacles – which seem to look very old-fashioned, like spectacles from the nineteenth century. Here is his pipe. I never saw him smoke a pipe: where is the yellow cigarette holder? I stare at these few artefacts, and at the text that identifies O'Connor as one of Ireland's greatest writers; and my eyes fill with tears. How archaic they look, these personal possessions of a man I once briefly knew and liked: as archaic as those fragments belonging to Yeats or Shaw! And I want once again to tell Frank I'm sorry; to take my silly speech back.

But now and for ever, this is too late. Frank O'Connor, like William Butler Yeats, like Michael Collins, like all past deeds and omissions, like the seagulls on the Liffey, exists in a dimension outside Time, never to be reached.

Eight o'clock. Brian and I walk up Baggot Street from our hotel. We're bound for O'Donoghue's, the pub at 15 Merrion Row.

Brian is still in his shorts, since his lost bag won't arrive until tomorrow; but although it's grown chilly, he seems not to feel the cold. He's full of anticipation, approaching this famous folk pub where he so often sang in the sixties; but he also has misgivings.

'I believe it's a tourist spot, nowadays,' he says. 'Most of the great singers I knew are gone. Don't expect too much.'

But when we go through the door into the bar, he's reassured, looking around him. He smiles delightedly.

'Nothing's changed,' he says. 'The old place hasn't altered since I sang here.'

So here is O'Donoghue's – famous on both sides of the Atlantic. I've never been in a pub quite like it. The immediate impression is one of smallness, age, and darkness. The dark front bar, narrow as a hallway, looks centuries old, and is crowded to the walls – walls which are a dim mustard-yellow: a colour not of this century. The ceiling is very low: it has perhaps been a nicotine colour once, but age and smoke have turned it almost black. Black and serious, it presses down, informing us that we've entered the past. Dark, ancient wood is everywhere: overhead beams and wall panelling, pickled by the tobacco smoke of years. Everything seems pickled here; that any redecoration has ever taken place seems unlikely. There are framed photographs and drawings of folk musicians around the walls, which I've not yet had time to examine. No sound of music at present. A poster says: *Dublin's Finest*. Another states simply: *Probably the Best Pub in the World*.

We edge our way through the crush, making for the long bar counter. This is of polished wood, with a low wooden rail running along the top, on the customers' side. A fair-haired, athletic-looking barman is at work here, moving with brisk efficiency: he looks friendly, but hard. Laughing, animated faces are all around us. Little lights glow everywhere in the gloom, through a screen of cigarette smoke: the new age's anathema on tobacco seems not to have been heard of in Ireland, and certainly not in O'Donoghue's. Brian orders drinks: a Jameson's whiskey for me and a Guinness for himself. He's devoted to Guinness, and says they only know how to pour it in Ireland. The barman lets it stand for a long time, before topping it up by degrees in the correct manner: a process as serious as the Japanese tea ceremony.

As I drink my Jameson's, everything around us is both deeply strange, and deeply familiar. The inverted bottles of spirits with black taps, suspended from a shelf along the big mirror at the back of the bar. An advertisement there saying: *Hackler: Pure Irish Spirit*. The red fluorescent tubing running along the top of the mirror, adding its glow to the larger glow. The many sourceless lights reflected there, in an intimate, storied twilight. I was here once, long ago. I know this looking at the mirror, which carries evidence of the pub's transatlantic nature. Police badges from all over America are fixed on the glass, donated, no doubt, by Irish-American cops on holiday. *Boston Police; New Jersey; County of Nassau; New York; Border Patrol*: runes from that great destination of the nineteenth and early twentieth century emigrants; the promised land of the Irish. Today, in this prosperous new era of the European Union, the Irish are coming back the other way; coming home. But just for now, in the dark of O'Donoghue's, we seem to be sitting in the old, dangerous, New York-linked Dublin of Michael Collins and Liam Tobin and Emmet Dalton – suspended in a dimension made from memory's deepest circles.

Music begins. A group has appeared at a table by the entrance: a woman playing a fiddle, a man with a squeeze-box and another man on mandolin. They are playing 'Carrickfergus': the music comes dimly through waves of voices and laughter that don't diminish, and Brian and I move nearer, across the bar. We come to the wall at the back, and are able to examine the framed drawings and photographs there: singers from the great days.

'Here they all are,' Brian says. 'Jesus – I'm surrounded by ghosts.'

His voice has dropped to a tone of awe, which is as close as he comes to sadness. He gazes up at the pictures like a man coming suddenly on old family photographs; and he points to them one by one.

'There's Tom Clancy; and there's his brother Paddy. Both of them dead, God rest them. And there's Bobby Clancy – *he's* not dead; still going strong, and ye'll meet him when we get down to Tipperary.' He points to a drawing of a bearded, pugnacious-looking man with a tower of curly red hair. 'And there's my friend Luke Kelly, from the Dubliners. Jesus, yes – there's poor Luke.'

Dead? I ask.

'Yes: dead of a brain tumour. And I'll tell ye what, Chris – you're looking at one of the best folk singers Ireland ever had. Every musician will tell you that: there was never a singer in Ireland better than Luke Kelly. Did I ever tell ye how he came with us on our honeymoon?'

'On your honeymoon?'

'True! When Phyllis and I got married in Galway, the Dubliners came to our wedding. Phyllis and I were booked on the Mail Boat from Dunleary next day, to go to England – so on the first night of our honeymoon we were to stay in a pub just outside Dublin. And Luke offered to drive us there. But we were drinking along the way, and things got a bit confused – and the car ran out of petrol. I don't know what happened to Luke at that stage, but Phyllis and I spent our honeymoon night in a barn, in the hay. Next morning we went and found the car – and Luke Kelly's mop of orange hair came up out of the back seat. "Jesus," he says. "That's the last focking time I come on someone else's honeymoon!" '

He laughs with me, and drains his Guinness. Then he looks at me solemnly. 'And I'll tell ye something else. The night of the wedding in

Galway, someone stole Phyllis's handbag, with all our money in it for the honeymoon in England. The lot. And the Dubliners took round the hat, and got seventy-five pounds together, and gave it to us as a wedding present. And Liam Clancy was there, and asked me how much more was needed to make up the rest. When I told him, he peeled off the lot in American dollars, and gave it to me. "Have a good honeymoon," he said. That's the sort of fellas they were.'

A man has loomed up beside us: short, massive, barrel-chested, in a checked shirt and leather jacket.

'Brian! Brian Mooney! It's been bloody years!'

He extends his hand, smiling at Brian with the joy of discovery. His large face is red in the half-light; his straw coloured hair is streaked with grey.

'Denis!' Brian says, and grasps the outstretched hand with the same easy joy. He turns to me. 'Denis is the best fiddler you're ever likely to hear. We did a few gigs together, in the old days.'

They exchange news for a time; then Brian says: 'Do you play in here, at all?'

'Now and then,' Denis says. 'But it's not the same, y' know. Dublin's mostly for the bloody tourists these days, and so is O'Donoghue's. I'm just over here from New York.'

'Are ye, now? Is there plenty of work there?'

'Plenty, plenty. They still love the music there, and they pay well. You should come over, Brian.'

'I will, some day. Right now we're travelling around Ireland, Chris and me. We'll go to Galway in a few days, and I'll look up old friends there. I'm planning to do a bit of pub singing and busking. Do ye know if the music scene's still good?'

'Aye, it is – I was there not long ago. You'll find plenty of places where the *craic* is good, in Galway. Give them my love in Taafe's hotel.'

'I will, I will. I'll be singing in Taafe's, right enough.'

When Denis has moved on, Brian says: *'That's* where you'll hear great music, Chris: in Galway! I've got so many friends there in the music game. And when we get to Tipperary, and you meet Bobby and Moira Clancy, they'll take us to little pubs where the really great stuff is still to be heard: not just in Tipperary, but in Kilkenny and Waterford. Just wait and see: it'll knock you out, I promise ye! Ah, you'll really like Bobby – I can guarantee that!' His eyes shine; rocking on his heels, he runs a hand through his tangled white curls, gazing at these prospects with the endearing excitement of a child. His unfailing elation at life's bonuses is something that age can't extinguish.

We have a little over a month in Ireland, and most of it will be spent in the West and the Lower Shannon: in Galway, Clare and Tipperary in particular. Galway is the county of Brian's family and ancestors, and it was in the West that he spent so many of his adult years; there, he'll visit his past and his friends. We discuss now how long we'll stay in Dublin, and when we'll leave for Galway. In two or three days, we decide.

'I don't know many people in Dublin, any more,' Brian says. He looks around the bar, and back at the pictures on the wall. Then he says again: 'I'm surrounded by ghosts.'

V

Brian has a relative in Dublin he wants us to visit: his first cousin, Freddy O'Donovan. Freddy and his wife Sally live in Howth, the seaside resort on the north of Dublin Bay. Now elderly, Freddy has been a successful theatrical producer, Brian tells me, and still produces an Irish show at Carnegie Hall in New York each year. Brian phones him from the hotel, and we're invited to pay a visit, late the following afternoon.

I know little of Howth, except that W.B. Yeats was a boy there, that he loved to wander on Howth Head, and that he once spent a day walking on its cliffs with the fatal Maude Gonne, and wrote 'The White Birds' in memory of that day:

I would that we were, my beloved, white birds on the foam of the sea!

Today, I learn from Brian, Howth has become a favoured residential area for Dublin's wealthy. I have no particular expectation of it. But the world of the *Sluagh Sidhe*, the people of the Faery Hills, is often to be glimpsed past the borderlands of banality; and this is the way it proves at Howth.

We catch the Dart, the electric train that runs around Dublin Bay. Howth Head – or the Hill of Howth – is at the northernmost limit of the bay, and I'm travelling in this direction for the first time. Long-ago Dun Laoghaire is in the opposite direction, to the south.

When we reach Howth station, Brian leads me out into bright afternoon sun, and we set off along an esplanade. It's five o'clock. A huge, clear blue sky: bright as though it were two o'clock in Sydney – and I suddenly recall how long the light lasts in this latitude. Broad spaces of lawn beside the esplanade, dotted with benches and a small number of people. Tall white lamp standards retreating into level distance, like the masts of the boats here; like all such lamp standards in all such seaside places. On our left, the harbour and the fishing boats. A marina, and a long stone breakwater. The marina, filled with the white nodding masts of pleasure craft, is like other marinas everywhere.

We walk north, Brian leading the way. Last night his missing suitcase arrived at the hotel, and he's been able to don more clothes: a long-sleeved shirt, a checked woollen jacket and jeans. Since the Irish summer is never really hot, I'm glad to see him warmly clad at last. He remembers only vaguely where Freddy's place is, but is sure he'll find it. I ask him the address, only to find that he doesn't know the name of the street, or the number of the house. He's navigating from memory.

'It won't be hard to find though,' he says. 'It's called Balscadden House. It was once W.B. Yeats's house. There's a plaque outside the door.'

I look at him in surprise: he's not told me this until now. This must be one of the cottages to which Yeats's father moved the family when William was about sixteen. I begin to look forward to visiting Freddy somewhat more than I did.

We walk. A line of commercial buildings on our right is overlooked by a high green ridge, up which more houses climb. Far at the end of the esplanade is the blunt-nosed Hill of Howth, where the young Yeats roamed in solitude, and where he walked with Maude Gonne. A squat brown Martello tower dozes on its top, against the sky. Apart from this famous headland, little here interests me; Howth seems like all such seaside resorts. But suddenly, everything changes.

Brian turns into a road that goes uphill onto the ridge. It's a steep, clean, narrow little bitumen road, running in a long curve. On its right-hand side, rising almost vertically from the bitumen, is a tall, grassy bank, which soon becomes a hill: a high, rearing, dark green ridge, empty of trees. On the top of this, standing against the sky, pleasant white villas can be seen, of a style suggesting the 1930s. We're walking on the left-hand side of the road, on a narrow stone footpath; and many of the houses here are hidden by high walls that stand flush with the path. Also set hard on the path are little cottages, probably of the last century, with prettily painted front doors and fanlights. I assume them to be modest, but Brian tells me that all of them would be expensive to buy. Certainly there's the odd, safe quiet here of a wealthy district. And yet it doesn't feel wealthy: just peaceful and removed, on its narrow little road. A car hardly ever passes.

In the middle of the bend, we come to a break between the houses on the left, spanned by a low stone wall. Beyond it is a scene whose beauty brings me to a halt. We are looking out over the Irish Sea. Small, racing waves are breaking on the rocks of a quiet little cove in the sun:

on bright, cream and orange stones that look like granite, a few feet below. On the far side of the cove is a long, low headland of rich green, lit in patches by the sun, with round, towering rock formations rising at the end, like prehistoric monuments. A small number of two-storeyed villas and long white cottages are scattered among the bushes, looking out to sea. Freddy O'Donovan's is one of these, Brian tells me; that's where we're making for. He asks me if I want to move on. No, I tell him, you go on, I'll catch you up.

I don't want to move from the wall. I'm surrounded here by a spell that's created by a change in the light, and I stare out over the cove and the sea, as Brian strolls on up the road. The Irish Sea! Brilliant blue-green in the delicate northern sun, it's lit up in patches like the headland, and its racing, foaming white-caps are transfigured by the light. The light of Ireland is always changing, but this change has crept in unnoticed. It's not the light of sunset; sunset has not begun. And yet the change is there. Clear and glassy as the light of vision, it floods cove and headland and houses in a warm, amazing radiance; in a pale yellow glow that's more Mediterranean than northern. Palm trees in gardens add to this illusion; and Ireland, suddenly, seems not quite a northern country. Startling, this balmy Mediterranean atmosphere, this blue-green sea, these villas flashing white as the waves. The glow holds the cove and its rocks and green headland in a daze: I'm in Ireland, yet not in Ireland; in a zone where north and south miraculously mingle.

A pretty woman of middle age is coming down the path, taking a spaniel for a walk on a lead. She smiles at me, and I smile back. People still seem to do this in Ireland, as country people do in Australia: one is not an object of suspicion. She stops a little way down the wall, and stares at the sea as I'm doing. We don't speak, and are perfectly comfortable. But it's time to move, and catch up with Brian. I walk off up the path.

The empty road continues to go in a curve, higher and higher. Still dark green, the grass-covered ridge towers above me on the right. And I find that I love this place, loving everything I see.

As I climb, I seem to be moving towards some private region of joy. Why? I can't yet say, but feel that I'll soon understand. Brian is still not visible ahead: the road is empty. The spell of the light isn't broken; its radiance deepens. It flares in the grass against the sky, picking out tawny tips on top of the dark green ridge. But now the ridge ends abruptly, falling in a cliff behind the roof of a house. I crane my neck to look up there. High, very high, Atlantic gulls wheel in the air above the ridge, and their cold, hungry cries come down to me. I go on, and sense that I'm nearing the top of the hill.

And here are the territories of the *Sidhe*. Looking ahead up the road, I recognise them immediately. To say that I've seen this place before would be wrong. Rather, I've expected it. Earlier landscapes in my life – landscapes which resembled it – have merely been its heralds: its distant, imperfect variations. There's nothing remarkable about it; it's simply an empty rise of yellow grass, standing on top of the hill against the sky: a low, dry-grassed rise, dotted with green bushes and heather. In my childhood, it stood on the eastern limits of Hobart, in a place where the town ended. It was called Lutana; but Lutana was only its phantom. Now, here is the true rise; and its grass glows with an uncanny tinge of gold. The little road has levelled out here; it runs as though through a tunnel between the walls of the houses on one side and the last of the steep green bank on the other, to disappear directly into the rise. Or rather, it gives the illusion of doing so: it no doubt turns a bend up there, to run out of sight. But the power poles beside it all seem to lead to the rise; and the sky has hugely opened up.

Ireland has a legendary frontier. There, where the real world ends, the four other worlds begin: the world of the *Sidhe*, the Many-Coloured Land, the Land of Wonder, and the Land of Promise. Here at Howth, I have come to the no-man's-land between. I know better, though, than to try and cross it. I don't set foot on its tawny grass. Instead, I follow the little road around the bend.

Brian is waiting for me, standing expectantly. He smiles, and calls out: 'We're here.'

At the end of the road, above a Tudor-style mansion of red brick, rises a round, sienna coloured hill of rock and heather, one of those monuments I saw across the cove. On our left is a long, high white wall beside the path. The sea is hidden. A shining new car passes; then the place is silent again. Brian points to the long white wall. This is Freddy's place, he tells me.

But no house is to be seen: there is only the long white wall, with a segment of grey-tiled roof rising just above it at the end. Brian leads me down there, and points triumphantly to a low, varnished door in the wall. A plate set just above it reads: *Balscadden House*. And a plaque in the wall beside it reads:

W.B. Yeats, poet, lived here, 1880–1883.
'I have spread my dreams under your feet;
Tread softly because you tread on my dreams.'

When Freddy O'Donovan opens the door and ushers us off the street into his hidden house, I have the somewhat comical sense of being taken into the Hill of Faery. He's a suitable guardian: a heavy, jovial, ruddy-faced man with a mane of greying brown hair and a theatre man's vivacity.

'Come in and welcome to you both,' he says. 'Sally will be with us in a moment. Come! It's so good to see you, Brian.'

We find ourselves in the hallway of a rambling, tastefully decorated Victorian cottage that smells of flowers and cooking. Freddy leads the way through a kitchen, and out an open door. And here, with a theatrical flourish, is the sea again, framed by a courtyard garden.

The courtyard is shielded by the wall that hides the street. Flowers and herbs and tomatoes grow in pots and tubs, and an old brown sheepdog lies on a cane chair, next to some climbing nasturtiums. He raises his head and wags his tail. A charming courtyard; once again, there's a sense of the Mediterranean. The cottage clings to the steep green headland we saw as we came up the hill, and looks straight onto Dublin Bay, which flares and unfurls below us, blue-green and mild. In the foreground, at the base of the courtyard's frame, the weird, globed heads of artichokes nod in a faint breeze, the colour of their spiky leaves matching that of the water. Out on the horizon is the humped, rocky islet called Ireland's Eye – streaked with bright green grass, a Martello tower tiny on its end. On our left is Howth Head again, standing quite close, and the edges of Howth village, and the breakwater going out into the harbour. Far beyond, on the other side of the bay, is the faint, grey-blue line of the Wicklow Mountains.

As Freddy is pointing out these features, his wife Sally joins us. 'They say on especially clear days you can see the mountains of Wales from here,' she says.

'I've never seen them,' Freddy tells us, 'but Sally claims she has. That's because she's Welsh, and *wants* to see them.'

'It's true,' Sally says to us, and laughs. She's a pleasant, dark-haired woman, with a soft voice. 'I've seen them; I know I have. But even if I've imagined it, I've still enjoyed it – so what's the difference?'

'Come and have a drink,' Freddy says. 'And something to eat.'

We're taken into the house again and led along to the sitting room, where we're seated in easy chairs and given glasses of white wine and salmon sandwiches.

'And so you and Brian are cousins?' I say to Freddy.

'That's right,' he says. 'My mother and Brian's were sisters.'

'Aye – and they were cousins to Paddy McGrath,' Brian says. 'Do ye remember, Freddy? Paddy fought in the Post Office in 1916, and was wounded there. He was shot in the head, and lost his right eye. And him only sixteen.'

'Well now, I knew he fought there,' Freddy says. 'But I thought he got that wound from the Black and Tans, later on. I was told they raided Paddy's house after the Rising, and found a British officer's cap there, and they thought Paddy must have killed him – so they beat him up pretty badly.'

'That happened too,' Brian says. 'But Paddy lost his eye in the Post Office, I'm sure of it. My mother told me that James Connolly was wounded at the same time, and he saw Paddy lying on some sandbags, and said: "Bring that lad over here." And they did, and laid him next to James Connolly, and Connolly comforted him – Paddy being so young.'

Freddy looks at me and smiles. 'Everyone's got a different story about so many things,' he says. 'You can never be sure, with Irish history. But the truth of 1916 is in the Yeats poem. A terrible beauty was born – no denying that.'

'And did Yeats really live here?' I ask. 'Or is that a myth too?'

'No, no, that's true enough,' Freddy says. 'He lived here with his family as a schoolboy. I've made his bedroom into my study. Come along and I'll show you.'

He leads me off into a large, airy Victorian room with green-striped wallpaper and a marble fireplace and glass doors at the end opening onto a verandah. Through these doors, beyond the verandah, the sea appears again, and the Eye of Ireland. I can see the little breeze moving through the tops of some bushes. The yellow in the light is deepening, now; it's nearly seven o'clock. There's a big oak table and a desk in here, and fine Victorian straight-backed chairs, and many framed photographs on the walls. Freddy is in most of these, together with famous show business figures of the recent past: Paul Newman; Bob Hope; Frank Sinatra. He points some of them out to me; but I'm distracted by that presence who lived and breathed in this room as a boy of sixteen.

He'd already begun to write his first verses. Did he stare out from the verandah to the distant Eye of Ireland? Did he ponder on this poignant, blue-green bay where so many raiders landed to set their mark on Ireland: Gael and Viking and Norman? Did he sit where Freddy has placed his desk? Was it in this room that he first began to dream of the host of the air?

The breeze outside, stirring in the bushes and the line of nodding artichokes, now seems to me a magic breeze. It comes, I feel sure, from the little dry-grassed rise beyond the road; and I'm remembering that *Sidhe* is Gaelic for both 'faery' and 'wind'; and that the tribes of Dana, according to Yeats, journeyed in the whirling air:

The host is riding from Knocknarea
And over the grave of Clooth-na-Bare;
Caoilte tossing his burning hair,
And Niamh calling Away, come away:
Empty your heart of its mortal dream.

VI

The time may be coming, in the century just being born, when Ireland's ancient, drawn-out hatreds – those hatreds which still rack the Six Counties of the North – will simply cease to matter in the Republic.

There are signs that this may already be the case where many of the Republic's younger generation are concerned. And though Irish traditional music still thrives here, the rebel songs that the Clancys and the Dubliners sang in the sixties have been quietly dropped from radio airplay; there's a policy of muffling the heritage of bitterness while the peace process continues in Belfast, and while the IRA and the Loyalists have put aside their guns.

The ancient, patriotic struggle has taken on the character of a dream. But it's a dream that lingers, and will not yet vanish, no matter how the world may weary of it, and grow sickened by its carnage. Only now, in this July, is the long, agonizing, undeclared war reaching its climax, with the uneasy ceasefire still in place in the North, the peace talks deadlocked at Stormont, and the IRA still refusing to give up its arms.

Tim Pat Coogan, the journalist and historian who is the author of a richly detailed biography of Michael Collins, is the world's foremost authority on Sinn Fein and its political wing, the IRA, and on the history of their struggle. He has studied the movement for over thirty years, and has interviewed its leaders and its soldiers in dedicated detail, in their homes, in their pubs, and in their reeking prison cells. I have an introduction to him; he lives at Dalkey, on the southern tip of Dublin Bay.

On the afternoon following our visit to Howth, I leave Brian to finish his painting of the Grand Canal, and board the Dart again. The train moves south around the bay, in the opposite direction from yesterday. As it does so, I glance through Tim Pat Coogan's massive and newly updated book, *The IRA*. That he's a passionate Republican and nationalist is clear; and although his book takes an objective standpoint, and doesn't condone IRA atrocities such as the bombing of women and children, what comes through is his deep emotional involvement with Sinn Fein, and his understanding of their passions and ideals.

I hope to discuss the current situation in the North with him, and what prospect he now sees for a final resolution there. And I hope as well to hear his opinions on those figures who still haunt the countryside of Tasmania: John Mitchel in particular, who broke with Daniel O'Connell and many of his Young Ireland comrades in rejecting the way of non-violence, and so anticipated the Fenians, and Sinn Fein. It was Mitchel, the Protestant gentleman, raging against the effects of the Famine, who called on the people to resist paying rents, to arm themselves, and to prepare for guerilla war: to tear up railway lines, and 'lay the axe to the root of this rotten and hideous Irish landlordism, that we might see how much would come down along with it'. Mitchel, transported as a dangerous terrorist for his writings and speeches, though he never took up the gun himself, was the ideological father of Michael Collins, and was seen as such by Sinn Fein. In O'Connell Street this morning, I discovered a statue of William Smith O'Brien, looking noble – but how many people in the street still know who he is? And is Mitchel still remembered here? These are things I want to ask Tim Pat Coogan.

Today is overcast, with showers that come and go. I look out the train window at the bay: metallic, this afternoon, and drained of colour. On its far side, tall smoking chimneys and cranes. The old grey industrial world; the hard-hearted landscape of fifty years ago, as we pass Dun Laoghaire and the East Pier. The past reaches out for me briefly, with its thin and coldly thrilling fingers; Nora Devlin must be a grandmother now.

I open a copy of the *Irish Times* I bought at the station. By coincidence, yesterday was something of a landmark in the history of the struggle in the North, and the front page headline reads: *Prisoner releases signal end of the Maze*. The story deals with the freeing of the final batch of convicted terrorists from the ill-famed Maze Prison in County Armagh – otherwise known as Long Kesh. Under the terms of the Good Friday Agreement, and as part of the peace negotiations that continue in Belfast, gunmen from both sides of the conflict – Ulster Protestant Loyalists and the Catholic Republicans of the IRA – are being set free, and the Maze will now close. A colour picture shows Sean Kelly, a tough-looking IRA man, embracing a woman admirer. Kelly is the Shankill Road bomber, who was responsible for the deaths of nine people.

Peter Mandelson, the Northern Ireland Secretary, is quoted as saying that he realises the releases are a 'bitter pill' for many to accept, but that the peace process will justify the pain. Extraordinary scenes of rejoicing are described, as men whom the *Irish Times* reporter describes as 'Loyalist cut-throat killers' and 'IRA sniper teams' are greeted outside the prison by their supporters and loved ones – in the case of the

IRA men, with champagne and confetti. The reporter states that the Loyalist inmates tried to disguise themselves, but that the Republicans made no such attempts. The IRA men who were released included the Canary Wharf bomber and the Baltic Exchange bomber. The IRA 'officer commanding' in the prison is reported as saying: 'We will walk free from this prison camp proud Republicans, unbowed and unbroken'.

A separate piece features interviews with relatives of the victims of the terrorists from both sides. A man whose daughter was killed in a bar in Greysteel by Loyalist Ulster Freedom Fighters says that such 'vicious thugs' should never be released. A young woman who lost her mother and father in the Shankill Road bombing blames the politicians for releasing Sean Kelly, whom she calls 'a psychopathic murderer'. Ultimately, she says, he will go before his judge and rot in hell.

It's raining when I get out at Dalkey station. I put up an inadequate little umbrella I bought in Dame Street, and set out to walk to Tim Pat Coogan's house in Castle Park Road, following directions he gave me on the phone. I find myself in the streets of a prosperous seaside suburb, filled with trees and gardens and stone walls. The big, gabled villas have a look of the thirties, as those in Howth did. Tim Pat Coogan's house, when I reach it, is pleasant-looking and rambling, and stands above the railway line. It's called *Eventually*. The name is on the gate, which I push open to walk down a garden path accompanied by a friendly Alsatian.

Tim Pat Coogan and I sit in big armchairs in a spacious, well-lit room lined with bookshelves: the room of a busy journalist and man of affairs. Papers are piled high on a table, and there's a phone on one wall which he frequently has to answer, taking calls from Dublin and New York. He's a large, rumpled man with a mane of thick grey hair and a broad, genial face. He pours two glasses of an excellent Beaujolais, making me immediately feel welcome, in the Irish manner. The rain has ceased for the moment, and a window at the far end of the room frames a scene so seductive my eyes keep going back to it. There are big trees in the garden out there, and their masses of shining wet leaves are filtering the rays of transient sunlight, creating an unreal radiance. Tim Pat follows my gaze.

'Lovely light,' he says.

His books are all about politics, and deadly, protracted violence and slaughter, and show little awareness of nature; yet he notices the light. It's something I'll encounter constantly in Ireland: an awareness and appreciation of the natural world, in people from whom one wouldn't normally expect it.

I tell him of my interest in the Young Irelanders, and of the relics they left in Tasmania. I ask him about Mitchel and his comrades. How well are they remembered?

'Well, they're *known*, of course,' Tim Pat says. 'Mitchel's *Jail Journal* is still known, and the Sinn Fein people would refer to him with approval, in the same way that they do to James Connolly and Wolfe Tone. Mitchel stood for the use of force against the British, and they respect that. But things moved on, after the Young Irelanders made their try. Sinn Fein is a grass-roots, proletarian movement – even though it does have support from the professional classes in Ireland – and the Young Irelanders were mainly gentry. Sinn Fein held the view that gentlemanly revolution wasn't enough. The Young Irelanders did leave a lasting heritage, though. The Irish flag, for instance – the green, orange and white tricolour – which Smith O'Brien and his delegation brought back from France in 1848: a gift from Lamartine. And Thomas Davis's Republican ideas were important. But it's not a very *explored* area, Young Ireland. And a lot of our historians dismiss them, today.'

I ask him why that is.

'The Young Irelanders are still victims of the British propaganda aimed at them at the time,' he says. 'The London papers set out to make them look ridiculous, calling the Ballingarry rising the Battle of Widow McCormack's Cabbage Patch, and Smith O'Brien the King of Munster – you know the sort of thing. And we now have a group of revisionist Irish historians who treat them in a similar way – calling them ineffectual, and their attempt at force misguided. They see Mitchel as dangerous in his ideas. They're quite comfortable, these Dublin academics, and doing nicely, lately – and they tend to disparage the sword. The fashion now is for normalization, as it's called, to help the peace process. It's been called "filtering out the trauma". So they don't see Mitchel as a hero. But to the IRA he was a hero. Their newspaper in the fifties and sixties carried the same name as his: *The United Irishman.* It occupied the office in Gardiner Street where the IRA's Dublin Brigade had its headquarters, and where Michael Collins used to hold his assignations.'

I turn the conversation to the present, asking Tim Pat Coogan for his views on the IRA today. The release of the terrorists from the Maze Prison is in my mind, and the fury of the families of their victims. I put it to him – choosing my words somewhat carefully – that a good many people in the world now see the military arm of Sinn Fein as callous killers and psychopaths. What would his answer be to such people?

He fills our glasses again and sits back, his face neutral.

'I'm an Irishman,' he says. 'To me that's a matter for pride rather than apology, and I've lived with these issues. The IRA are rough and bloody men – no-one would deny that. But they are first and foremost idealists, with an idealism so high it's their main motivation. People talk about them as a Mafia – but all the money they steal from banks or extort goes to the war effort. That's not a Mafia. When I've gone into the kitchens of IRA leaders, I've seen precious little sign of wealth. They're highly disciplined, and any individual member who tried extortion for his own gain would very likely be knee-capped. As to atrocities – the IRA see atrocities as civilian casualties in a war. And what they've never ceased to argue is that they are soldiers, not criminals. Their view is the traditional Republican view: that since the British invaded and occupied their land, the Irish have a moral right to wage war. That's what Bobby Sands and his comrades died on hunger strike for, in the H Blocks of Long Kesh. It was in Long Kesh in 1980 and '81 that they showed the world the Provisional IRA's capacity for endurance. They were prepared to suffer torture and finally to die for their cause. And the death of Bobby Sands was as powerful in its effect in Northern Ireland and the world in general as the 1916 Rising.'

I ask him about the situation at present. Is the IRA doing all it can to achieve a final peace?

He says he believes it is, and that Gerry Adams is now a moderate, who is exerting all his powers to keep the negotiations for a final peace on course.

'The difficulty lies with the splinter groups,' he says. 'In particular, Continuity IRA and the Real IRA. The Real IRA is the most danger- ous. They see the Good Friday Agreement and the peace process as a sellout of 1916. They say the British have no right to be involved in a settlement. But I see them as wrong: the treaty is a good thing, and should have come earlier. Young Ireland's Thomas Davis was right, all those years ago: we need a non-denominational nation, as an extension of the family. Sinn Fein now say we've passed beyond the military phase; and I say they're right.'

The phone rings again, and he goes to answer it.

When he comes back, I thank him for giving me his time, and he accompanies me out the door, and up the garden path to the front gate. As we prepare to part, I ask Tim Pat Coogan if he sees the contempo- rary Irish Republic as lacking some of the idealism that still drives the fighters of the North.

He makes a face. 'In some ways, yes,' he says. 'It's a very material- istic society now. Idealism isn't so popular any more. Greed and corruption are in.'

I point to the sign on his front gate: *Eventually*. What does it signify?

He smiles. 'Eventually we'll be one country,' he says.

We shake hands, and I walk off down the road, putting up my umbrella against a fresh shower of rain. He waves to me as I go: a stocky, kindly-looking man who has spent half a lifetime dealing at close quarters with fanatical belief, with youthful idealism, with extremes of hatred and cruelty, with the daring and ruthless actions of guerilla war, and the maiming and destruction of the innocent. The penalties of history: things we don't yet suffer, in Australia

VII

Afternoon tea in Bewley's Oriental Cafe in Grafton Street; a Dublin institution. I'm sitting on a little bentwood chair at a marble-topped table, a pot of tea in front of me, eating a slice of apple pie. The apple pie in Ireland, I'm discovering, is beyond compare. I'm waiting here for Bernard Share, an Irish writer. We have a mutual friend in London who suggested that we meet.

A vast hum of voices: Bewley's is extensive, with many rooms and levels, and attracts crowds of tourists. I'm in a little annexe off the big main room on the ground floor; there's a certain intimacy here. Well-dressed middle-aged women are taking tea and coffee and cakes all around me, with parcels and shopping bags beside them. Waitresses in traditional black dresses and white aprons clear the tables. Most of them are young, and their faces have a nineteenth century appearance, like old photographs; perhaps it's the uniforms. They fascinate me, these faces of the young Irish women: they're familiar yet unfamiliar. Over generations in Australia, Irish features have changed, somehow: been watered down. Now, here it is, the pure Irish face: usually fair-skinned and blue-eyed, with a downward slant to the upper lids, and well-defined cheekbones. And they are quick, quick as birds, these young women, in a way that their Australian cousins aren't: the heads darting and turning, and the smiles quickest of all, flashing into being in a split second. Two of the waitresses pause for a moment, carrying their trays; one says something to the other, and the lightning Irish smiles flash on; they lean towards each other, like two birds about to touch beaks, and their expressions are benevolent. People are often benevolent towards each other in Ireland, despite their reputation for belligerence; or so it seems from their faces and gestures.

Here in Bewley's, it might be 1920, or 1890. In the main room outside, the walls and pillars are painted ochre and orange; other walls are red. There's much dark wood, and an outsize Arabian Nights amphora elevated in the centre for Oriental effect. A staircase goes up to further levels, which I explored before I sat down. On the stairs, there were portraits of the Bewley family, and shelves of old books: half-forgotten authors like Alton Locke and Sir Phillip Gibbs; a set of *The Ecclesiastical Review*. On an upper floor, I discovered on the wall a framed newspaper clipping from 1910, reporting that the Council of Europe voted Bewley's Cafe 'one of Europe's greatest, worthy to be put by the side of Sacher's in Vienna and the Cafe Flore in Paris'. Bewley's had come second in an international competition; but I doubt that it would do so today, pleasant though it is.

It's reminiscent now of the old Lyons Corner Houses in London. The waitresses who clear the tables don't wait on you: it's necessary to stand in a queue for your food, which is displayed behind glass, and to pay for it at an elevated cash-desk, where immigrants from the Balkans, Spain and Africa look down on you. Bewley's has joined the fast food century.

'Old Ireland's disappearing fast,' Bernard says. 'You won't find many thatched cottages, unless they're tarted up for tourists. It's really quite recent, this process – it began about ten years ago. But you'll still find a bit of traditional Ireland, if you hurry. Certainly in the West.'

He takes a last small mouthful of cake and smiles at me encouragingly as he chews. He's a big, handsome, bearded man with light, greying hair and a mild demeanour. He speaks softly, without emphasis, but everything he says is worth listening to. He's published novels, travel books and works of history, and survives, as I do, through the precarious business of writing. We've talked about literature, and the traditional difficulties of our craft; now the subject of his country's modern transformation has come up, and he runs through the facts that make the Republic the economic star of Europe, after its centuries of depression – facts which are discussed in every magazine and newspaper I read here. No other economy in Europe is growing so fast. Foreign investment is massive. The per capita income has overtaken Britain's. The cost of housing has risen phenomenally, and there are fifty per cent more cars on the roads than there were ten years ago. Last year Ireland overtook the US in exports of computer software.

'The European Union's had a lot to do with it,' Bernard says. 'We've done very well out of the EU. Quite a few overseas Irish are coming home, for the first time since the Famine. And a lot of foreign workers are coming in, as you must have noticed: East European; Asians; Africans. The Americans see this country as a bridgehead for their firms – it gives them access to the European Union. But there's a price for all this, of course. We're getting quite a few refugees – you'll have seen the Romanian beggars in the streets – and some racial problems are appearing. This has always been a white, Catholic country – very homogeneous – and there are people who feel threatened by the change. And the new prosperity doesn't have entirely pleasant effects.'

I ask him if it's changing people.

'I'm afraid so. Now that people are more affluent, they're getting more self-centred. It's a constant topic of discussion here. And I guess you know about the scandals involving our politicians and the banks – we've got this Moriarty Tribunal going on at the moment, in Dublin Castle. You must have seen the uproar in the press.'

Indeed I have; to read the papers here is to be made aware of this enquiry all the time. *Tribunal season reaches fever pitch of revelations. Haughey faces grilling on £8.5m money trail.* Headlines like these greet me every day. The former Prime Minister and one-time leader of the still-ruling Fianna Fáil party, the aged Charles Haughey, is currently being grilled at the Castle about his financial affairs during his years of power, from the 1970s until the early nineties. Over a seventeen-year period, he seems to have been the recipient of gifts of money totalling over eight million pounds from businessmen and friends, and to have been allowed to run up huge overdrafts with the banks. The enquiry has been trying to establish what sort of favours Mr Haughey's rich friends received in return for their money; but the answers seem to elude them. And Mr Haughey has not been alone in this suspicious behaviour; some senior members of Fianna Fáil who were serving in the eighties and nineties have recently been forced out of office because of similar charges. Most of the donations they received came from development companies.

The old man who talked to me in Foley's on my first day here seems to have been right about such things. It all sounds like the bad old days of Tammany Hall in New York; and the newspapers talk of a Mafia style of government. The once-popular Mr Haughey seems to be the symbol of modern Irish greed and corruption: a scapegoat who's generally vilified. His lifestyle is what most attracts attention; he apparently lives like an Ascendancy earl. He owns a private island off the coast of Kerry, complete with luxury home, and another grand house in Dublin. His disaffected mistress recently went public about his luxurious way of life, including such details as the hundreds of Charvet shirts he had tailored for him in Paris. The shirts arouse particular outrage. Yesterday, the *Irish Times* reported that Haughey was greeted by protesters as his car entered the yard of Dublin Castle. They rained coins on the black Mercedes, chanting: 'Your island, your yacht, your shirt, you're caught.' And: 'Charlie Haughey, what's the score? One law for the rich and one for the poor.' The accompanying picture shows a white-haired old man sitting inside the car whose face betrays no emotion, and whose pale eyes stare straight ahead. He does look like an aged earl; yet his Republican lineage is impeccable. His father was a member of the IRA who fought in the Anglo-Irish war, who smuggled arms into the North, and was a close associate of Michael Collins.

I ask Bernard now how deep the public corruption runs.

'Very deep,' he says. 'And it's made people pretty disillusioned. There's a feeling that all politicians are bad – and also the banks and the judiciary. This is a small society, and some of the corruption was known about before – but up until recently, people were scared to say anything, because of our ferocious libel laws. Then, almost by accident, and because of a couple of crusading lawyers, these things started to come out. It's had a domino effect, with one tribunal after another. But there's a high level of public cynicism – because no-one's yet gone to gaol for tax evasion or bribe-taking or anything else. There's certainly a perception that there's one law for the rich and another for the rest of us, in modern Ireland.'

'Well, it's the same in most countries,' I say. 'We say the same thing in Australia.'

'Sure,' Bernard says. 'But in a small society it has a greater impact. There's disillusion with the Catholic Church, too. All these priests being involved in sex scandals was a blow to the Church, which used to be the rock-solid base of Irish society. There used to be a moral smugness, here. We thought we were better than most other countries – more morally sound. Now we find that isn't so.'

'What about your patriotic tradition? Are people still conscious of the line of patriots and heroes, from Wolfe Tone to Parnell and de Valera?'

Bernard shakes his head, and puts down his coffee cup.

'There's only the dimmest apprehension of it, I'm afraid. You're being romantic, if you think otherwise. People are living in the present now; we've joined the consumer society with a vengeance. You've got to realise that a twenty-year-old in the Republic is living in a country that's been an independent nation for over seventy years. People are less and less inclined to celebrate the men of 1916. There's respect – but we've all moved on. We're much more pragmatic. In a sense, the Irish in Australia and America have fossilized those things. But the younger generation here is scarcely aware of the Famine – or even of the hungry thirties. And the oral tradition is dying. Grandmothers are no longer passing the story on.'

That's sad, I say. Why has it happened?

'The big watershed was rural electrification,' Bernard says. 'It came here in the countryside very late – in the 1950s. Before that, people were still sitting around the hearth in front of their peat fires, telling stories. Electrification meant a total change: the lights came on, and the radio and TV. There goes your oral tradition. Now it's on its last legs.'

With a sinking heart, I ask about traditional music. Is that threatened too?

'No,' he says. 'The music's proved very resilient; there's been a great revival in the past thirty years. It truly is a living tradition; it's constantly evolving, and it's taken off worldwide lately, as you know.' He smiles encouragingly. 'So it's not all bad news I'm bringing you. You and Brian will hear plenty of great music in Galway and Connemara.'

I ask him for more good news. Why does he prefer to live in Ireland, despite its new age faults?

He raises his eyebrows, looking through the door to the milling crowds of tourists in the main room, and is silent for a moment. He's a calm, unhurried man who knows how to sit still, and gives the impression of being neither perturbed by life, nor deceived by it. Finally he says: 'There's still a freedom of the spirit here: a liveliness; a willingness to engage. From being inward-looking and navel-gazing, we've turned outwards – and being Irish does give you some advantages. The diaspora gave us an extraordinary position in the world, considering our size. America; Australia; Argentina; Britain: they're all areas of Irish influence. We're not some little place like Liechtenstein; we're part of a much wider picture. It's still a lovely environment to live in; and our people are coming back.' He smiles again. 'That says it as much as anything, doesn't it?'

After we've parted, I walk through the evening crowds down Dame Street.

I pass one of the Romanians Bernard spoke about. I've noticed her before, about the streets: a tall, powerful-looking woman with black hair drawn back in a bun, carrying a baby in a sling. Her brightly coloured clothing is like that of a gypsy: long knitted jacket, long skirt and sandals. Outlandish as some vivid tropical bird in the grey-blue dusk of Dame Street, she pretends to sell newspapers, muttering and accosting passers-by: clearly a cover for begging. Most people ignore her. There's a good deal of resentment of these Romanians, I notice: Irish charity and tolerance seem to be wearing thin, in their case. People complain angrily that they all collect Government pensions, but continue to beg.

Thinking of what Bernard has told me, I try to see other signs of the new, variegated Ireland. But apart from the Romanians, and the first black African faces passing now and then, as they passed in England in the fifties, the signs are few. In fact, I begin to realise what it is in Ireland that keeps taking me back into the past. This is still an almost entirely northern European society, and northern European faces and blue eyes predominate. I once took it for granted that such faces would always surround me in Australia; now we're a multi-racial country, like America and Britain, and like many of the countries of continental Europe. Is this the direction Ireland is moving in?

At present, the Republic is still a tight-knit family, with a family's common memories. The negative side of this is parochialism; but there's a positive side. The people have an unusual gentleness with each other, and are almost unfailingly friendly to strangers. This seems to spring from the fact that they have an old-fashioned family's sense of security: a security not always assured in multicultural nations, whose colour and diversity make them otherwise so attractive. And this gentleness and ease does much to give Ireland its charm. One encounters it immediately on arrival: a calm, good-humoured easiness. Even the officials at Dublin airport have a relaxed friendliness as they check your passport; and there's an underlying tranquillity in the terminal, despite its ceaseless activity. A tranquil and relaxed air terminal! Where else could you find such a phenomenon?

Tomorrow, Brian and I leave for the West.

FOUR

The West

I

A T EIGHT IN the morning we take a taxi from the hotel to the Busáras: the bus station on Store Street. It's a grey, overcast day. Making for the big glass doors of the terminal, I hurry ahead with my two small bags. Then, looking back, I see that Brian has come to a halt, red-faced and perplexed.

He's lost control of his multitudinous gear. his big lost-and-found suitcase; his guitar; his concertina; his round case of paintbrushes and colours; his camera; his plastic shopping bag of tin whistles. Attempting to carry it all, he looks like a member of a travelling circus troupe; two of the items are slipping from his shoulders, and he's put down the suitcase to stare at it with an air of hopeless bafflement, as though he may decide to abandon it. He'll more readily abandon his clothes, I feel sure, than any of the tools of his trade. He's deeply attached to the concertina in particular, in its ancient varnished box: it's an antique, he tells me; he's had it all his life.

Ashamed of my thoughtlessness, I hurry back to him, and tell him to give some of the items to me. His look of anxious perplexity instantly gives way to a smile.

'Can ye manage some, Chris, as well as your own bags? Ah, I'd be very grateful.'

Loaded more evenly now, we enter the terminal. It's a big, resounding place, with long lines of people waiting at the ticket windows. Doors at the far end open onto a yard where the long coaches of Bus Éireann, the national company, are receiving passengers. Having bought our tickets, we join the queue for the Galway bus, and soon all Brian's gear – except for the camera and bag of tin whistles, which he retains – is loaded along with mine into the compartment underneath. It's all very easy and efficient, and there are no signs of the impatience or officiousness that are often met with in such organizations in other countries. Irish good humour prevails; yet Irish muddle, like Irish poverty, seems to be a thing of the past.

The coach, with its logo of a running red setter on the side, swings out of the yard. Most of the people on board are Irish, but there's a party of male and female Spanish students. Lively and elated, but in no way rowdy, they laugh and talk together, up and down the aisle: the youth of the new Europe. Ireland is a favourite destination with them, now that movement about the EU is so easy.

Side by side in the comfortable seats, Brian and I relax, and his infectious enthusiasm returns.

'Ye're going to like Galway, I know it,' he says. 'There are so many old friends there I can't wait to see, and introduce you to. Ah, the Ireland I love most is in the West!'

The coach speeds along the four-lane freeway out of Dublin, embarked on its journey across Ireland, from the East coast to the West.

The green and white road signs are the same as those everywhere, on the freeways of the global society. One of them reads: *The West*. As always in setting out on a journey to places unknown, the most ordinary objects and vistas are fixed in a dimension of strangeness: a sign reading *Texaco*; neat new houses beside the road, with cream stucco walls and orange-tiled roofs. We are soon past the city limits, and billowing, luxuriant, light green beeches come down to the road on either side. Here are some two-storeyed villas with grey-tiled roofs and little front gardens, Germanic in their trimness, and in fact, this could easily be Germany or Denmark. Where is untidy old Ireland? Not to be found, apparently: Bernard Share was right.

But now we are deep into the country. Fields appear, with neat stacks of hay; and there is a square Norman church tower, quiet and grey and crusty beside a grove of sycamores and larches. We are driving into cloudy weather; the summer is vanishing, and a misty rain begins. Power poles become spectral, and Brian says: 'Let's hope we haven't lost the summer.' He grins at me slyly. 'Ireland can do this sort of thing for weeks. But maybe it'll be better in Galway.'

The radio on the bus is tuned to a station called Today FM. Van Morrison is singing 'Daring Night', filling the bus and the landscape with an extra charge of speed and expectancy. Today FM has its counterpart in Sydney, and the announcer has an Irish-American accent, just as our announcers have Australian-American accents. Now a newscast has come on.

'This is Today FM noos. The Deputy Prime Minister, Mary Harney, has come out against further European integration. The Tanaiste said she was opposed to a more centralised Europe, with decisions being taken at Brussels level. She favoured a Europe of independent states, not a United States of Europe. She laid great emphasis on Ireland's relationship with the United States, and its attractiveness to American business. "The figures speak for themselves," she said. "Ireland, with just one per cent of Europe's population, accounts for twenty-seven per cent of US greenfield investment in Europe. And spiritually, we are a lot closer to Boston than Berlin." '

We have come into County Meath. Sycamores and beeches, massed behind old stone walls; beyond them, a slim grey church spire. More far fields, with cattle grazing. Dark lines of pines on the rim of the land. Open tracts of gorse and purple heather, and stands of young, pale spruce. High green banks beside the road, with little yellow flowers: the sweet roadside banks of Europe, unchanged by the global freeways that pass through them. The soft rain comes and goes, and distances open up: the low, rolling country of the Midlands. Round little hills appear: fairy hills, which remind me of those in other midlands: the Midlands of Tasmania. And I begin to see why the Young Ireland exiles found their gaol colony both sombre and surprisingly beautiful. Thomas Meagher, on his arrival in Van Diemen's Land, was carried by coach through the Midlands to his place of exile in the Campbell Town district, and wrote:

> As the morning dawned, the fresh and beautiful features of the country gradually disclosed themselves. One by one they seemed to wake up, and, shaking off the dew and mist, scatter smiles and fragrance all along our road . . . For a long, long time I was in raptures with my drive, and almost forgot I was hurrying away still further from my own poor country.

Brian's voice rouses me. The Hill of Tara is not far north of here, he says: the seat of the High Kings of Ireland. He speaks with an unaffected reverence, his voice low. We are passing through the valley of the Boyne, and he talks of the famous battle of 1690: the War of the Kings, when William of Orange defeated the Catholic forces of James the Second. Not for the first time, I'm struck by the bitterness in his voice when he refers to these ancient struggles with the English; they might have taken place only six months ago, and are the only thing that can make his customary cheerfulness give way to a hint of smouldering anger.

The newscast has been replaced by rock music again, at low volume. And now an interviewer is talking to an Irish pop star whose name eludes me:

'Your new album is an overnight success. Are you happy?'
Silence for a moment. Then:
'Good question. I'm not sure.'

The bus speeds on; we are in Westmeath. The rain comes and goes, and the sky remains steely. But there's a strange yellow light on the horizon, leaking through the grey: the sun's huge presence behind. I don't tire of studying this Midlands country, which is never dramatic, but infinitely various and delicate. Nor do I mind the weather, which also recalls Tasmania, where neither sun nor rain can ever be relied on for long, and sometimes coexist in the landscape. The frail, tantalising light is the product of such weather, picking out features on distant knolls or slopes so that they light up in a way that makes them revelations. It's windless and tranquil out there, following the latest shower. Dark veils are hanging over fields and trees that are tiny and far off, the light striking through them like news of some unearthly event. Every tree and bush is electric; everything waits for magic. The light picks out stick-thin, radiant power poles, and a paddock where five small foals are running in joy. A cottage on a ridge is lit blinding white by sun, and becomes an enchanted dwelling; then the sun leaves, and returns it to the ordinary world. Nothing is ever still, in this landscape. No wonder it seems full of presences; no wonder that George Russell thought that the *Sluagh Sidhe* might some day emerge from the mountains.

We slide through the narrow main streets of a series of small towns. Plain, tall, Georgian buildings of three and four storeys are set hard on the pavements. Secretive pubs succeed each other endlessly, their signboards repeating: *Guinness; Heineken; Harp.* Nearly all the shops and houses have vivid summer flower-boxes, and are painted in surprisingly bright colours for a northern climate: mustard yellow; red; pink. Does Ireland yearn to be further south? But already the grey-tiled roofs are shining with more rain.

Afternoon, and we are crossing the border into County Galway.

Brian sits up eagerly, pointing things out to me. We are passing through Ballinasloe, the chief town of East Galway. Big, three-storeyed, slate-roofed buildings: the Duck Inn and Murphy's Food-store and Dooley's Bar, all grey in the rain. Net curtains fussily drawn in upper windows, like those in Australian country towns. Next, the little village of Aughrim, and Brian's face darkens: this is where the Williamites defeated the Irish and French forces in 1691, cementing the English Protestant ascendancy. A grey church steeple; fields of sheep in the mist; then the shadowy, storybook sorrow of Aughrim is gone.

Gone too, the rain, as we move into the spaces of East Galway. Patches of blue sky appear; the yellow light floods the land everywhere, together with long scarves of mist, and our hearts lift. Brian is back in his native country, and his face is lit with delight.

'The West is full of stones,' he says, as though describing treasures. 'Ye'll see stones wherever you go.' It's true: we're moving through an open, moor-like country of pale dry grass and boulders, of stone barns, and drystone walls; and these walls and the spaces of tussock grass tug at my memory. What do they remind me of?

After a time, Brian points: here is Galway Bay. Through the low, fleeting mists and the revelatory shafts of light, a long silver inlet appears on our left. Lowlands can be seen on its far side, and a military barracks. The levels of tussock grass and long stone walls continue – and now I remember. It all resembles the east coast of childhood, which is also a region of tussock grass and boulders, and of similar drystone walls, built by the pioneers.

Was this why my grandmother so loved Coswell – and why I loved it too? Were deep-sunk memories called up by those landscapes around Great Oyster Bay – memories not our own?

II

I'm roused by knocking.

I pick up my watch from the bedside table and examine it blearily. Half-past nine: very late to be sleeping, but Brian and I had a late night in the pub. I remember where I am: in a tiny place called Claremount, outside the village of Oughterard. I wonder if Brian's awake, and will answer the knocking; but the cottage remains silent. Outside my curtains is the silence of the countryside, broken only by the bleating of sheep.

The knocking sounds again: it's at the front door. I jump out of bed, pull on the ski-jacket that serves me as a dressing gown, and plunge out of the bedroom. All is quiet from Brian's room next door; he's a heavy sleeper. I hurry down the hallway and open the door.

A thin young man in his thirties, in a white, open-necked shirt and tan trousers, is standing in the bright morning light. He's fresh and shaved and trim: a reproach to my slovenly, lie-abed condition. He has fair hair and a keen, narrow face with a long, firm chin: the austere style of Irish physiognomy, like that of a young priest. I stare at him in confusion.

'I'm Terry O'Flaherty,' he says. 'I was told Brian Mooney's here – is that right?'

I tell him it is.

He smiles. 'They said in the Anglers that Brian was in there last night, and asking after Mick Maguire,' he says. 'They gave me this address. So the old Brian's back in Galway – that's great. Is he not awake, yet?'

Probably not, I say. But I'll wake him.

Terry holds up his hand. 'No need,' he says. 'I've got to be getting on, just now. But tell him there's a session in Powell's at around three o'clock this afternoon, and he'll be very welcome. Yourself as well. I'll be playing, and so will Mick Maguire. Mick can't wait to see Brian again. Ask him to bring his guitar, okay? We'll have good *craic*. See you.'

The village of Oughterard is half an hour's drive from Galway city. It's described in the guide books as 'the gateway to Connemara', and stands on the shores of Lough Corrib: the largest lake in the Republic. Since this is the height of the season, when the whole of Galway is filled with international tourists, we booked our cottage before leaving Australia, and will stay here for a week. We plan to hire a car, and to use Oughterard as a base for exploring some of the West. After that, when we journey to Tipperary, we'll take our chances in bed-and-breakfast guesthouses.

Tourists usually want to rent traditional thatched cottages – which are now being built for them by the hundred, with every modern amenity, and will soon be the only surviving specimens of their kind left in the country. Ours is not one of these. Instead, it's a plain suburban bungalow, with a front path, a lawn at the back, and a roof of the grey synthetic slates that seem ubiquitous in modern Ireland. It stands in a little cul-de-sac of similar bungalows, all with neat and pretty front gardens. Claremount is a sort of suburb of Oughterard – if so tiny a complex of houses can be called a suburb. At the end of the road, and behind the house, the spaces of the countryside begin.

Brian and I arrived here in a taxi last night from the bus depot in Galway city, through light but steady rain. We were greeted by Mrs Fogarty, the owner of the cottage: a lean, friendly old lady in a hat, of the kind I used to see at Mass as a child. She gave us the keys, demonstrated the workings of the house, showed us where the turf was for the fire (peat still being a main source of fuel), and departed in a little red car for her home near Galway city. A fire would certainly be needed, since the evening temperature was chilly, despite the season.

The house might not be fashionably quaint, but we found it was comfortable enough, giving us a large bedroom each, and a reasonably modern, pink-tiled bathroom – rather like those found in Australia in the 1950s. But it had no phone, so that we would have to call our wives in Australia from public call boxes, reversing the charges. Another disadvantage was its location: without a car, we faced a ten-minute walk to the village in the rain to look for dinner. We trudged into Oughterard nevertheless, sharing my small umbrella. In a green and white pub called the Anglers, an excellent Irish stew and some Guinness did much to improve our outlook, and Brian made enquiries about his friend Mick Maguire. He was told Mick was still living here, which cheered him greatly. We called our wives from a phone in the bar, and finally faced the rain and the walk back to bed.

This morning, coming out the door to set off for the village again, we're made still more optimistic. The fine weather is back, with a blue sky and small white clouds. It's very quiet here, except for the bleating of the sheep I heard on waking, and the sound of a car starting up across the road. And now I discover that the pasture at the end of the cul-de-sac runs away to a deep green hillside, dotted with heather and stones, flanked by leaning trees, where the sheep are grazing – and that what looked like a mundane suburb last night is actually a last little oasis on the edge of an extending, enigmatic countryside: the wooded Hill of Doon, and the boglands and wilds of Connemara – hidden but not far away to the west. There's a strangeness about this.

We walk down the road to Oughterard again. Last night it was enveloped by darkness and rain, and was mainly invisible to us. Now it's revealed in full summer dress, shaded by huge beech trees and rimmed by a low stone wall above a glinting, bottle-green, fast-flowing little river. Brian is delighted. ('Look at these trees, Chris! Just look at the *density* of them!') Discovering Oughterard's beauties all over again, after a visit three years ago, he's already planning sketches.

The village has a long main street called Main Street, with a square halfway down. It beckons to tourists from one end to the other: thatch-roofed gift shops and craft shops, an information centre, money-changing establishments, restaurants, and pubs. It advertises itself as a centre for anglers, since Lough Corrib is famous for fishing, being filled with brown trout, salmon, pike and eels. At lunch time, we eat in a cosy yet capacious pub called O'Fatharta's, in Main Street, with many tables and nooks and crannies for a quiet meal, attended by kindly waitresses. And now I discover the advantage of being by Lough Corrib. We order trout, and it's the biggest and finest trout I've ever eaten: a transcendental trout, whose taste is like the essence of the country, accompanied by honest hunks of soda bread.

O'Fatharta's is filled mainly with local couples and their children; and also with grandparents, teenagers, and friends of the family. I'll soon discover that this is typical. All ages mingle, in traditional Irish pubs like this one; there isn't the age segregation that's observed in Australia and elsewhere. These pubs are not just for drinking: they're also family and general meeting places. No wonder they're so inviting. With their fine polished wood, comfortable seats, knick-knacks on shelves, and soft little lamps along the bar, they're like private parlours available to everyone: a national art form. Children and infants wander among the legs, in O'Fatharta's, and their intermittent cries mingle with greetings and laughter that erupt continously. Yet none of this noise is jarring; it's somehow muted, and makes up a smooth-rolling wave of Irish gladness, powered by Guinness and beer and good food.

A euphoric well-being enters me, and Brian and I smile at each other in understanding, raising our glasses. Here we are: this is what we've been waiting for, ever since we arrived at Dublin airport. But O'Fatharta's is merely a low-key prelude to Powell's Hotel.

At three o'clock, the appointed time, we emerge and make our way down the street. Brian is armed and ready for the music, carrying his guitar and bag of whistles; I carry his concertina.

'Powell's is very old,' he says. 'I've heard it's one of the oldest pubs in Galway. I used to sing here in the old days.' He grins. 'The crack'll be mighty, I promise ye.'

Crack – or *craic*, in Irish – is a versatile and subtle noun, I'm finding. It means good talk, good music and good drinking – all in happy combination. It's what the Irish love most. It can also be used as a verb, as in: 'We were crackin' on all night.'

We come to Powell's. At first I don't recognise it as a pub at all. It's a long, single-storey building with an aged-looking thatched roof, and small, secretive, deep-set windows, rather like an old farmhouse. A single narrow door stands open on the street: a door so low that Brian instinctively ducks as we pass through. Inside, it's crowded and dim: so dim, despite the bright afternoon outside, that I must blink to adjust my eyes. We are greeted by a wave of voices: the same sort of muted, happy clamour as the one in O'Fatharta's, mingling male and female laughter with infant squeals and babble. Above this, and happily co-existing with it, rides another, larger wave: the wave of the music, bringing me to a halt.

It comes from the end of this long, barn-like room, where two musicians are seated behind a big, polished table that's covered with glasses and bottles. On their left, a vast, antique barrel is set against the wall, like the barrel in a nineteenth-century tap-room. Behind them is a big black dresser, whose mirror reflects them. They work without a mike, and don't need it. One of them is our visitor, Terry O'Flaherty, still looking crisp and respectable in his well-pressed shirt. He plays a melodeon: a small accordion whose strap goes across his shoulder; and he plays with great skill. The other musician, who is singing and playing guitar, is Mick Maguire: a lean, haggard, long-haired man of around forty, with a fox-red beard and moustache, who looks like a hard drinker.

Encountering a born ballad-singer, one knows it immediately. Mick Maguire holds me fixed where I stand. His voice has a plaintive, passionate colouring; and Terry's melodeon, elaborate and inventive, running and dancing and singing in response, matches it perfectly. The song is *Down by the Glenside*, and none of the noises in the room can subvert its forlorn power and beauty:

'Twas down by the glenside I met an old woman,
A-plucking young nettles, she ne'er saw me coming.
I listened a while to the song she was humming:
Glory-o, glory-o, to the bold Fenian men . . .

Brian peers at me, smiling and nodding as he sees my rapt expression. 'This is what ye came to Ireland to hear, isn't that right?'

I offer to buy our first drinks, and go across to the bar counter. Brian walks over to the polished table, carrying his guitar, and sits down opposite the musicians. Terry grins and winks at him, but Mick's eyes are closed, as he sings. Pub performances in Ireland are very casual, I'll find: there's hardly ever a stage or platform, the musicians simply sitting at a table that suits them, and performing from there. Powell's is more casual than most.

It really does resemble a huge barn. It's divided by the long, enclosed bar counter into two rooms, both of which are packed, throbbing with voices and laughter. The back room – which I examine as I stand in the crowd at the counter – is filled with young men and girls in their teens and twenties, talking and playing snooker. The customers in the big front room, where the music takes place, seem mainly to be couples with children, or else the middle-aged and old. Casually furnished with unpainted wooden benches and tables, and with pieces of antique furniture ranked around the walls, it has a high cathedral ceiling of dark, stained boards. The thick stone walls are finished with rough stucco; where they reach the angle of the ceiling they form a shelf around the room, high up, on which many oddments have been placed: a ladder; old bottles; an ancient sewing machine; a valve radio. Attic-like windows up there let some afternoon light in, as do the other small windows at ground level. A little more light penetrates the dusk from overhead lamps hanging on chains, and from other red-shaded lamps on wall brackets. The walls are crowded with more decorations, all of which are relics from the early years of the departing century: old farming implements, framed prints, a mirror lettered *Player's Please*, and a pair of archaic black bicycles, hung fifteen feet above the floor, one of them with a rifle strapped to its carrier. I don't understand the bicycles. There's also a framed, idealised portrait of the Kennedy brothers, John and Robert, at the height of their youth and beauty, smiling in dual profile towards their destiny. They are clearly icons, and I will see them in many another pub in Ireland.

Carrying a Guinness for Brian and a whiskey for myself, I reach the polished table where Brian is sitting. I feel disinclined to sit beside him; the table is clearly musician's territory. So I place his drink in front of him and sit on a bench a little to one side, under the huge old barrel that looms beside the wall of the bar. *Down by the Glenside* is just finishing:

I passed on my way, God be praised that I met her,
Be life long or short, I will never forget her.
We may have brave men, but we'll never have better:
Glory-o, glory-o, to the bold Fenian men . . .

Applause from the room, as Terry slips off his melodeon, and Mick puts aside his guitar. There's a cluster of emptied Guinness glasses in front of them; one is still half full, and Mick picks it up and drains it. Terry, I notice, is drinking only mineral water. I was right in my first impression; he's the abstemious type of Irishman. Brian gets up and greets them, and Mick clasps his hand and shakes it long and fondly; then Brian introduces me.

Many songs and hours have flown by. The narrow little doorway to the street frames a young, jade-green tree across the road, fixed in another land of treacle-coloured light. In here, in the sounding dusk of Powell's, Brian has begun to sing, accompanying himself on his guitar, a mouth organ hung around his neck. It's the song of the '98 rebellion, in which his long-lived great-grandfather took part: the song of the Wexford rising that was led by Father Murphy, the fighting 'croppy priest' whose body was burned on a rack. Brian sings with pride and an underlying fury, as though the rising took place only yesterday. His big, rueful voice has lost none of its power, and rises easily above the laughter and the squeals of the children:

Then Father Murphy from old Kilcormack
Spurred up the rocks with a warning cry:
'Arm, arm,' he cried, 'for I've come to lead you;
For Ireland's freedom we'll fight or die.'

When he finishes, after a burst on the mouth organ, there's prolonged applause; the room is delighted by him. I've had a good many glasses of Black Bush, my favourite whiskey, and now make my way somewhat unsteadily through the back room towards the toilets, glad Irish faces swimming past me as I go. A small, large-headed old man with wide-set grey eyes addresses me genially from behind, and I smile and nod foolishly; he has a very strong accent, and I understand nothing of what he's said. Standing at the urinal, I find him beside me at the next stall, and he speaks to me again. This time I realise that he's not speaking in English, but in Irish. It's the first time in my life I've heard Gaelic spoken, and I nod enthusiastically, and smile again. As I weave my way through the back room to the front again, I become aware that other voices are speaking in Irish, as well; and I recall that we're on the border of Connemara, where Irish is used as commonly as English.

Mick Maguire is now singing the hauntingly beautiful *Night Visiting Song*. How he sings it! He's truly become the wandering lover, this red-bearded bard with the ravaged face; and Terry O'Flaherty's melodeon follows him faithfully, gliding and singing and winding with lyric skill:

I must away now, I can no longer tarry,
This morning's tempest I have to cross;
I must be guided, without a stumble
Into the arms I love the most . . .

A figure out of Brueghel's *The Peasant Dance* has appeared in a chair beside Terry's at the table, head cocked to one side, leaning at the same angle as Terry does as he plays, and swaying in harmony with him.

It's the old man I encountered in the toilets, his wide-set eyes gazing into the music; into bliss.

When the song is done, the big, middle-aged publican hurries to the table, setting down three more glasses of Guinness for the musicians. He keeps them supplied constantly, free of charge, and there are now many more empties in front of Mick and Brian; none in front of Terry. But this time, Terry allows himself a Guinness. Then he begins a solo piece on the melodeon. As he does so, Mick Maguire comes over and sits on a bench beside me, Guinness in hand.

'Well now, are ye enjoying the music, Chris?'

His reddish, foxy beard juts at me; so does his beaked red nose. He has bitter blue eyes with pouches under them, a small mouth that appears to have lost some teeth, and an appealing, vulnerable smile. A face with hurt in it somewhere, and one that's capable of signalling fast and dangerous swings of mood. I tell him truthfully that the music gave me great joy, and he smiles more widely.

'That's good, that's good. Sure, Powell's is a grand old place. We've been singing here for years.'

Mick has a very strong Galway accent; so strong that I can only just understand him; even Brian has to ask him to repeat things. I ask him about the vintage bicycle on the wall, with the rifle on the back. He gives me a significant sideways look.

'Black and Tan bicycle,' he says.

He says no more; but his narrowed blue eyes are watching me as he sips his Guinness.

'Good riddance to them,' I say.

His smile returns, filled with warmth; he nods at me, telling me I have passed his test.

We talk of the days of the Black and Tans; of de Valera and Michael Collins; of the Civil War. And then he begins to talk of the IRA hunger strikes in the Maze Prison and elsewhere. He speaks more and more passionately, his speech growing thicker. He is telling me a story, a story that possesses him; we have both had quite a bit to drink now, and I struggle to follow. It concerns a young IRA martyr called Frank Stagg, who was a native of Mayo, here in the West. Mick perhaps knew him, in his youth; he speaks with the sort of emotion that suggests he did. Stagg went on a hunger strike in Wakefield prison in Yorkshire, in 1976. He demanded to be treated as a political prisoner, Mick says, and to wear his own clothes; but this was refused, and he starved himself to death.

'He was blind, in the end,' Mick cries, looking at me fiercely. His small blue eyes have become red-rimmed; he seems on the verge of tears. 'Blind, and all that he weighed was four stone. Can ye *imagine* that?'

What followed seems to have been an extraordinary struggle over the nature of Stagg's burial. The Provisonal IRA were determined that when the body was flown to Dublin, they would take it in a military funeral procession all the way across the country to the West, where Stagg would be buried in Mayo, in his native town of Ballina, with full IRA honours. This had been done with a comrade of his, Michael Gaughan, also from Ballina, who had died two years before in Parkhurst prison, on the Isle of Wight. The funeral procession had resulted in worldwide publicity for the Provisionals; but it had caused embarrassment for the Irish Government. The Government, it seems, didn't want a repeat performance in Stagg's case. It didn't want to deal with the pressure that would be brought to bear by London, and nor did it like the IRA flouting its authority.

'So they diverted the focking aeroplane to Shannon,' Mick says. 'The cunning bastards. The focking Government knew what it would mean to face the Provos at the airport in Dublin: the boys would have taken Frank's coffin away, and no stopping them. So the Government got the coffin straight to Ballina, and they buried Frank near Mick

Gaughan – but it was not in the Republican plot he had wanted. *Not in a Republican plot* – do you see?'

Terry O'Flaherty is playing a reel now, his melodeon dancing and happy, and the laughter and talk around us seem to have grown louder and merrier. Mick leans close, raising his voice to penetrate the noise; his mouth works, and his face is filled with outrage.

'They buried him under a concrete slab,' he says, 'so that no one could move him to where he wanted to be. Under a focking *concrete slab*!' He seems torn between rage and weeping. 'The focking police put a guard on the grave around the clock,' he says, 'and our bloody Prime Minister did nothing! I ask you: what sort of a Republican is that?'

The shining, angry eyes study mine. I'm in unknown waters here: I shrug, my expression neutral. He nods, apparently satisfied, and goes on.

'But the Provos beat them in the end,' he says. 'One night six months later, they dug a tunnel under the concrete and got the coffin away. They had a priest with them, and he blessed the body. Then they buried Frank in a Republican plot.'

He goes back to the table, and picks up his guitar again. He and Brian will sing many more ballads, as the light through the door fades, and gives way to dusk. When it comes time to go, and we are all much tipsier, Mick comes up to me to say goodbye. He takes my hand and holds it, and will not let go. Swaying, he regards me with a sort of yearning tenderness.

'Now tell me, Chris: how did ye like it? Did ye have a good evening? How did ye like the music?'

I see no rage in his face now; only gentleness, and a deep-buried hurt. I tell him with truth how well I liked it, and how greatly I liked his singing.

He sang many good songs; but the one that won't leave my head, as we go off up the road, is *The Night Visiting Song*. Certain songs define the singer: there's no telling why.

III

We have hired a car. It stands in the driveway of our cottage in Oughterard: a bright blue Japanese Nissan. We picked it up yesterday at Budget Rent-a-Car in Galway city, and the transaction was my first experience of the claws of the Celtic Tiger.

In Budget's tiny office, Brian and I found ourselves sitting at a desk in front of the manager, Mr Lynch, rather like boys being given an oral examination. Mr Lynch was of the second of my two Irish types: the pale, tight-mouthed, unsmiling kind that once went into the Church, and which now seems to enter the ranks of the new millennium's hard-driving businessmen and corporate executives. There was an air of impatience about Mr Lynch, as though we were here on a frivolous mission. When he told us the cost of hiring the car for a single week, we gaped in disbelief. With the addition of many little extras, it all added up to six hundred and twenty-six pounds: roughly the cost of a flight to Australia.

I had been told hiring cars was expensive in Ireland, but this was insane. I began to argue; to ask whether a mistake had been made. But Mr Lynch's thin lips grew thinner, and he adopted a bullying tone.

'You wanted an automatic. That's the cost of it, and it's the last one I've got. Do you want it or not? There's plenty of others waiting if you don't.'

There was nothing to be done: this was the height of the tourist season, and Mr Lynch could do what he liked. I signed the papers, and a few minutes later Brian and I drove away in our immensely valuable, bright blue capsule.

Now here it stands, shining in the nine o'clock sun. Having cooked and eaten our bachelor breakfast of bacon and eggs, we stand looking at it in a bemused manner. The wounds inflicted by the tiger are still bleeding, and we have many rough things to say about Mr Lynch. But we begin to cheer up: it's another fine day, we have our transport, and we're bound for the wilderness of Connemara: the utmost west of Ireland.

Driving out of Oughterard, we cross the invisible frontier immediately. I'd feared that the roads would be filled with tourist traffic, as so many are in Ireland in summer; but they're almost empty.

We're entering a high, open, empty land of dark little pine woods and rocky, treeless hills. We pass through Maam Cross, a crossroads where a big hotel sits by the roadside, and a few tourist cars are parked; but then the road runs straight and level and far into a moorland where scarcely a car passes, and where there's no sign of life at all, except for an occasional farm cottage. Huge, charcoal-tinted rain clouds sail overhead, so that the light is beginning to wax and wane in the classic Irish manner, and the hills to darken. Soon it will rain, Brian says: it always rains in Connemara. We're driving directly west, and he points out the features of the land to me; he knows this countryside well. On our right are the foothills of the Maumturk Mountains, and out on the horizon ahead of us are the blue peaks called the Twelve Bens. These are the two great ranges that dominate Connemara, sitting on the rim of the land. Nearer, the whole empty country is filled with little lakes, gleaming like a hoard of silver in the rolling, silent flatlands and knolls of dark green grass. These are the bogs.

I pull the car over, and we get out. The highway is deserted. No sounds but the crying of curlews, and the bleating of black-faced sheep, wandering free on the grass flats and the road verge. On a grassy bank across the road, two plump brown ponies are grazing. Connemara ponies, that roam wild. In the background on that side of the road rise high, stony hills and granite mountains, bare except for grey-green grass and patches of brown bracken, their ultimate colour in the distance an elusive silver-violet. We're entirely alone here; when a single van whizzes by, it's startling. Then the huge silence resumes.

I'd always imagined that the Irish bogs would be dreary. The reverse is true. They're very beautiful; or rather, they're beautiful if your spirit is of a kind that is drawn by open, lonely moorlands or waste places that retreat into inscrutable distance. Such places resonate with a high, single note of mystery: a singing that's only just audible, like wind in a wire. Their melancholy quiet is filled with waiting; with the nearby presence of something remarkable, just beyond the reach of the eye and the mind. Here on the edge of the boglands, I understand why a knowledge of the Otherworld was always so strong among the Irish: that profound understanding which Yeats said married them through myth to their native rock and hill, and which now is in danger of being lost – withered and stunted by the rays of our video machines, and the babble of the global culture. This is a landscape that's filled with the supernatural.

Brian and I step across a low stone wall, and wander onto the dark green turf among tawny tussocks. In front of us is one of the silver lakes. On its far side, a green-black line of pines, and a small, peaked, violet-grey mountain, rising there quietly. The sky has turned a very strange colour: an unnatural, luminous grey-green. Little white daisies flare bright in the grass, and Brian points out a purple-pink heather growing among the lichen-covered stones: St Dabeoc's Heath, which grows only in Connemara. In this darkening light, as the rain clouds advance, the colour of every bush and flower has a final, arresting brilliance, as though flaring up before extinction. The entire countryside is like a theatre. And now its effects intensify.

A light shower of rain has begun, and we turn and make our way back towards the road. By the time we reach it, the rain has already passed on; but the land in front of us has turned dark in a way that scarcely seems possible by day: so dark, that the banks on the other side of the road have become almost black. But then thin shafts of sun strike through, from somewhere in the grey-green canopy, and one of them lights up a single, bare, round-topped mountain, not far off. Alone in the night-dark landscape, lit by a miraculous zone of daylight, the mountain is transfigured: violet and pale umber, it seems to glow with summer from within. Then the sun moves visibly towards us, lighting up a line of electric pylons that are stepping through vacancies beyond the road: picking out a gorse bush; a rock; a single slope of green.

Dark and light; dark and light: Connemara is a country in a dream.

We drive on, in our blue Nissan, and I notice that the occasional road signs are entirely in Irish. As the rain showers come and go, and the windscreen-wipers swing and hiss, Brian talks to me of Connemara.

It was always left untouched by the world, he says, because no-one wanted it. Despite its beauty, it's a land composed of little else but stone, and it kept the people poor. They scratched out a living in tiny fields that were nothing but cleared rock; on these they spread thin layers of soil, carried in baskets by the women.

"This was where the Famine hit hardest,' Brian says. 'Every second one of them headed for America – and it was the money they sent back that kept alive the ones who stayed. The people here weren't interested in the rest of Ireland – they looked out across the sea to America. I've heard it said that Connemara had two capitals: the town of Clifden, and Boston, in the United States.'

Because of its poverty and remoteness, as well as the hard weather, the old ways of life lingered on in Connemara much longer than anywhere else. Still Irish-speaking, it's the largest of what are called the *Gaeltacht* areas. Even today, Brian says, it doesn't do much to cater for tourists, and its great tracts of bogland wilderness still remain empty. And the handsome, dark-haired people here are the real, ancient Irish, he says: they retreated into Connemara long before the Normans came, and in Brian's opinion are the original Milesians, who mingled and interbred with the tribes of the goddess Dana: the people of the Faery Hills.

'If I could have brought ye here when we were young,' he says, 'ye'd have still seen the donkey carts, and barefoot girls in their red skirts carrying baskets of seaweed and earth: girls who knew nothing of what was beyond Connemara, and who'd have stared at us like we had two heads. No electricity, no cars, no shops. The cows would have run away from the car because they'd never seen one before. It's not like that now; but it's still a long way from the rest of the world.'

The sober green moorlands roll by. The houses remain few; but even here, I notice, they're roofed with the new synthetic tiles. Meanwhile, the tall wooden power poles that stride beside the road are carrying the fatal spark that links even Connemara to the global nervous system: to radio and television and the internet; to the knowledge and pseudo-knowledge and vices and despair of Dublin, London and New York. And the Danaan voices fade.

But now Brian points to a cultivated field going by, with a little hill in its centre crowned with stones. It looks as though the farmer piled the stones there simply to get rid of them; but Brian identifies this is a *rath* – a fairy fort. In the old days, he says, the farmer would never plough a hill like that, since it was known to belong to the fairies.

Perhaps he still leaves it alone for that reason. Or simply in memory of that reason.

In the early afternoon, after many halts to wander by the road, we are nearing the coast.

We come into Clifden: a market town, founded in the nineteenth century, when it was decided that wild Connemara needed civilizing. The rain clouds are gone, and the sun is out in a high blue sky, lighting up Clifden's two stone church spires and its big, solid white houses. The houses wander around a hill that slopes down to the estuary of the River Owenglin. The green, stony moorlands roll away outside, and the blue, shadowy peaks of the Twelve Bens encircle the town in the distance. It's a pretty town, quite small, dwarfed by this wide, ethereally lovely landscape. But it's geared for tourism, with a jumble of craft shops and pubs and restaurants around a central square, and disco music drumming from the doorways. This is not what Brian and I want today; we want the lonely places. So we eat a quick fish meal in a restaurant on the square, and then drive north-west on the Sky Road.

The Sky Road is a seven-mile, circular route running high above Clifden Bay and the sea. It's a very narrow road, with a fence of tipsy wooden posts and rusty barbed wire on the side that falls away to the bay: a cliff grown with purple-flowering heath and rusty yellow grass. We meet only one other car as we climb, and must pull over to let it by. Then we go on to the road's highest point, and get out. Brian has urged me to come here; now I see why. There is no further west that we can go: here is where Ireland ends. Here is where Europe ends.

We're looking out over the North Atlantic, from Connemara's utmost edge. There's only a faint breeze here, and the sky remains deep blue, with brilliant white clouds on the horizon. Like the rest of the countryside, the peninsula we're on is bare of trees, so that nothing impedes the view, and land and sky are vast. We're standing at the centre of a landscape whose distances, at all points of the compass, seem infinite, and which pulses and shimmers with colour: a landscape like mirage. At our feet, dark green turf and purple heather. Behind us, in the east, the pale, pale green of the boglands behind Clifden; and beyond these, the blue and mauve of the Twelve Bens, low under the huge sky, dwindling and fading into that land of enchantment the eye always seeks in such distance, no matter how old we grow; no matter what voices of rationality drone denial in our brains. To the south, straight below us, is the long, deep blue channel of Clifden Bay, dotted with a few white boats, and bounded by a faded green spit with a scatter of tiny houses. Past that, the blue and aquamarine of Mannin Bay; and beyond that again, south around the coast, more land and more low peaks: far, dim territories of mystery, going off to the limit of vision.

But always one's gaze is drawn back to the west, and the ocean beyond the bay. Here, where the water becomes a pure and profound aquamarine, and the long, rolling waves break white on some reefs, is the hard, final line of the horizon. Here is the Atlantic, and beyond it is America: that Land of Wonder which human feet may stand on. Gazing at this horizon, one understands all the nineteenth century's hopes; all the wistful songs of emigration.

We drive south, through the waning afternoon. Our destination is the coastal village of Spiddal, at the southern edge of Connemara, on Galway Bay. Here Brian has musician friends he's not seen for years; he's confident they'll still be there, and that with luck we'll find good music in the evening. He's brought his guitar in anticipation, and we won't return to Oughterard tonight; instead, we plan to stay in a bed-and-breakfast guesthouse.

Spiddal is on the main road: a drive-through town. In the main street, we find a pleasant B and B, with only one disadvantage: we must share a double room. We'll find that single rooms are almost unknown in these establishments, everywhere in Ireland: presumably they don't return enough profit. But our homely upstairs double, with its two big beds and dwarf-size ensuite bathroom, is pleasant and clean. It looks down on the street, where tourists and locals are strolling, and I stand at the open window, breathing the soft evening air while Brian rummages in his bag. Opposite, in the twilight, is a Catholic church; on an empty lawn at the side, a Carmelite nun kneels in devotion in front of a grotto in which a blue and white plaster statue of the Virgin Mary appears, as she appeared to Bernadette of Lourdes. The nun is so lifelike that at first I think her real: but then I see that she too is of plaster.

After a meal in a restaurant, Brian and I join the throng in the main street. It's now nearly nine o'clock, but the long twilight continues, and the air is very still and balmy. Soon we'll seek out the pub where Brian hopes his friends will be found; but first he wants to take me to the nearby bay.

We walk down a little road that runs out of the village, passing a few white cottages and a drystone wall that borders open fields. We come to a halt on the edge of a broad, sandy beach. The twilight is fading rapidly, and has reached that point where things grow uncertain, but where colours are still discernible. Lights have come on in the cottages. A car pulls up, but then goes away again. The only sounds are the barking of a dog, the sharp, urgent calls of children and gulls, and the soft hushing of water. The children can be seen paddling at the far-off water's edge; they carry shrimping nets, like figures in Victorian illustrations. A long, high sea-wall, black and sinister in the failing light, extends into the bay; and Galway Bay is calm, immense and flat. Outside it, in the west, is the Atlantic, and the invisible Aran Isles. On its southern side, very far off, is a long, low line of violet-grey hills, only just possible to make out, where little pinprick lights are glimmering. Brian points.

'That's the Burren, over there, in County Clare. We could go down to Clare the day after tomorrow, if you like, and have a look at it. Then we'll look for that Big House your ancestors lived in.'

The Burren! I've always wanted to go to that strange, bare lime-stone plateau in northwest Clare. Now, looking across to the violet line of land and its mysterious little lights, we might be sighting a country in another dimension. It seems remarkable that we may actually drive there in a day; but nowhere's very far in Ireland.

Tigh Hughes has always been a great music pub, Brian says; music sessions have been going on there for well over a hundred years. He used to sing there in the old days, when he lived in Galway; but that's over fifteen years ago, and he hasn't visited Spiddal since.

'I hope the old crowd will still be there,' he says.

This doesn't seem to me to be very likely; but I hold my peace.

Carrying his guitar now, he leads me back into the town's main street, and then into a very narrow side street lined with two-storeyed Victorian and Georgian houses, standing flush on the footpath.

'The first thing to do is to find Mary Daly,' he mutters. 'Mary used to live a couple of doors down from the pub. She's a great little singer, and knows everyone. If I can only find Mary, we'll be right. I think I can remember the house.'

He comes to a halt, frowning at a two-storeyed house: one of a number in a red brick terrace.

'This should be it. Yes, I'm pretty sure this is the one. Only one way to find out.'

He puts down his guitar, raps with the iron knocker, and then stands back, smiling: waiting for someone he's not seen or heard of for fifteen years. We wait for some time, and he knocks again. This time the door is thrown open by a woman in her fifties: stocky, with copper hair streaked with grey. She stares at Brian blankly, and he smiles.

'Hello Mary – it's me. Brian Mooney.' He puts a hand on his hair. 'Maybe ye don't know me. I've gone a bit white.'

Recognition dawns in Mary's eyes. She shrieks, and smiles in extravagant delight; then they embrace. She has warm brown eyes, and a shrewd, good-humoured face.

'*Brian*! Jesus, Brian! No, I didn't know ye – it's been so long. Jesus! Where in the fock did ye come from?'

'We're here from Australia, Mary – me and my mate Chris.'

'You're very welcome, Chris.'

Mary takes my hand and holds it with immediate, glad warmth. Many Irish people display this warmth on first meeting: it can make you feel that you've known them for years, and that you'll discover great things together. Critics of this style ask how much depth lies under the veneer, and point to the speed with which Celtic enthusiasm can be replaced by hostility, or even by deadly attack. Perhaps. But I see it as the style of a people who are at ease with themselves, for whom enjoyment of life is the paramount virtue, and whose first response is to open their arms to what life brings – including the stranger. Implicit in this is that if they are given reason, the gift of hospitality will be smartly withdrawn. It's a style that was taken to Australia, and I'm happy to enjoy it without question.

'We're wondering if there's a session on at Tigh Hughes,' Brian says. 'Will there be some singing there tonight, Mary?'

'There will of course,' Mary says. 'Isn't there always? And I see you've brought your guitar, Brian, so *you'll* be singing – no getting out of it.'

'Well, I might if you do, Mary. It'll be great to hear ye again. I've been telling Chris how good you are. Will ye come with us?'

'Just let me change my dress. I wasn't going tonight, to tell ye the truth – we did a bit of drinking at Paddy's place last night, and I'm just getting over it. But with Brian Mooney back, how can I refuse? Jesus, it's so good to see you!'

Tigh Hughes, like Powell's in Oughterard, is the sort of Irish pub that you pass without noticing: a long, two-storeyed house of a stealthy mustard colour, with window frames painted a dark raspberry-red, and a low, medieval door of the same colour. For many good reasons, the old style of Irish pub had no great wish to be noticed, or to seem to entice customers; and Tigh Hughes looks positively forbidding. Nothing, as it turns out, could be more misleading.

Once through the little low door, we encounter a surging wave of voices, laughter, and bodily warmth, filtered through a universal veil of cigarette smoke. It's a snug, family sort of warmth, its density increased by the pub's low ceilings. Tigh Hughes is a fishermen's pub, and the decorations are marine: a ship's bell hanging by the door; a brass ship's clock on the wall behind the bar; pictures of fishing boats on the dusky yellow walls. There are two front bars, divided by a doorway, and a big back room. All are packed. Here in the larger of the two bar-rooms, stools are set along the counter, and there are tables around the walls; but most people are standing, and we must edge our way through the crowd to get to the counter. There are men and women of all ages here; and although it's nearly ten o'clock, the usual infants and children are piping and wailing and scurrying in the background. Many of the customers greet Mary Daly as we go by, and I have the impression that I'm in a private house where families have gathered, all of whom know each other, and many of whom are related. In this, I'll find, I'm not far wrong.

As Brian orders drinks, I try and attend to the voices around me, and to pick up conversations. But I find I can't; it's as though I'm listening to a radio that's not properly tuned to the station. Then I realise that I'm not hearing English: nearly all of these people are speaking Irish. Sometimes they break briefly into English; but then they return to Irish again. The sensation is very strange, since so many of the faces look familiar: faces I've known all my life. It's as though friends and neighbours have suddenly begun to speak in tongues.

As soon as our Guinnesses are poured, Mary leads us over to a big round table in a corner, next to the wall of the back room. This will turn out to be the table of the singers, and Mary calls out to a group of people who are sitting around it on stools and chairs.

'Liam! Bernadette! Sean! Here's Brian Mooney back! Look here: it's Brian!'

We are suddenly surrounded by a group of delightedly smiling men and women, all of middle age, shaking Brian by the hand, thumping him on the back, and staring at him as though he's descended from the clouds.

'Brian! Jesus, it is! It's Brian Mooney!'

'Sure, it's Brian! You're back then, after all this time!'

'How have ye been, old son? And where's Phyllis?'

Not for the first time, I see what affection Brian inspires. He recalls the wandering bard in *The Parting Glass*, who sings of all the comrades he's had, who were sorry for his going away; and of all the old sweethearts who would wish him one more day to stay.

We're all seated around the table, and Mary Daly is singing.

She is singing in Irish, unaccompanied, sitting in a chair beside

Brian. Once again, I'm startled: here she sits, this greying, pleasant-looking woman in her pink cardigan and plain blue cotton dress – the sort of woman who's very familiar to me, and who might be sitting in a pub anywhere in Australia – singing in ancient Gaelic, the language which is native to her, and which is as strange to me as Swahili. There's a good deal of noise in the bar, and more coming from the back room through an open window in the wall beside us, where laughing and shrieking young women are framed drinking at a table. But as Mary sings, much of the noise dies away, except for the noise through the window. The air, which is unfamiliar to me, is beautiful, and Mary's soprano voice is very true.

When she's done, the group applauds with great enthusiasm, and so do others nearby. Brian urges her to sing again, but she shakes her head.

'Ah, there's too much noise,' she says.

A large, curly-haired man on the other side of the table leans over and slams the window to the back room shut. The shrieking girls disappear.

'Now there isn't,' he says.

After some urging, Mary sings again, as beautifully as before. Then she points at Brian.

'It's time for Brian to sing. He's brought his guitar.'

As Brian tunes up, I go over to the bar counter to buy another round of drinks. Waiting for the Guinnesses to settle, I look across to our table in the corner, where the group is visible through the dense blue screen of cigarette smoke. There's a good deal of laughter there. It's grown quite hot in the throbbing, laughing room, which seems to have little ventilation, and Brian has decided to get rid of some clothing before singing. This entails taking off his plaid woollen shirt and removing a black t-shirt he wears underneath, before replacing the shirt. Bare to the waist, a white Irish giant, he flexes his biceps amid cheering and clapping, before resuming the plaid shirt: at home among his friends of fifteen years ago.

He sings *The Wild Colonial Boy*, which is applauded enthusiastically, and follows it with a drinking song, *Rosin the Bow*. His mouth organ is hung around his neck as usual, fixed on its little holder in the Bob Dylan manner so that his hands are free, and he finishes with a rendering of the melody on this. As he does so, a small, very drunk man resembling a jockey staggers over to us from the bar, a glass of whiskey raised in his hand like a flag. He has wavy red hair and very blue eyes, and plants himself directly in front of Brian.

'Brian!' he cries. 'Brian!'

Brian, blowing, signals with his eyes that he recognises him, is delighted, but is helpless to speak.

'Brian!' The little man jigs from foot to foot, pointing. 'Jesus, it's Brian Mooney! Can you believe it now!'

Mary and the others in the semi-circle at the table begin to laugh, and Brian brings *Rosin the Bow* to an end, breaking into his big grin and holding out his hand.

'Paddy! Is it you? It's good to see you, Paddy.'

Brian introduces me to Paddy, who seems filled with friendliness, but is too drunk to say more than a few words. He doesn't stay; he seems to keep hurrying about.

'Paddy's a fisherman,' Brian tells me. 'He's a great little bloke; but you won't get much sense out of him tonight.'

The evening roars on. Paddy comes and goes, calling, 'Brian! Brian!' – always on a note of discovery. Then he goes off into helpless laughter. Brian and I talk to Mary. The big, curly-haired man, whose name is Liam, is talking to Bernadette, a pleasant, somewhat masculine-looking woman with short-cropped brown hair, sad dark eyes and a weathered, drinker's face, who is smoking a thin cigar. They are holding hands, in a friendly, affectionate manner. There's much hand-holding and touching, here in Tigh Hughes: these people are very close and tender with each other.

An old man comes in, and joins our circle at the table.

He's quiet, and says little after greetings are exchanged; but he's shown great respect, and chairs are moved aside to make a space for him next to Mary. He's urged to sing, but at first merely shakes his head. He has dark, greying hair gone bald on top, low-set, bushy black eyebrows, and sharp, grey-blue eyes glinting from under them. I never catch his name, but seem to recognise him; then I realise that he resembles Charles Culley: the Labor politician who was my grandmother's brother, and Margaret O'Meara's grandson. He's a strange, enigmatic, self-contained old man, with a pale, bulbous nose, jutting chin, and a fierceness in his eyes: a face from the nineteenth century. It's not a drinker's face, unlike many in here; I notice that he lingers over one glass of beer, and there's a sober, even monk-like quality about him.

'Come on, now,' Liam calls to him. 'Give us a song or two.'

'Do,' Mary says. 'Sing for us, now. I'll be sad, if you don't.'

The old man looks at her sideways, from under his brows. He takes her hand, and smiles for the first time. 'I will then,' he says. 'Since it's you that asks, Mary.'

He doesn't move from his chair; holding Mary's hand, he simply begins to sing, and there's instant quiet. He sings in Irish, and I sense that he's shown the respect due to a bard. He's a wonderful singer, with a deep, effortless voice and clear delivery. He sings emphatically, with the authority of an artist, and as he does so he continues to hold Mary's hand, squeezing it for emphasis in rhythm with the words. He goes on to sing other traditional songs in English. He sings *Carrickfergus*, and *Eileen Aroon*; he sings of lost love, and of war with the Saxon stranger. And then, quite suddenly, he stops. He stands, and announces that it's time for him to go.

Mary protests. Everyone protests; they implore him to stay. But the old man sets his chin, looking about him fiercely. He must go, he says firmly; and he wishes us all goodnight. He turns and disappears: a stern and abstemious visitor from the past.

Everyone is now very merry: there are many empty Guinness glasses on the table, and there's a good deal of laughter and happy shouting. Paddy hurries by, calling: 'Brian! Brian!'

Brian looks up. 'Hullo, Paddy, are yez all right, then?'

Passing behind my chair, Paddy leans down to my ear, resting a confidential hand on my shoulder. 'I've never been so happy in me life,' he says. Then he passes on and is gone.

Brian is talking to Bernadette and Liam; I'm talking to Mary, and to a friend of hers called Grania: a thin, pretty woman in her forties, wearing jeans and a royal blue jacket of crushed velvet. She has shoulder-length brown hair, a narrow, smiling face and dark blue eyes. She asks me how Brian and I met. Brian is a fine singer, she says, and we talk about the ballads. When she finds I know them, her smile becomes tender, as though we're talking about her children.

'The young people don't care about them,' she says, and her voice is soft and wistful. 'They listen to rock and roll.'

'Time that you sang, Grania,' Mary says. 'Sing a song for Brian and Chris.' Then she says something in Irish, and they both laugh.

With complete naturalness, and without a word, Grania gets up and stands behind her chair, still smiling. Sad-eyed Bernadette looks across at her and then smiles back, taking the cigar from her mouth. 'Grania's going to sing,' she says, and hisses to the others for silence. Then she calls out something in Irish, and they all become instantly quiet.

Grania sings *The Bard of Armagh*: the song of Phelim Brady, the aged bard who is farewelling his youth and his talent. She sings in English, but she introduces thrilling and protracted quarter-tones, in a way that makes the song into a Gaelic lament. The words have always seemed to me to have an Elizabethan nobility, and never more so than now:

And when Sergeant Death in his cold arms shall take me,
And lull me to sleep with sweet Erin-go-bragh,
By the side of my Kathleen, my young wife, O place me,
Then forget Phelim Brady, the Bard of Armagh.

At one point, singing, Grania looks down at me and smiles, and lightly touches my shoulder. She is telling me that her song is a gift to the visiting stranger. Like Mary, like the stern old man, she's transformed as she sings, and is no longer a woman of today in a blue velvet jacket, but a visitor from that old, lost century of pain and hard usage and beauty. All of these people in Tigh Hughes are a family, and all are transformed by their art: by a still living ritual, by that unity which Yeats said was engendered by mythology and the land. Tigh Hughes is no nostalgic folk club; no cabaret for tourists. Tigh Hughes is essentially private, and alive. Here in Connemara, at modern Europe's farthest western point, a life that's rooted in Western myth and memory still survives, for those in middle life. But for how much longer, as the wind hums in the wires that loop across the bogs?

Across the table, Bernadette is watching Grania sing with absolute intentness, her thin cigar suspended in her hand. Her eyes have lost their sadness, and are half-closed in ecstasy: the high and pure trance the Otherworld brings. The Irish need this trance, whose door is opened by music; they are borne up by it, and cannot bear to lose it. Descending, they seek out the substitute trance of drink.

IV

Ten o'clock on a bright, clear morning, two days later. The blue Nissan, which is attempting to reconcile us to its horrendous rental cost by performing smoothly, is on the road again — heading south out of Galway city on National Route 18, bound for County Clare. Irish roads are often narrow but always well paved, and I find driving here relaxing: even on a major highway like this one, the traffic seems never to be too heavy.

A very short run has taken us to the southern side of Galway Bay, where the Lower Shannon region starts. Still in Galway, we're headed for the Burren: the violet land we saw from the beach at Spiddal. When we reach it, we'll have crossed the border into Clare. We plan to linger in the Burren region, and will spend tonight in a fishing village there called Ballyvaughan. Tomorrow, before going back to Oughterard, we'll move further south into Clare, and will search out the village of Sixmilebridge. There, I hope to find Deerpark.

I turn off Route 18 at a town called Ardrahan, and now we drive west on a highway that runs beside Galway Bay towards the Burren. Soon, we come to an inlet of the vast bay, very blue in the bright morning, with a high sky over it and deep green grass running to its edges, littered with dozing rocks, its far shores looking very tiny and remote. Here is Kinvarra, a little fishing port, with the small black Galway fishing boats called hookers moored at the quay, and a cluster of pubs and restaurants, and little throngs of tourists. But Kinvarra is still in Galway, and I don't stop. I want to cross into Clare, whose invisible frontier is just down the road. I'm impatient to reach the Burren, which unaccountably draws me: that vast, extraordinary plateau I've pored over for years, in photographs and passages of description. Now at last I'll see it, and I'm filled with anticipation. Driving, I speed along the straight, empty road, watching through the windscreen. The Burren extends for two hundred and seventy square kilometres: why haven't we sighted it yet?

Brian smiles indulgently beside me. It's here, just up ahead of us, he says.

I stop the car at a crossroads, and we get out to look about us. Low, flat, open country here, with power lines looping through it in long cadences. Very quiet, under the high, clear sky with its white stratocumulus clouds; and the space here seems limitless. Part of Galway Bay is still visible behind us: a green channel. Delicate sunlight, and a light, steady breeze through waving dry grass. Few other cars go by, and there are no people to be seen. Like Connemara, this is a land of stones: piles of stones in a field in front of us, and drystone walls extending into the distance. Scotch thistles and blackberries and many little field flowers skirt the road. There are very few trees; the scene is almost stark. But nothing is ever wholly stark in Ireland: on the southern side of the road there's a field of grain, and beyond that a line of beeches, out in full leaf, and beyond that again, some far, dark green woods. And I find that this open, rocky landscape at the crossroads fills me with the same strange joy that Howth did. Here is another aspect of that lost, unvisited otherland which was first glimpsed in childhood.

But where is the Burren?

Brian points ahead to the west. There, he says; and now I see.

On the other side of the stony field stands an inviting, two-storeyed farmhouse with a glassed-in verandah, next to a little grove of trees. And just behind it, quite close, rising out of the flatland to loom above its roof, is a low, violet-grey barrow, entirely treeless and bare, with a few mossy patches of green. It's at first unremarkable, except for its colour, and not very high; I took it for a mere low hill. But now I see that it's part of a single vast formation of rock, extending to the south until it runs out of sight, and fading to a strange yellow-silver. This is the mysterious Burren, which Lutana once hinted at, in the same way that it foretokened the little rise at Howth: another entrance to the world of the *Sidhe*.

We get back in the car and drive towards it. As we do so, we cross into Clare, and the country of the spirit.

We come into Ballyvaughan: a prosperous-looking little town of solid stone houses and slate-roofed cottages. It's on the coastal road, and is filled with tourists. We've booked two rooms in a big, sprawling old hotel here, and check in and deposit our bags. We eat a fine lunch of cod and fried potatoes in the busy dining room, with most of the languages of Europe babbling around us, together with resonant American-English. Outside in the street, the Burren can still be seen, rising beyond the town, empty as ever.

After lunch, we drive off down a highway whose signposts announce places called Lisdoonvarna, and Doolin. But we won't go there; we're heading only a short way inland, to the Burren. Some two kilometres beyond Ballyvaughan, we pause at Newtown Castle: a circular, simple, sixteenth century tower, constructed of the local silvery stone, and sitting right under the plateau. Nobody here but ourselves and an elderly Irish couple, who are walking about the towerhouse. It was built as a stronghold by one of the O'Brien clans who dominated the Burren; the region is known as O'Brien country. The Burren seems very low here, and its summit looks near enough to reach in minutes. Its highest parts – or so I've been told by our hotel landlord – are no more than three hundred and fifty metres.

We walk on to a little slope at its foot, just behind the tower. Lush grass and bushes go up to a certain level, and then abruptly stop. After that, the violet limestone rocks begin, bare as some alien desert ridge: strange. We won't climb up here, however, since Brian recommends that instead, we drive up a zigzag route just down the road which will take us to the Burren's highest point. He came here often with Phyllis when they were young, he tells me; on the way, he'll show me a Burren ring fort they used to visit: a *rath bóirne*. Constructed by the Iron Age Celts, it's more usually called a fairy fort, and most local people believe it to be fairy-haunted. So does Brian: he's a firm believer in the existence of the *Sidhe*. All his life, like me, he's been aware of the presence of elementals in the landscape; in this, we have a perfect and instinctive understanding.

So we take the zigzag route up a pretty, wooded hill called Corkscrew Hill. Halfway up, Brian directs me to pull over, and I follow him across the road towards the woodland. It's now mid-afternoon, and the delicate sun continues.

Stepping off the road, and passing between some trees, we come almost immediately to a grassy bank, about four feet high, running in a circle around a glade. Richly spreading beeches and chestnuts also enclose the glade – growing both inside and outside the bank, but not in the centre. The centre consists of an open space of soft green grass and wildflowers, perhaps two hundred yards across, and almost as level as a lawn. A modest fairy ring stands on one side of it, made not of stones but of tree stumps. And this is all that's here. This is the *rath*: the fairy fort, or ring barrow.

We walk around the top of the barrow, which time has worn down and eaten gaps in. The glade it encircles is entirely hushed, and patterned with sun and shadow. Our voices become hushed too; the place imposes it.

'I tell ye,' Brian says, 'when I come here, I always feel they're close: the Good People, I mean. Phyllis felt the same. Ye can't doubt it, can ye?'

He smiles, but I know him to be serious. No, I say, you can't doubt it.

We're entirely out of tune with our time, of course, and are glad to be. This post-Christian era in the West, despite its desertion of rationalism and its automatic reverence for alien religions, is not one that's open to Faery, as Yeats and his circle were; as Keats was, and Coleridge, and Shakespeare. The idea of Faery has become absurd: an infantile whimsy, of little interest even to the juveniles of the computer age, who are preoccupied instead by pseudo-legendary warriors, fighting and maiming in those screen-bound computer games whose rays appear to create a Circean enchantment, tedious as the halls of Hell. Legend, exploited and reinvented in the animation studios of Hollywood and Tokyo, is supremely fashionable, and makes money. But not Faery; not those spirits in trees and streams and hills that the Greeks knew, and the Elizabethans, and even the Victorians. Perhaps this is because the interest in Faery was also bound up with Beauty; and Beauty in the Platonic sense – as an archetypal Form, as an absolute and perfect essence – has lately been driven into the street and mocked, and left to wither. Beauty as a grail to be pursued is a notion that's absent from the West's postmodern salons, and even from its poetry, since Beauty and studied irony make poor companions. But this empty *rath* on the Burren is filled with its presence.

While Brian continues to pace along the top of the bank, I step down into the glade.

There's a soft, endless hissing and sighing here, as the afternoon breeze moves through the ring of guardian trees. Nothing else; just an empty space, surrounded by an earthwork that's overgrown with grass: all that's left of a settlement of Celtic cattle lords. Much of the floor of the glade lies in a green-black shadow that's cast by the trees. But where the three o'clock sun gets in, coming through the canopy of leaves, there are bars and patches and coins of blazing gold, turning the green of the grass to a blinding, whitish yellow. Walking into the centre, through this brilliantly spangled shade, is to walk into a dimension like hallucination. The multiple greens of leaves and grass are so intense that one might be under water, and the *rath* seems to sit outside the present, and perhaps outside the real. It resembles a medieval tapestry, the trunks of whose stylized trees are pale with a magical light. Inside the tapestry is an atmosphere that's difficult to define – that's somehow both intense and nebulous. All that one can know is that its origins are very far away.

I climb back onto the barrow, and continue to walk around it. Reaching the western side of the glade, where Brian is standing by a gap in the trees, on the barrow's outer edge, I find that we're looking out from our pool of shade onto sunlit woods and fields that fall away below us: a glowing patchwork of greens and yellows; a land of silent peace. It's the lowland we've just left. The far-off, tiny silver tower of the O'Briens can be seen, and cattle grazing: a pastoral, from the secondhand Europe of my childhood books. The lowing of the cattle floats up to us, and the bleating of sheep. Nothing else. Great clouds come and go, hiding and then releasing the sun.

We linger, in the utter quiet of Fairydom. We are very reluctant to go.

It takes only a few minutes for the car to reach the level, open roof of the Burren. The road runs right onto the top.

Only one other car is here, and its two occupants can be seen walking away up the road. When we get out, silence encloses us again, and the sighing, fugitive breeze. Here at last is the *Boireann*: Gaelic for 'the land of stone'. There are no trees here; nothing to obstruct the gaze. This is the terrain famously described by Oliver Cromwell's surveyor, General Ludlow, as 'a savage land, yielding neither water enough to drown a man, nor tree enough to hang him, nor soil enough to bury'. It was into this barren country that Cromwell drove the defeated Irish Catholics whom his forces had stripped of everything. It was not a land that anyone would covet; yet its emptiness, I know, is an illusion. For thousands of years it has had its visitors and inhabitants: early Christian mystics, for whom its simplicity suggested the Holy Land, and gave rise to visions; megalithic farmers; bandits; Celtic cattle men. Now, only a low drystone wall separates us from its surface; it lies open and waiting, in bright and glittering light.

A desert of smooth limestone pavement, shattered and serrated and broken in fantastic ways, extends into a distance that has no visible limits, under a huge sky. The pavement fills the entire horizon, and resembles the surface of the moon; its colour is silver-grey, tinged with whitish yellow. The violet hue of the Burren has vanished, close up, but reappears in the middle distance like a mirage, where giant rock monuments stand against the sky: deceitfully significant. Brian has no great desire to walk these pavements; he prefers to stroll on the road. But I'm filled with eagerness to be out there. I get over the wall and step onto the surface, and begin to make my way across the limestone slabs.

The breeze increases to an exhilarating wind: I'm surrounded by wind, and by glittering, truthful light. I'm forced at times to leap and clamber, as one does around the rocks on a seashore, since between the smooth slabs are the deep, long crevices called grykes. These are said to harbour the most varied flora in Europe: Mediterranean and Alpine, growing together. The plateau is a desert only from a distance: the rock is stitched with flowers, and full of colour. In spaces between the limestone walls and slabs, tender green grass makes little lawns, where dandelions grow, and many small holly bushes. In the grykes, maidenhair fern and flowers that are mostly unknown to me are growing. Two I'm able to recognize from pictures: the pink geranium of the Burren called Bloody Cranesbill, and a yellow rock rose. Butterflies flutter above the stones.

And now I come to a place where the rock and shale stop, at a little cliff; and once again I'm confronted with the Burren's double landscape. Below me, suddenly, on the other side of a line that's quite definite, the green, pastoral countryside of the lowlands opens up: the woodlands and pastures of peace we looked down on from the barrow. So sudden! This is the secret of the Burren: that aridity lives next to fertility, and hard, stony emptiness coexists with gentle life. And even the rocky Burren has a kindly side, I've learned; there is no severe frost here, the grass grows all the year, and the limestone actually stores warmth. This peculiarity means that it's warmer up here in the winter than it is in the valleys – so the cattle are brought up from below to graze, and then taken down again in the spring.

I wander on across the flowering stone, through the glittering wind and light, not wanting to go back.

V

Next morning we leave Ballyvaughan, and drive back along the road to Ardrahan. There, briefly inside Galway again, we rejoin National Route 18, and head south, bound for the heart of Clare. But before we cross the border, we stop in the small town of Gort.

'I'd like to drop in to Flanagan's Hotel,' Brian says. 'I used to sing there, fifteen years ago. Mr Flanagan's probably still in charge: he ran sessions every week. It was a great pub for singing.'

Gort has a somewhat severe town square, made more severe by today's overcast sky. A giant, crowned statue of Christ the King stands on a plinth in the centre. Coldly handsome, three-storeyed, slate-roofed buildings enclose the square on all sides, their attic windows staring down. Most of them are shops or pubs, and one of them is Flanagan's, which looks newly decorated: white, with a pale blue trim on its windows and gables. We go into a small bar lounge at the front which is empty of customers.

A pale, serious-looking middle-aged woman with blonde hair and a crisp white blouse is standing behind the counter and writing in an account book. A radio is playing very softly, and a percolator of coffee stands on a hotplate at one end of the counter. I order a cup, while Brian asks for his inevitable Guinness. We sit down on plum-coloured banquettes at a table by some windows on the square. The sun has come out without warning, and a beam strikes through these windows to light up our table. It's a very pleasant little bar, expensively fitted out and soothing to be in, at ten o'clock in the morning with the sun appearing. The counter and its set of high stools are of dark, polished mahogany with decorative carving, and the beer-pulls, with their oval badges, are set in a mahogany box that sits on top of the counter like a little coffin. The mirror behind the bar is tastefully lettered with the legend: *Flanagan's Hotel, est. 1962.* Black and white china Scottie dogs sit on a shelf: Irish bars have pleasant *kitsch*.

It's only now, looking about me, that I see that we're not alone here after all. At a table not far from ours, in a corner, a bald, plump, elderly man in a white shirt and black waistcoat is finishing a breakfast of bacon and eggs. Brian sees him at the same time, and calls: 'How are ye, Mr Flanagan?'

The man looks up at him through his spectacles, unsmiling. He shows no surprise, though Brian has appeared in front of him after an absence of fifteen years.

'Not too bad, not too bad,' he says. He speaks in a rapid, terse, precise mutter, rather like old Australian men of my grandfather's generation.

'We've just been in the Burren,' Brian says. 'It's been pretty good weather for us.'

Mr Flanagan considers, expressionless. 'The weather isn't great, but it's dry,' he says. He pops a last forkful of bacon into his mouth, and chews.

The quiet, pale waitress brings a cup of coffee to his table, moving softly, as though approaching a dignitary.

'Put it there,' Mr Flanagan orders, 'and you can clear this away.' He gestures at his plate: a squire in his own domain. Softly and respectfully, the woman obeys, taking the plate and cutlery and moving towards the bar.

'The place is looking nice,' Brian says.

'Yes – I had it all done up.' Mr Flanagan looks around him with sober satisfaction, spooning sugar into his coffee.

Brian tells him that he's been away for many years in Australia, and that he's showing me the country. We hired a car in Galway city, he says.

'Expensive, was it?' Mr Flanagan glances at us both sideways.

Brian says it was, and tells him what we paid.

Mr Flanagan raises his eyebrows, silent for a moment. Then he says: 'He saw *you* coming.' He sips his coffee, and shakes his head: still not smiling, but looking as though he's considering a smile. He seems to be a man who enjoys the misfortunes of others. 'Yes, he saw you coming,' he repeats. 'I could get you a car around the corner for half that price.'

Brian says cheerfully: 'Ah well, it's a pity we didn't know that, and could have come and seen ye. But there it is.'

Mr Flanagan looks at Brian again, more carefully this time. 'I remember you,' he says. 'I remember when you used to play here. Time's going on.'

'It is, it is,' Brian says. 'I've changed a bit.' He claps a hand on his white hair, and grins.

But Mr Flanagan doesn't grin back. 'I've no live music now,' he says severely. 'Only the radio and tapes. I can't afford you now. There's not much music in pubs any more. We don't need it. We've a nice steady trade without it. And people won't travel far to a pub – the breathalyser killed that. There's more Gaelic music in London now than there is here. The Irish over there get homesick.' He gives a short, toneless laugh. 'I used to own two pubs in London: music going all the time, like we had here. But that's all gone now. The young people aren't interested in the old music. They don't care.'

He drains his coffee, and pushes away his cup. 'All the changes,' he says, and stands up.

He moves away out of the bar, without looking back.

We drive down through Clare, where we'll go in search of Deerpark. As we near the county town of Ennis, I think about the Ascendancy, the Normans, and the many complex threads in the weave of Irish ancestry.

Among Catholic Irish, I've discovered, one doesn't talk too much about being of Protestant Ascendancy descent. It isn't popular; the old, subterranean hostility remains, though the Ascendancy as a ruling caste has gone into history, and its families have quietly melted into the general population. But were they not truly Irish? Surely they were, unless Irish patriots are prepared to expel from the pantheon some of their most revered heroes – men such as Wolfe Tone, Robert Emmet and Thomas Davis – and many of their greatest writers as well, such as Swift, Goldsmith, Sheridan, Oscar Wilde, William Butler Yeats and Elizabeth Bowen. The trouble is that the true nature of the Ascendancy is somewhat ambiguous.

Mostly, of course, the Protestant Ascendancy is seen as that Anglo-Irish upper class that established itself at the turn of the 17th century, following the Cromwellian conquest and the final defeat of the Jacobites at Aughrim. The noted Irish historian Roy Foster (himself from one of the great Ascendancy families), says that the definition of the term, which comes from that time, revolved around Anglicanism – and that this in turn defined a landed and professional elite. But the origins of this elite were varied, as Foster points out. Many had arrived in the Cromwellian period; but others had roots much deeper in Ireland. A good proportion of the Ascendancy were descended from the 'Old English', as they were called – those first conquerors who had arrived in the reign of Henry II, and who included Norman nobles and minor English gentry. And some – a very few – could trace their pedigrees to the ancient Gaels. The Young Ireland leader, William Smith O'Brien, was of such descent. The O'Briens of Dromoland had eventually become Protestant baronets; but they were directly descended from the Gaelic High King of Ireland, Brian Boru.

The Ascendancy was focused on the Irish House of Commons, and you could join it by converting to Protestantism, if you had the achievement and money to qualify. Many of the prosperous Old English and Gaelic families did so; and Trinity College, that symbol of Ascendancy privilege, was a seedbed of native Irish causes, and produced such activists against British rule as Wolfe Tone and John Mitchel. Trinity was attended by the sons of landowning peers and professional men – but it also received the sons of successful builders, distillers and butchers. Essentially, the Ascendancy was an aristocracy of self-made men.

Its story really begins with the Norman invasion of the twelfth century, when Richard de Clare, known as Strongbow, landed in Wexford with a small force of knights – among them my ancestor, Philip Devereux. Should one be furtive about this kind of Norman ancestry? Should it disqualify its descendants from being seen as proper Irish? I think not, on both counts. The Normans may have been ruthless, but they were surely one of the most extraordinary groups of people in European history – transforming themselves in a few generations from Viking raiders to a warrior caste possessed of both military and administrative genius. It was this administrative genius that permanently transformed society and government in France and England; and it did the same in Ireland. Its mark is still there, everywhere you go in the countryside; and the Irish can no more expel the Norman from their genes than the English can.

The most generous defence I've read of the Norman role in Ireland's history was written by an Irishman: Sean O'Faolain, who fought for de Valera in 1921. In his brilliant short history of the Irish, O'Faolain rejects out of hand the notion of the Normans as foreign enslavers; instead, he says, they did much to create the modern Irish nation, and taught Ireland the art of politics. They founded the first towns; they built the roads and the ports. They began civic life in Ireland; and O'Faolain sees their castles and their abbeys, whose ruins still dot the countryside, as relics of *Irish* civilization, and as part of a truly Irish inheritance – since the Normans and the Irish commingled. A new sweetness and a new urbanity, he says, were introduced by the Normans into the old Celtic world of blood and feuds – and he speaks of Norman civilization 'lying like a drowned glory beneath a little Irish village', and of what he calls a masked Norman influence still hanging palpably in the air, where only a ruined abbey or hump of grass may remain. At least a seventh of the commonest Irish names are Norman, he points out; and many others are Norman but masked: Burkes are Norman de Burgos, and Power, Coady, Costello, Butler and Joyce are all Norman names. The Normans were not only integrated with the Gaels, they were thoroughly Irishized, in the end; and London began to see the threat of a Norman-Irish island balancing the Anglo-Norman island across the Irish Sea. It began to fear Norman-Irish power and independence, and took measures to quell it, such as forbidding the Normans to wear their hair long, like the Irish. This, O'Faolain says, anticipates the fight of the eighteenth century Ascendancy against the Union of Ireland and Great Britain. The Normans were the first Home Rulers, he claims, and many Norman families opposed the forces of William of Orange: 'Norman gentry went down at the Boyne with the last peerages of Gaelic blood'.

It was the eighteenth-century Anglicans, O'Faolain says, who erected the barriers again. Yet he's generous as well towards the national contribution of the new, Anglo-Irish Ascendancy. It left as its monuments the grace of Dublin and the Big Houses of the countryside, he says; it produced such patriots as Emmet and Davis and Parnell; and in the nineteenth century, native Irish and Anglo-Irish worked side by side to preserve the Irish language and traditions, and to produce the Gaelic revival.

I've touched on these things with Brian, from time to time, but mostly we tend to skirt around them. He's a man of unfailing tact and gentleness, and would never initiate confrontation, or seek to give offence. But the traditions of his family and past make him less than warm towards the Ascendancy; although he never says so, I'm aware that he still sees that class as the traditional enemy. He's less hostile towards the Normans as such, and points out Norman towers to me whenever they appear; but he points more warmly to the old round towers of the Gaels. He's long accepted the fact that my great-great-grandmother Devereux was from an Anglo-Norman family who were Protestants; he's happy to help me look for her grandfather's Big House, and is politely interested in the search we're on today; but I still remember the time, many years ago, sitting over a convivial whiskey late at night, when I first told him of my Devereux ancestors.

He seemed to turn pale, and looked at me with a sort of horror: the only time I'd ever seen him wear such an expression. Then he said: 'You're never descended from *Essex*?'

He was referring to Walter Devereux, first Earl of Essex and Earl Marshal of Ireland, who set out to colonize Ulster for Queen Elizabeth in 1573, and is still remembered for his appalling slaughter and treachery.

No, I said quickly, no: there was scarcely any connection. And I hastened to assure Brian that the Irish branch of the Devereux family, descended from Philip, was separate from the Herefordshire branch that produced the 16th century Earls of Essex. He was mollified, but only just. He looked troubled for some time afterwards, and I've sensed ever since that he warms to a discussion of Margaret O'Meara, but cannot feel warmly towards Jane Devereux. The old barriers are too strong.

Three o'clock in the afternoon, and we're deep in the Clare country-side. According to our road map, we're somewhere between Newmarket-on-Fergus and the village called Sixmilebridge – still on Route 18, which has become quite narrow. We had lunch in prosperous Ennis, in a sumptuous hotel dining room where waiters in black and white hurried about, and lavish sides of meat oozed juices behind glass, and the well-dressed business people of the new Ireland sat talking and laughing over bottles of French wine. Then we explored the streets for a time; but I was anxious to get on and find Deerpark, and Brian had no objection.

The sun is out, and the country through which we're driving seems very quiet and far from the world. Yet it's not: the Shannon, and Shannon airport, are not far from here, on Clare's southern boundary. The luxuriant trees of summer come down to the roadside; occasionally we pass a house, or the gate of a farm. It's a level, pastoral country, with cattle grazing in the fields, and long green hills lying low in the east.

If we find Deerpark, I will be the first Australian descendant of the Devereux family ever to visit it. My only guide is a page photocopied from a book called *Houses of Clare*, by Hugh Weir, published fourteen years ago, in 1986, which says that Deerpark is some three kilometres south-west of Sixmilebridge, on a byroad north of the Hurlers Cross Road. A line drawing of the house is featured, and some account of the different families that owned it, beginning with the Devereuxs. It states that in the eighteenth century William Devereux of Deerpark was married to Margaret Atkins of County Cork – which tallies with the information in Great Uncle Walter's family tree. Great-great-grandmother Jane was William's granddaughter. Her uncle Robert seems to have begun the process of losing the estate by leasing it out; a process which Aunt Averina completed by her demand that it be sold entirely. This would have been around 1814.

Among the succeeding owners were another old Norman family, the Maunsells; and Weir's entry says that during the Famine, Edward Maunsell dispensed gruel to the starving families in the area. The entry says that the walls of the house are some three metres thick – an indication that it probably incorporates an earlier fortified building. A Mass Rock on the estate was used during penal times, and Masses were held there when Dr Kennedy, Roman Catholic Bishop of Killaloe, was living at Deerpark in the early 19th century. The house is now un-inhabited, the entry says, but the original gateway and utility buildings are still standing. It once faced a well-wooded park, but the demesne is becoming a modern housing estate.

Coming near to Sixmilebridge, we see an old man walking by the road, and stop to ask directions. I ask if he's heard of a house called Deerpark; he thinks for a time, and then says he has. But in giving directions, he becomes like the old rural Irishman of the well-worn jokes. 'Ye go down this road to the turn, but don't turn yet. At the next one, turn left, and left again at the junction. Then ye must go up a side road . . .' Thoroughly confused, we drive away, turn down various side roads, and become quite lost. But we are not much concerned, since this is a very beautiful country to be lost in, and the afternoon remains bright, sunny and still. We are driving now down a narrow little road like a lane, with steep, grassy banks on either side and sycamores and beeches leaning over it: a tunnel of green. There's only just room for another car to pass. No car does: we seem to have the country to ourselves. Brian sights the stone gates of what looks like an old estate; perhaps this is Deerpark.

He pulls the car over. We get out, and find ourselves enclosed by an absolute peace, here in the tunnel of the lane. Its warm, still air encloses us like sleep, alive with the hum of summer insects and the sharp, small cries of birds. The trees cast big shadows on the road, and the sun strikes through their leaves to light up the mustard-coloured wayside grass. A few yards off down the lane there's a break in the trees, with an iron gate locking off a pasture where black and white cows are grazing. Distances open up across this green pasture, and the long, soft, low-lying hills are seen on the horizon again, patchworked with trees and other pastures: the distant fields of bliss. Just by the gate, there's an old stone barn with a rusted iron roof, and nettles growing by the door. Nothing else; and yet, as I stand here, I'm filled with the pain of an inverted exile. This is the ancestral Arcadia which some parts of Australia try and duplicate – never quite succeeding, if only because the intensity of the green can't be duplicated. I have a sudden, irrational longing to stay here for ever, and say so to Brian.

He grins. 'Of course ye have. Ye're in the county of your ancestors.'

We go through the high stone gates of the estate, and walk up the drive between low, clipped hedges. A two-storeyed house of eighteenth century vintage appears as we come round a bend. When I compare it with my drawing of Deerpark, it doesn't look quite right; but we decide to ask. We knock at the front door. No-one answers. We walk around to the back, where long stone stables and a courtyard appear, and a parked tractor; we call out, but there's nobody here. We go back down the drive, baffled. It could be Deerpark, but somehow I don't believe so.

Four o'clock. We're still driving about on our search, without success. Hurlers Cross Road doesn't appear on our road map, and there seems to be no way to find it. This is a district of farms and fields and little woods, where occasional small bungalows appear beside the road – most of them of modern construction – and where a few people are going by on foot. We've asked a number of them whether they've heard of Deerpark, or Hurlers Cross Road, but nobody has. One woman says that she thinks there's a district here called Deerpark, but she knows of no old house of that name. We talk to a group of road-menders working at a crossroads; they've not heard of Deerpark, but point to a service station nearby: we should ask in there, they say.

The woman behind the counter knows where Hurlers Cross Road is, but she's never heard of Deerpark. She advises us to go next door, where there's a tiling business, and ask for the owner. 'Tom Fitzgerald will be able to help you, sure,' she says. 'Tom's really keen on local history, and he can tell you about every old house around here. Ask Tom.'

We go into a clean little shop filled with samples of coloured ceramic tiles. A girl asks us to wait, and goes out the back. When Tom Fitzgerald emerges, he proves to be a young man in his thirties, with brown hair in a fringe and a narrow, thoughtful face. Quiet but friendly, he seems more like a scholar than a businessman. He listens attentively as I explain about Deerpark.

'I know the place you mean,' he says. 'And I know where it is. They've built a small new housing estate there, and they've called it Deerpark. But I've never actually seen the old house. It's well off the road, and not easy to find. I'll take you there.'

We tell him we don't want to take up his time, but he assures us that it won't take long, and that he's happy to do it.

'I'm curious,' he says. 'I'd like to see the place myself. Get in your car and follow mine.'

We obey, and follow his red car down the road. He takes a couple of turns, and now we are going along a level, narrow road where some new bungalows appear, roofed with the usual grey synthetic tiles. He stops, and we get out; it has only taken about five minutes. It's a pleasant little road we're in, still rural, bordered by fields and groves of trees; but the bungalows make it look quasi-suburban. There's no sign of any old mansion.

Tom Fitzgerald walks back to us, and points across the road. 'We have to get through here.'

We're looking at a border of such dense undergrowth that nothing can be seen of what lies beyond it. A small, ugly pink bungalow stands some yards away down the road, but there are no other houses nearby. Tom leads the way; we get across a ditch, make our way around some clumps of blackberries, and wade through grass, thistles and nettles whose tops come almost to our shoulders. I follow Tom, with Brian bringing up the rear. Then, emerging from a thicket, we come to the edge of what looks like a disused field.

It's a large field, overgrown with tall, wild grasses with feathery yellow heads, and dotted with big old trees: beeches; firs; ash trees. Because of the trees, its extent is difficult to judge; but it seems to run to a strip of woodland. I guess that we're looking at the remnants of Deerpark's 'well-wooded park', and I struggle a little further through more grass and nettles, catching up to Tom. He's come to a halt, with his back to me. He points without speaking. Out in the middle of the field are what appear to be some old stone stables and outbuildings, of a pale dun colour. They are no different from the other old stables we've seen today, but a sort of shock runs through me. Half-hidden by a stand of beeches, they seem to wait there, as though seen across a belt of time. We have found Deerpark.

We advance a few more paces through the shoulder-high grass; and now the grey roof and chimneys of a big, two-storey, eighteenth century house come into view beyond the stables, partly obscured by the dense, spreading beeches. There's something immensely sad about this silent, grey slate roof and dun-coloured gable, even from a distance: seeing it there, in its abandoned parkland, I have a fathomless pang of grief. Out in the open field now, and bathed in sun, we go on through the feathery yellow grass towards the stables and the back of the house. And as we approach, I see what has happened. Deerpark, the ancestral house of the Devereuxs, which figured so largely in Great Uncle Walter's noble dreams, is derelict.

It isn't beyond repair: both the great stone house and its outbuildings still appear basically intact. But it has obviously deteriorated considerably since Hugh Weir wrote his entry for *Houses of Clare* – calling it 'delightful', and speaking of the yards and walled gardens that were once here. All these are gone. Gone, the orchards, lawns and fishponds; gone, the greenhouses and beehives and kennels; gone, the deer park. The stucco is breaking away from the stonework of the house, the glass has gone from the upper windows, which stare like dark eyes, and those on the ground floor are boarded up. Small trees are growing through holes in the roof of the stables, and a sapling can be seen coming up through a break in the roof of the house. Grass and bushes sprout from its chimney pots, and great dark masses of ivy, like creeping bloodstains, cover large areas of its walls.

We stop by the entrance to the cellars, and Tom peers up at the gaping windows above us.

'What a pity,' he says softly. 'What a pity. They've really let it go. It's the Shannon Development Corporation that owns it – and I'm told they won't repair it. It'll be too late to save it soon.'

I say something about the senseless loss of such a building. Does nobody care?

He shakes his head. 'This is what's happening to eighteenth century houses all over Ireland: the Government can't save them all. It needs a private buyer to come along. I wish I could afford it myself.' He points to the upper windows. 'You can see the situation: kids get in here and vandalize it. I don't think *we* can get in, though, unless you fancy climbing up to the top floor.'

We decide that we don't. We go down into the dim stone cellars, which are like catacombs. I find nothing there but an old wooden butter churn. Then, while Brian lingers by the stables, making a quick sketch, Tom Fitzgerald and I walk around to the front.

The house faces south-east, looking over a long, gentle slope of the feathery yellow grass, bordered by more big trees. Here, Deerpark is seen as it is in the drawing. For all its shabbiness and disrepair, it's still imposing: a typical Anglo-Irish Big House, hip-roofed, massive and plain, with triple chimney pots on its great stone chimneys, and an arched front door in the Venetian style so often used in such houses, with a wide fanlight. Above all, it's plain; what Roy Foster has described as the classic, tall, plain Irish house. 'The beauty of Irish Georgian architecture', he says, in his *Modern Ireland*, 'is that it is never pretty.' This is undeniable: dun-coloured Deerpark is almost stark. It rears against the sky with a sort of sullen stubbornness, recalling those sad, archaic men (still encountered in my youth, and now entirely extinct), who had come from prosperous backgrounds but were now descending into failure, and were 'keeping up appearances' by always presenting themselves in their last, good-quality but disintegrating suits.

The house seems to fascinate Tom Fitzgerald, who surveys it in silence. He roams away through the grass by himself, studying the building and the field from all angles, as though in search of something. I'm glad of this, since I welcome solitude, just now. The three of us seem to be wandering in a dream here, through the yellow, waving grass; we have lost vital contact with each other, as one does in dreams, and have been struck dumb. This is natural; we have wandered into the past, whose invisible film surrounds us, and whose impotent, soundless lament hangs in the buzzing air. I stare at the facade of Deerpark, and its dark, glassless windows stare back at me. They have a stealthy look: they cause me to recall what Elizabeth Bowen once said about the Anglo-Irish: *Their existences, like those of only children, are singular, independent, secretive.*

And I'm remembering *Bowen's Court*, the history of her family and their house in County Cork, where those existences are distilled and preserved, though Bowen's Court itself is gone. The Big House of the Bowens from 1775 until 1959, it was lost when Elizabeth Bowen was finally forced to sell. She saw its new owner raze it to the ground. It was a clean end, she said; and perhaps she was right. Unlike Deerpark, Bowen's Court didn't linger to become a ruin; it lives, instead, in her words:

The great bold rooms, the high doors imposed an order on life. Sun blazed in at the windows, fires roared in the grates. There was a sweet, fresh-planed smell from the floors. Life still kept a touch of colonial vigour; at the same time, because of the glory of everything, it was bound up in the quality of a dream . . .

The land outside Bowen's Court windows left prints on my ancestors' eyes that looked out: perhaps their eyes left, also, prints on the scene? If so, those prints were part of the scene to me.

'I'm trying to see which way the driveway ran. It must have come up here in a curve.'

Tom Fitzgerald has wandered back to me; he points to the roof of a bungalow at the bottom of the slope, showing through the trees by the road.

'You can see what they've done,' he says. His quiet voice has no particular expression; it's neither regretful nor approving. 'They've taken out the gates and what was left of the drive down there, to put in that new house.'

So the 'tall columned ashlar gateway' that Hugh Weir saw fourteen years ago has gone since. I remember the ugly pink bungalow, and imagine more bungalows creeping up the hill, and feel faint and foolish rage.

'What a pity you can't buy the place,' I say. 'You seem very interested in old houses.'

'I am,' he says. 'My father's an historian, and I'm interested in history myself. I bought an old schoolhouse near here, and restored it for my own home. But I couldn't afford Deerpark.' He looks at me. 'So some of your ancestors lived here.'

I explain about the Devereuxs, and he looks into the grass, listening, this quiet descendant of the Norman Fitzgeralds. 'Yes,' he says. 'I see. The name hasn't survived in this region. There are some Devereuxs in

Cork, I believe. Some of the Ascendancy families – like mine – blended in. They took over whole regions, and became completely Irish. Others didn't. I don't think the Devereuxs ever did.'

Brian joins us, and we make our way down the slope, heading towards the road. On the way, we pass through a grove of beeches and sycamores. Their leaves are brightly lit, and circles of sun lie on the carpet of nettles and grass underneath them. Suddenly Tom stops, and stares at two sycamores. Their trunks have grown together, so that they form a Gothic arch that could be walked through.

'Look at that, now. That's very unusual,' he says. His face shows the same deep interest as it did when he looked at Deerpark, and he turns to me. 'They're very old, those two trees. They would have been here when your ancestors were here.'

We go on towards the road. I look back only once at the grey, ruined house of the Devereuxs.

VI

The front bar of Taafe's Hotel, a traditional music pub in Galway city. It's nine o'clock at night: our last night in Galway. Tomorrow we'll quit our cottage in Oughterard, return the blue Nissan to Mr Lynch, and leave for Tipperary on the bus.

I'm seated on a stool at the bar, drinking with an old friend of Brian's called Sean Doherty. People are crowded three deep behind us, and there are few stools to spare: Galway city teems with tourists, and so does Taafe's. But despite the crowd, it's pleasant here, and cosy. The long bar has a polished wooden canopy, and the light is reddish. Brian has been singing, and will sing again. He's sitting with a crowd of fellow-musicians over by the street door, in a sort of performer's preserve: a red-upholstered banquette that runs along the wall, behind a barricade of low wooden tables and a forest of Guinness glasses.

Behind them, a window looks on to Shop Street, framing the medieval steeple and clock of the Church of St Nicholas, in the last pale twilight. And Brian is blissful, seated among his fellow-musicians. He's spoken nostalgically about Taafe's since we left Australia: it's where he performed more than anywhere else when he lived in Galway, and the musicians are all old friends.

The instrumental group who are performing now are impressive: a big, fair-haired man on accordion; a red-haired woman playing the fiddle; a bearded man on uillean pipes, and a black-haired, brooding man playing the bodhran: the Irish drum. This is music from Ulster: the war march of Hugh O'Neill, the brilliant and tragic Earl of Tyrone, defeated by Mountjoy in 1603; music that calls up memories of the last stand of the Gaelic aristocracy, and the Flight of the Earls. The sound is both stirring and menacing, and Sean Doherty drums his fingers in time on the bar, his expression meditative.

He's a regular in Taafe's, it seems: a friendly and talkative man who knows almost everyone around us, and has made me welcome. But despite his gregariousness and surface affability, he isn't easy to categorize; I sense that he's one of those men whose centre is coldly guarded. His age isn't easy to guess. He's lean and athletically built, wearing a dark blue bomber jacket with a checked shirt underneath. He has white hair, close-cropped in the military style, but his long face is youthful-looking; perhaps he's in his early fifties. Brian says he was a schoolteacher for a time, but what he does now isn't clear. He's a native of Galway, but lived for some time in Belfast. He's typically Irish in appearance, but there's something about his face that's also Germanic. Perhaps it's the set of his eyes, which are light blue, with a hard and steady stare: the sort of stare which might be unnerving, if it were not accompanied by a smile. When strangers come up behind us to order drinks, he always puts the same question to them: 'Where are you from?' He puts his question directly, but in a winning manner, and in this way he's so far exchanged pleasantries with a middle-aged engineer from Oregon, a young Dutch couple, and a Jewish lady from New York.

He establishes very quickly that I'm of part-Irish descent, and a Catholic, and seems to warm to me. He talks to me about Galway city, and somehow we pass on to Oliver Cromwell.

'That focking bastard did more destruction here in Galway than anywhere else in Ireland,' Sean says. 'It's been said the curse of Cromwell lies heavier on this town than any other. It's only now beginning to recover from what his army did to it. He destroyed its people; he destroyed its trade; he drove its merchant families into exile. And this was one of the greatest merchant cities in Europe before that, trading with England and the Continent, and especially with Spain. No other ports could touch it, except Bristol and London. You've seen the Old Quays, and the Spanish Arch? Once you'd have seen the big Spanish wine barrels, stacked along the wharf.' He points towards the window, and the fading square tower and steeple of the Church of St Nicholas. 'You see that church? It goes back to the fourteenth century. Cromwell even vandalized *that*, and stabled his focking horses there.'

His pale eyes are baleful, now: the thought of Cromwell seems to stir murderous rage in him, as though we're discussing an oppressor who only died last week. To steer him onto other topics, I ask him whether he thinks the deadlock in the North will soon be resolved. He's noncommittal, and plainly unwilling to discuss it. I offer the opinion that the worst animosity between the Catholic and Protestant factions appears to have died down, and that the people here in the Republic don't appear to care much any more about the old issues.

He glances at me quickly, his expression guarded and withdrawn; then he picks up his Guinness. 'You're right there,' he says. 'They don't care.' There's a note of bitterness in his voice, and I don't pursue the subject.

I order another Guinness for Sean, and a Bushmill's whiskey. When it arrives, Sean looks at it and says: 'Did ye know that's a Protestant whiskey?'

No, I say, I didn't know.

'Bushmill's used not employ Catholics, in the old days.'

'Is that so?' I say. 'Well, it's still a beautiful whiskey.'

He looks at me for a moment as though debating something; then he shakes his head, and grins.

A middle-aged man comes up behind us. He's stockily built and balding, with a reddish, Scottish-looking face. He raises a finger to the barman, and orders a beer. Sean turns to him, smiles, and puts his question. 'Where are you from?'

The man frowns. 'Where am I from?'

'Yes. Where are you from?'

'That's a pretty personal question.' His accent, too, sounds Scottish: an Ulster accent.

Sean continues to smile. 'Personal?' he says. 'It's not meant to be personal. It's just a friendly question. I haven't seen you in here before, so I ask you where you're from. Where *are* you from?'

'I believe that's my business.'

The Ulsterman reaches over and takes his beer from the barman, putting his money on the counter. He's a hard-looking man, and I expect Sean now to be embarrassed into withdrawal. But instead, his pale and level stare remains on the other's face; he continues to smile, in a way that begins to look insolent. 'I meant no offence,' he says. 'This is a friendly pub. Everyone talks to everyone here. I ask everyone that question: Where are you from? People come here from all over the world. That lady over there's from New York. My friend here's from Australia. Do ye see?'

I expect the Ulsterman to grow angry, or at least to walk away. Instead, he stands stolidly with his beer, just behind my stool. He takes a couple of swallows, not looking at Sean. Then he says briefly: 'I'm from Belfast.'

'Ah,' says Sean. 'Yes. I knew you were from the North.'

The Ulsterman ignores him. He turns to me, and his expression becomes quite friendly. 'From Australia, are you? I've relatives out there. Do you know Sydney?'

I tell him that I live there, and he says that his relatives live in the west of Sydney, and that they earn good money as tradesmen. Meanwhile, Sean continues to stare at him, his insolent smile in place. He sways, and I see that he's perhaps a little drunk.

'No offence then,' he says. 'Right?'

The Ulsterman looks at him. 'Look,' he says. 'You ask me where I'm from when I walk in here, and I don't feel bound to tell you that. It's personal. That's all.'

When Sean goes out to the toilets, the Ulsterman addresses me again, in an amiable manner. He tells me that he's just come here to Galway, and has a job with a big manufacturing company: he's an electrical engineer. He volunteers this without my asking him anything; he seems quite happy to talk to me, and his demeanour has changed entirely, to one of easy friendliness. He's on his own here in Galway, he says; he knows nobody yet, and just dropped in to this pub for the first time. He's happy to be out of Belfast, he says; the place depresses him, with its endless troubles.

I ask him whether he thinks an agreement will finally be negotiated in the North between Republicans and Loyalists.

'Christ knows,' he says, and his tone is one of disgust. 'I'm sick of the whole fucking thing. They should give the Loyalists and the Catholics racing cars and put them on a track, and make them settle it that way.'

He finishes his beer, and says he must leave. He shakes my hand, and is gone.

Sean appears a few moments later, sliding onto his stool. 'Gone has he?' he says. 'Stiff-necked bastard. He's a Prod, of course – a bloody Loyalist. I picked him straight away.'

We have a few more drinks, while Brian sings. Sean's eyes are hooded now, and there's a slight slur in his speech. 'To hell with it,' he says suddenly. 'This pub is the best place for me. The rest of the world can go to hell.'

An hour or so later, Brian and I take our leave. Sean grips my hand, and his dangerous eyes hold mine. 'It was good talking with ye, Chris,' he says. 'I hope you'll come back. You'll always be welcome in Taafe's.'

We drive back along the road to Oughterard, to spend our last night in the cottage. Dark trees loom beside the road, and the lights of little houses and shops flare up and then are swallowed in the blackness. Rain has begun. I talk to Brian about Sean, and of the strange and instant hostility between him and the Ulsterman.

'Not surprising,' Brian says. 'Just between you and me, Sean was an IRA gunman. He got into a bit of trouble up North, a few years ago. I'm not entirely clear about it, but he and some of the boys were involved in a shoot-out with some Loyalists in Armagh. Sean did time in the Maze – but that's all behind him now. He's a nice fella.'

FIVE

The Golden Vale

I

Mild, quiet air receives and bathes us: the air of a country town. It's ten o'clock in the morning in Carrick-on-Suir: a fine, bright day of sun and shadow. Released from the Bus Éireann coach by an obliging driver, we stand in Well Road. This is where our bed-and-breakfast guesthouse is located: an establishment called Clareen House. Well Road is a section of National Route 24, which has brought us to Tipperary from Limerick this morning, and which goes on through Carrick on its way to Waterford.

I have an immediate sense of peace. There are masses of fine, big trees a little way off down the road, and bird calls mingle with the distant, wild shouts of children. Two young women go by pushing infants in prams, both of them in jeans and bright-coloured camisole tops. Clareen House is straight across the road: it was known to the bus driver, and its name is fixed above the door. We telephoned its proprietor from Limerick city last night and made a booking, having picked it out of a guide book. It's a tall, two-storeyed nineteenth century building with an arched stone gateway at the side which would once, no doubt, have been the entrance to the stables. We pick up our bags and Brian's gear and make our way across to the front door, where I press the electric bell.

The door is opened by a gaunt, smallish man of middle age. His thick black hair is streaked with grey, and a lock of it falls over his brow. Alert greenish eyes peer at us from behind heavy-framed spectacles, lingering with some curiosity on Brian's musical and painting equipment. Then he says: 'You'll be the gentlemen from Australia? I'm Martin Feeney: just call me Martin.'

Brian and I introduce ourselves, standing in the high old hallway, which leads to a staircase with dark, polished bannisters. The house has a clean smell of furniture polish and flowers.

'You were wanting two single rooms,' Martin says, 'and I'm sorry I can't oblige you, as I told you on the telephone – we just don't run to single rooms, I'm afraid. But when you see the double I've got for you, I think you'll be happy, gentlemen. It's a fine, big room, and you won't be crowding each other. I'll show you up there now, if you like. Later I'll show you the breakfast room. My wife's at work, so I'm doing everything. It's no fun being a housewife, I can tell you.'

He grins confidingly, soliciting a laugh, and leads the way up the stairs. Slightly stooped, in a brown cardigan, blue shirt and woollen tie, he has something of the look of an old-fashioned academic. But his manner is theatrical rather than scholarly, and his raised, thick, humorous eyebrows and flopping black forelock put me in mind of an actor of the old days – or a music-hall comedian, perhaps, in the London of the fifties.

Our double is on the top floor: an attic room. It's as large as a loft, well-lit and handsomely furnished, with a ponderous nineteenth century dressing table and wardrobe, various little tables and chests of drawers, two beds, one at each end of the room, and a big ensuite bathroom. Its high open window looks out over the yard of the house at the back, and distant roofs and trees. The mild, sunny air flows in through this window, and once again I have a vivid sense of peace.

'There you are, gentlemen – plenty of space, as you see,' Martin says. 'Do you think this will suit you, now?'

We assure him that it will, and he asks us how long we'll be staying. Perhaps as long as five days, I say. Perhaps more; we'll let him know. I have a premonition of happiness here, and the feeling that I'll want to remain longer, if Brian is willing. This is entirely irrational, since I've so far seen almost nothing of Carrick-on-Suir at all.

'Of course,' Martin says. 'Certainly. Stay as long as you like, so long as you give me a day's warning.' Elaborately courteous, he manages at the same time to hover on the edge of a mysterious amusement, his mouth fastened tight over the edges of a saucy smile. He appears to be playing a part, to divert himself: a comic butler, perhaps, out of an old drawing-room comedy. 'Sure, and you're lucky with the weather,' he says. 'You may not realise how unusual it is. We've not had a summer like this for years. But I hope you won't be bored here, gentlemen. It's a lovely place, Carrick, but it hasn't the number of beauty spots or monuments you'll find in other parts of Ireland.' He cocks his head on one side. 'Would you know anyone in the town at all?'

'I'm an old friend of Bobby Clancy's,' Brian says. 'We've come to visit him. Maybe you know him?'

Martin raises his eyebrows higher. 'I do of course,' he says. 'Everyone in town knows Bobby Clancy: he's one of our famous men. Well, well, so you're a friend of Bobby's.' He glances at Brian's guitar. 'And you're maybe a musician yourself, now?'

When Brian tells him he is, Martin nods and looks arch, adjusting his spectacles. 'And you'll be out playing in the pubs with Bobby, I've no doubt? You'll have some good times, then. He's a night owl, our Bobby – I don't know how he keeps it up. I'm sure *I* couldn't. Well, gentlemen, if there's anything you need, you've only to ask. Give me your washing, and I'll put it through my machine – it's no trouble. And now I'll leave you to settle in.'

He gestures at the beds, only one of which is a double.

'I'll let you fight it out between you who has the biggest bed.' He winks at Brian. 'You're a big fella – maybe *you* should have it. But don't let your friend jump in with you.' Then, hastily, holding up both hands to take back his words: 'But that's all right: *I* don't mind, I'm sure.'

A last little smile and he's gone out the door, closing it gently behind him.

Five o'clock in the afternoon, and I'm dozing on the single bed.

We've spent the day exploring the town, and got back half an hour ago. Brian has gone out again to make a sketch by the River Suir, but I've succumbed to a wish for solitude, and to a pleasant languor. The day's mild warmth continues, filtering through the high, open window. The people here call it a heat wave, but it's hardly what Australia terms heat; rather, it's like Sydney in the spring, before the real heat begins: the mild, delicious summer of the temperate zone.

I'm asleep, and find myself standing in an empty lane. It's bright with sunlight, and bordered on both sides by blossoming hawthorn hedges. Bird calls sound here persistently, and somewhere there's the barking of a dog. I'm not sure where this place is; but I think perhaps it's near New Town, the suburb of Hobart where I lived as a child, and where the big old houses of Bay Road looked down towards a bay of the Derwent, and across to Mount Direction in the east. A little way upriver, at Risdon, the prison hulk *Anson* once lay, where Margaret O'Meara served her time of gang probation. I'm somehow aware of this, in the dream, and find that I've become a child again. Then I hear my name called, in a woman's voice.

It calls me on three long-drawn syllables: *Chris - to - pher.* This is the way my mother used to summon me, when I was off around the district with my friends and she wanted me in for tea – her voice floating out across the neighbourhood's gardens and backyard fences. I look down to a bend in the lane, expecting to see her. A woman appears there: smallish, dark-haired, pale-faced, light-eyed, in a fawn dress with a pale blue shawl about her shoulders, similar to one my mother used to wear. But it isn't my mother – though it's not unlike her. It's no woman I recognise, yet she smiles and calls my name again, in her high, musical voice; and now I become aware that her accent is Irish. I would like to go to her; to walk down the lane. But as happens so often in dreams, I stand frozen, unable to move. The birds twitter, and the dog barks.

I'm awake, in this big, pleasant attic in Clareen House. The birds go on twittering, and the distant dog barks at intervals. My watch says five-thirty; but the sun is as bright through the window as it was this morning. The long Irish twilight has yet to begin.

I lie thinking about Carrick-on-Suir. Its peace, though gentle, has proved to be oddly magnetic, and my premonition has already been confirmed: I want to prolong our stay here. In fact, in the ten days that are left to us in Ireland, I doubt that I'll want to take up residence anywhere else – and have said so to Brian. He's agreeable: since we'll be seeing Bobby and Moira Clancy, he's more than content to stay. But my wish must have seemed a little strange to him: as Martin Feeney has pointed out, Carrick-on-Suir has few particular beauty spots or monuments. My guidebook confirms this, baldly stating that this sleepy market town has no outstanding sights other than its fifteenth century Norman bridge across the Suir, and Ormond Castle: the fine Elizabethan mansion built by 'Black Tom' Butler, the tenth Earl of Ormond – this being a region once dominated by the powerful Ormond Butlers. And the book goes on to point out that Carrick has been in decline since Tudor times. At the end of the 18th century, its population was 11,000: today, it's only half that. But none of this matters: tourist 'beauty spots' and ancient monuments have never mattered much to me, and have little to do with the effect that this place has on me.

In the course of the morning and this afternoon, wandering about the town and along the river, Brian and I entered a territory of trance, mild yet profound, coloured by the extraordinary summer weather. The trance gave birth to my dream; and *I know where I am* – though we've yet to explore very far. A country I've glimpsed only in books now lies all around me, filled with the murmuring of the past. Carrick-on-Suir (*Carraig na Siúire*, or Rock of the Suir), tucked into Tipperary's southeast corner, is unremarkable as a town. But it was once the theatre for remarkable events, and lies at the heart of great beauty, in a landscape that resembles the valley of the Loire. It's close to the border of Waterford, where the Comeragh Mountains stand, seven miles off to the south. To the north, also quite close (and nothing is very far here), are the soft hills and vales of Kilkenny. And in the northwest is one of Ireland's loveliest and most fertile regions: the Plain of Tipperary, or Golden Vale, at whose heart rises the giant Rock of Cashel, seat of the ancient Irish kings. Out there, visible from the town, is the small round mountain called Slievenamon: the Mountain of the Women, where Finn mac Cumhal and his warriors of the Fianna met the host of fairy maidens, and did battle with the fairy hordes – and where the leaders of Young Ireland held their last mass meeting, on the eve of their doomed attempt to wrest freedom for their country from the British.

Yes, I know where I am, here in the valley of the Suir. This is the edge of the heartland of Munster, where William Smith O'Brien and Thomas Meagher and their comrades staged their hopeless, romantic rising, in 1848: the gesture that would see them transported as felons to my native island. This is south Tipperary, the region that was home to Margaret O'Meara – transported for a far less exalted crime than that of the exiled heroes, just three years earlier. And thirteen miles upstream from here is Clonmel, Tipperary's chief town, where her trial took place.

Was Clonmel where she lived? Or somewhere else, nearby? Did she live here, perhaps, in Carrick? This might account for the effect the town has on me: for the feeling of tranquillity and joy which is almost like that of homecoming. Is this why I have such a reluctance to leave? Whatever the facts might be, I know one thing: she is in the air around me.

Brian knows Carrick quite well, from visits in the past to Bobby Clancy. After we'd unpacked this morning, he took me down to the river.

Clareen House is on the western edge of the town, taking its name from Clareen Well, an ancient source of water. A byway off Well Road led us within minutes to a towpath along the Suir: a relic from the days of horse drawn barges, taking traffic from Carrick to Clonmel. It was now nearly noon, with no sign of a break in the weather. Under a soft blue sky, the river flowed by on its way down to Waterford, some 28 kilometres to the south.

I take deep and wistful delight in the rivers of the northern hemisphere, coming as I do from a country whose waterways are either sluggish or in devastating flood – and the Suir was a classic northern river. It ran swift and broad, its water a clear and clean blue-green, with scatterings of silver. There were many little eddies and currents in it, since the Suir is a tidal river; and the spot where we were standing was close to its upper tidal limit. Reeds swayed in its eddies, and long, canoe-like skiffs lay moored at intervals: fishing boats, Brian told me, known locally as cots. We followed the towpath downstream, where it ran along a curving quay: a low stone wall above the water. On the inner side of the path was a bank, lined with tall trees and hedges of blackberries; behind these, pastures could be glimpsed. A little way ahead, the bank was replaced by a high brick wall; further on, the old gabled buildings of the town could be seen, and a long green hill behind, and a little Norman church, and the old Norman bridge that a Butler had built, before Columbus sailed to America. I counted eight stone arches, and Brian told me that the arch on the opposite shore had been blown up in the Civil War of the 1920s, and had been rebuilt.

Only a few people were walking on the path: women and children, mostly. From somewhere distant came the shouts of boys, dwindling quickly in the bright, wide air. Very still. A faint breeze moved the leaves of the trees, and an intimate warmth enclosed us as we walked. It was strange and euphoric, this warmth, acting like a drug, making the towpath seem a byway into bliss. It enlarged the tiny twitterings and stirrings of the natural world, and made its creatures distinct as things seen in childhood: a white butterfly, dancing up and down in the grass; a dragonfly hanging poised on a reed above the water. There was a sense of waiting; but a waiting that was abstract, remote from the material world. The regular chugging of an engine came from nearby: a pump, perhaps. No other man-made sounds. Peace enclosed the river and the town; peace, and the burgeoning splendour of summer in Europe.

I paused, to look across the river. Over on that opposite shore, there was little sign of settlement: nothing but gently sloping pastures, gold-green in the sun, where groups of very sleek cattle grazed. The fields were marked out by lines of trees, coming right down to the river. Behind was a backdrop of thickly wooded hills, long and very low, running for the length of the horizon, their rims dark with pines. A row of giant beeches grew near the shore: so dense, so sumptuous, that the shadows at the heart of them looked black, while their heads glowed like clouds of green smoke.

I went on, and caught up with Brian. The voices of the boys called louder, and now we sighted them, out in the middle of the stream. Some half a dozen were crowded on a rubber raft: Irish Huck Finns, gesturing and chattering like a group of white-skinned monkeys. Catching sight of us, they waved and cheered. A group of little girls ran past us, laughing. A woman in a big straw hat walked a golden Labrador on a lead.

'He'll be wanting a swim,' I said; and was suddenly conscious of how Irish this construction was: a construction I'd used all my life.

She smiled. 'Sure, he's had one already.'

We went up into the town, turning left at the Old Bridge.

Carrick sat on a little hill. It was quiet, as I expected, and sleepy contentment hung in its air; yet it also had a look of prosperity. Main Street ran along the top of the rise, following the curve of the nearby river; yet the river was hidden from view. The town was immaculately tidy, and busy without loss of serenity. The people bustled and smiled, and there seemed to be a legion of young mothers pushing prams and strollers. Most of the old shop buildings – none of which appeared to be of any later vintage than the nineteenth century – had been recently renovated, and painted in the bright pastel colours that Irish towns like. But there was no abortive modernization: the buildings had been treated with respect. The old wooden frames of the display windows were in primary reds and greens, and nearly every upper window had its flower-box. Baskets of flowers dangled above doorways. It was a town that made you cheerful, as the people did; a town that appeared to be cherished.

At the old Carraig Hotel, we paused. Daniel O'Connell once banqueted here, after a Repeal mass meeting; and it was here, on the street outside, when the Carraig was called the Bessborough Arms, that the young Thomas Meagher had rallied the people of Carrick, in the hot and crucial July of 1848: a summer that must have resembled this one. The great meeting on the slopes of Slievenamon had taken place on the 16th; in response, six days later, the English Government had suspended habeas corpus. Forced into action before they were ready, the Young Ireland leaders had 'come out', as they put it – and Meagher, William Smith O'Brien and John Blake Dillon, all with charges of sedition hanging over them, had moved through the countryside with their comrades, preparing to launch the rising that had come too soon, but which they hoped would put all Ireland in their hands – recruiting a peasant army of half-starved men who brandished pikes, guns and pitch forks. They could take Kilkenny, they thought. They could take Waterford. They could take Tipperary. They were told that the country along the Suir was ready to take up arms at once; and so they entered Carrick.

It was a high point in Meagher's life. In its aftermath, a few months later, incarcerated in Richmond Prison in Dublin, he would muse on that moment in wonder, in his *Narrative of 1848*:

Though many months have passed away since, I am still as perplexed
about that strange scene as when I stood in the midst of it . . . It was
then more like a dream than an actual occurrence; and it now seems to
me the same.

A torrent of human beings, rushing through lanes and narrow
streets . . . whirling in dizzy circles, and tossing up its dark waves, with
sounds of wrath, vengeance and defiance; clenched hands, darting high
above the black and broken surface . . . eyes red with rage and despera-
tion, starting and flashing upwards through the billows of the flood;
long tresses of hair – disordered, drenched and tangled – streaming in
the roaring wind of voices, and, as in a shipwreck, rising and falling
with the foam; wild, half-stifled, passionate, frantic prayers of hope.

It was the Revolution, if we had accepted it.

They were his, that night, and he led them down to Waterford. But
outside the city, in the early hours of the morning, they melted away.
The fact was that Meagher and his comrades were trying to lead a
people who were exhausted by the Famine, and whose priests were
warning them to do nothing – telling them that the British would
decimate them. So the revolution died stillborn; it must await the
Fenians and de Valera and the deadly Michael Collins to be brought
into being. And as punishment for their poetic and ultimately bloodless
revolt, the patriotic gentry of Young Ireland would spend years of exile
in a crude yet tranquil British gaol colony, on the utmost rim of the
earth.

I stood in peaceful Main Street, the far-off cries sounding in my
head, thinking of young Tom Meagher: that privileged, high-spirited,
witty and irrepressible man who scarcely took life seriously, yet who
was prepared to cast all his privilege away in the pursuit of national
freedom. A quintessential man of 1848, with its fevered nationalism,
he's become an entirely archaic type in every way: a flamboyant
romantic hero for whom failure could be a sort of grandeur; a warrior
cheated of his battle and his glory. Carrick would remain at peace –

though there would be blood enough here when the 1920s arrived – and Meagher would find war and fame in the end on the fields of the American Civil War: those terrible battlefields where the modern world was born, with its mechanical and unromantic slaughter.

Six o'clock now, and Brian comes in. Throwing down his sketchbook and his round case of paints, he comes over to my bed and grins down at me, hands on hips.

'Time to get moving,' he says. 'I got through to Bobby Clancy on the phone.'

He first telephoned Bobby from Galway some days ago; so the Clancys have been expecting us. But there was no answer on their phone this morning or early this afternoon.

'He and Moira were out visiting friends,' Brian says. 'But they're happy to see us now – Moira's asked us to tea. And this evening, they'll drive us down to a pub in Kilkenny. Bobby says it's a really special little place, where music's bound to happen. There'll be good crack there with Bobby around, I can promise ye.'

We walk into the town by way of Well Road, which soon becomes Greystone Street, which brings us to West Gate: once the entrance to the walled medieval town. Here we turn left, passing by the solid square tower of the eighteenth century Town Clock, whose hands have almost reached seven, and which is topped by a weather vane in the form of a salmon, signalling Carrick's identity as a river town: a fishing town. It's still bright daylight; only lengthening shadows indicate the remote possibility of evening, and the pollen-coloured sunlight continues to hold the valley and the town in a delicate, musing calm, as though refusing ever to dissolve. We turn right into a street where the old town wall once ran, passing the St Nicholas Burial Ground, and so come into the shadow of St Nicholas Church: a grey, massive, nineteenth century building with a tall, Italianate tower. Here, in narrow William Street, is the home of Bobby and Moira Clancy: a two-storeyed town house.

This is the family home where the Clancys grew up: the brothers who were largely responsible for launching traditional Irish music into world popularity. Bobby and Moira have a big house on the coast in Waterford, Brian tells me; but they still use this home in Carrick. Tom and Pat Clancy are dead now. Liam is the sole survivor of the three brothers who made up the original group in America with Tommy Makem. Bobby occasionally went over to America in the seventies to do concerts with his brothers, but chose mainly to live and work in Ireland. He achieved national popularity in the sixties with a regular television programme, and he and his sister Peg collected traditional ballads over many years, performing as a duo on radio and television. Now seventy-two, Bobby still does occasional concert tours in America, and makes recordings.

'Every one of that Clancy family was musical,' Brian said. 'And there were nine of them altogether. The most musical of all was the mother, so they say: she grew up listening to the old songs, and passed them on to the boys. Well, here we are.'

He puts his guitar down on the footpath, and knocks on the door.

Nine o'clock. Moira Clancy has served us a dinner that was perfect in its simplicity: superb fresh mackerel fried in butter, with boiled potatoes and cream and a green salad, followed by apple pie. Now we're on our way into Kilkenny, in Bobby's car. It will take us less than half an hour to get to the promised pub, which is called Shirley's.

We've already crossed the Kilkenny border; it took only a few minutes. The twilight has at last begun, but the colours are still in the trees and the fields. As Bobby speeds down a narrow, deserted little road that passes through some woods, Moira leans close to him, and murmurs:

'Are you all right to drive, Bobby? We've had a good bit of Guinness.'

'Of *course* I'm all right, Moira.' Bobby turns his beak-like nose towards Brian and me in the back, and winks at us. 'This car practically drives itself to Shirley's, it's been there so often. And it'll bring us back again, even if I'm blotto.'

Moira turns to us, eyebrows raised, and smiles. '*I'll* be the one who drives back,' she says.

She's a pretty, brown-haired woman, friendly and gentle-voiced, with a soothing calm about her. Her grey eyes have a humorous glint. And a memory has come back to me. I've owned for years an ancient copy of the *Clancy Brothers Irish Songbook*, published in New York in 1969: among the many photographs in it there was one of Bobby and Moira's wedding party. He and she, bride and groom, glowing with youth and happiness, were marching down a road in the countryside here – somewhere near Carrick, no doubt – flanked by the brothers, Liam, Tom and Pat, and followed by a great crowd of people. All four Clancy brothers were in formal dark suits, and all of them were joyously singing as they went, while Liam strummed a guitar. Moira, in her wedding dress, smiled just as joyously, holding Bobby's arm: a classic, dark-haired Irish beauty. She was the prettiest woman for miles around, Brian once told me, and the picture bore this out. Moira comes from Ring, the Gaelic-speaking region of Waterford, and her maiden name was Mooney. She and Brian speculate that they may be related.

Bobby turns again, darting another swift glance at Brian and me. He's the lean, dark-eyed type of Irishman, with fine features and rapid, precisely articulated speech. The mop of dark hair that appears in the photograph has gone white now: sparse in the front and swept straight back. Like Moira's, his brown eyes shine with a lively amusement. Sharp and vital, he's continuously cheerful, and his life-force seems that of a much younger man.

'I tell you, you'll love this pub,' he says. 'It's in a little village called Kells. Mary, the woman who runs it, is an old friend. Shirley's hasn't been spoiled – it's off the beaten track, and we all know each other there. So many of those old places are gone, now. You remember how it used to be, Brian?'

'I do, sure,' Brian says. 'Great times we had in those days, Bobby.'

'Yes – those little pubs,' Bobby says, and his voice, in the dimness of the car, becomes tender and elegiac; yet it never loses its underlying, matter-of-fact cheerfulness. 'Just as they'd been a hundred years before, with a big fire, and we'd crack on all night. But now the plastic and the TV sets and the piped music have taken over, in so many of them. It's sad.'

He points to a lone house on a rise, as we pass: a chalet-like building with a tiled roof, that appears to be of recent construction. 'Take that place,' he says. 'That's a really ancient pub that got modernized. We all used to go there often, years ago. We called it the Whispering Pub.' He laughs. 'We called it that because it was run by two old ladies who'd never speak above a whisper. So everyone found themselves whispering too. You'd go into the bar there and you'd be *whispering*. You didn't dare make a noise. If anyone had spoken out loud, those two old ladies would have been horrified.'

Laughing, we drive through the woods and deserted fields of the Nore Valley: a rich, green and amber landscape that seems buried too deep for the contemporary world to find. Perhaps this is why Bobby likes it.

When we reach Kells, sunset is almost over. Kells is a very small village indeed, sitting above the banks of the Nore. It's not the place where the Book of Kells was found, Bobby tells us: that is in County Meath. Shirley's pub, where he parks the car, is a long, low, farmhouse-like building standing on a junction. A little road goes down from it to a stone bridge over the river, and an ancient stone water mill. Twilight is advancing fast; but before we go into the pub, Bobby and Moira lead us off down the road.

'You've got to see Kells Priory,' Bobby says. 'You won't see another place like it. It's not far.'

We come to a spot where dark green fields extend for miles, in the final heavy rays of sunset. Tiny woodlands lie beyond, like those in a tapestry. And here are the ruins of a whole medieval walled city: square, sombre grey towers, a long broken wall, a ruined church, and a gatehouse; a Norman settlement, all laid out on the edge of these empty, pondering, dark green pastures. No-one else is here. We all grow quiet, wandering along the wall; as we do so, the sun finally sets, and the gold disappears from the trees. Dusk makes the ruins illusory; our faces grow pale and unlikely, and even Bobby's brisk comments seem to come from a distance, as though heard in memory.

We turn away from a past that's too stony and far to touch, and walk up the road towards the warm amber lights of Shirley's.

The aged, low-ceilinged bar-room takes the form of an L. There's much old wood; pastries and cakes sit in baskets along the bar. Placid voices murmur, and there's an occasional soft laugh. I'm becoming accustomed to the intimate, domestic atmosphere of Irish country pubs, but this one seems more private than usual. There are no more than twenty people here, all of whom clearly know each other. Their eyes turn towards us with a polite, cautious friendliness, and I guess that we're expected.

A number of people greet Bobby and Moira Clancy, and she and Bobby wish everyone good evening. Mary, the owner, comes from behind the bar to greet us, and is introduced to Brian and me. She's a plump, vivacious woman, with the lightly-worn air of authority that all successful inn-keepers have, and she points out a table for us at the top of the L, next to a sort of internal courtyard. Bobby leads the way, carrying his banjo in its case; Brian follows with his guitar. I suspect that this is the unofficial musicians' section; but no music is being played at the moment. Extra chairs are brought for us, and we sit down at a table with a group of men and women all of whom seem to be known to Bobby and Moira.

The people at the table glance at Brian and me with veiled curiosity, but nobody makes us feel that we should account for ourselves; everyone is easy yet reticent. Bobby is treated as a friend, not as a celebrity, though his arrival here is clearly a happy event. He has the unmistakeable air of a seasoned entertainer, and moves with a straight-backed briskness which is almost military. It's a style that brings back a memory of his brothers on stage, all those years ago: they moved in the same way, professional discipline and vitality combining with irreverence and humour.

The singing begins quite naturally, without urging or discussion. It's opened by a large, elderly woman in a black silk dress, sitting at the table next to us with her daughter: a young woman in her twenties. Side by side, glasses of Guinness in front of them, they have been entirely silent; but now the mother suddenly begins to sing, unaccompanied. Surprisingly, she sings 'Danny Boy', which many Irish singers have come to avoid, since its beauty has been defiled by all too many drunken amateurs. She has a fine, pure voice which has once been a big one. People in pubs like this simply sing when the spirit moves them, and are listened to respectfully. This is how it must have been once in England and Australia, until somewhere in the mid-nineteenth century. Then it was lost, as the oral culture was lost. If the woman in the black dress sang in an Australian bar-lounge, she would cause laughter or embarrassment or both; and she would scarcely be heard for the thundering of the poker machines, the television set over the bar, and the general din.

When she's done, we applaud. 'Lovely,' Bobby calls. 'Lovely, Josie.'

But the woman shakes her head sadly. 'Ah no, my voice has gone,' she says.

'Well, if that voice has gone,' Bobby says, 'I'd love to have heard it when it was here.'

A big, black-haired man leans over to Bobby. 'You'll sing for us, Bobby?'

'I need no persuading,' Bobby says. 'You know me, Tommy – any excuse to crack on.' And he opens the case that holds his banjo.

The long-necked banjo is an exciting instrument in the hands of a professional. Bobby plays it with an American crispness and panache, and with the same electric liveliness that's in everything he does. The sound fills the room, and people begin to move towards us from the far end, and to gather round our table. He begins by singing 'The Barnyards of Delgaty' and follows it up with 'The Real Old Mountain Dew'. Fast jaunty songs like this seem to suit his nature: he's a jaunty man. I'm struck by the power and ease of his delivery, and say so to Moira, who sits next to me. I tell her what a pleasure it is to hear one of the Clancy brothers, after listening to their recordings for years. But she shakes her head, and faint sadness comes into her face for a moment.

'Ah, but his voice isn't quite what it was.'

I can detect no trace of deterioration, and say so.

Bobby then introduces Brian, who sings 'The Rocks of Bawn', and 'Bold Jack Donahue'. He's regarded with warm curiosity, like an emigrant returned after many years of wandering. People grow easy and friendly with us both, and ask us questions about Australia. After more drinks and conversation, Tommy leans over to me, and speaks in a confidential tone, his lean face serious.

'Are you enjoying yourself, now?'

I assure him that I am, and he nods solemnly, seeming reassured. 'That's good. You're an *inward* sort of fella, I'm thinking.'

A short, sandy-haired man sitting next to him is looking at me fixedly. 'I've seen you before. Now where is it I've seen you?'

'You can't have seen him, Michael,' Bobby Clancy says. 'He's just here from Australia.'

'But I have, I have,' Michael says. 'Or else he reminds me of someone.' He snaps his fingers. 'I know! It's Senator George Mitchell!'

'By God, you're right,' Tommy puts in. 'I've been thinking the same myself. He's the double of Senator Mitchell! Isn't that so?'

He looks around the circle of smiling faces, all of whom are studying me, and there's a murmur of agreement. 'Sure, I thought so the minute he walked in here,' someone says.

It's agreed: I'm the double of George Mitchell, the Irish-American senator who acted as a peace envoy for the United States in Northern Ireland, chairing the historic 1998 peace negotiations, and doing a good deal to forge the power-sharing agreement that ended decades of bloodshed in the North. I've never seen a photograph of Senator Mitchell, but I'm happy to accept the honour; and happier still when attention turns elsewhere.

At midnight, the singing is still going strong. The doors are shut, but no-one makes a move to leave; and now Mary serves free sandwiches and sausage rolls. This is clearly in honour of Bobby's visit, but it's done without fuss or explanation. Bobby sits down next to Moira, and leans to speak in her ear, his words just audible to me. 'Nice of Mary to do this for us, Moira. Nice.'

Somewhere near one in the morning, the session draws to its end. Bobby, Brian and Tommy sing 'The Parting Glass' together: most haunting of all Irish drinking songs, and the traditional farewell of the Clancy family:

> Oh, all the comrades that e'er I had,
> They were sorry for my going away.
> And all the sweethearts that e'er I had,
> They'd wish me one more day to stay.
> But since it falls unto my lot
> That I should rise and you should not,
> I'll gently rise, and I'll softly call:
> 'Good night, and joy be with you all.'

Listening, enfolded by the warmth and noise of Shirley's, and seeing in my mind's eye the cold stone towers of Kells and the deep fields of night outside, I'm filled with a delight that's unique in my life. Moira glances at me, and smiles: a smile which has understood me.

'You're home,' she says.

II

Breakfast, in the quiet ground-floor dining room in Clareen House. It's nine-thirty, and all the other guests have eaten; Brian and I slept late, after our evening at Shirley's. But although we're half an hour outside the time limit, the obliging Martin Feeney brings us the usual huge breakfast that's expected in an Irish B and B: bacon, eggs, sausages, tomatoes, and soda bread.

'There you are, gentlemen, you'll be needing the sustenance. You've been out jarring in the pubs with Bobby Clancy, I've no doubt? They drink a lot, these musicians.' He winks at me, and jerks his head at Brian. 'Your friend must be a very good musician, to play with Bobby. But they live and play hard, don't they? I'll get you some coffee, gentlemen: that should restore you. Anything else that you need, you've only to say.'

Watching us with his air of mysterious amusement, he seems to be guessing at wild nocturnal orgies.

At four in the afternoon, we're in the back seat of the Clancy car again, being driven north from Carrick. Martin Feeney is right: Bobby is a night owl, and likes to start his day at around this time.

Once again we have perfect July weather; and there are many hours of daylight ahead. Moira and Bobby are taking us to Ballingarry, about half an hour's drive away, on the edge of Tipperary's Golden Vale: the little village where the ill-fated rising led by William Smith O'Brien came to its climax. Yesterday, telling Bobby and Moira how important Smith O'Brien was in Tasmanian folklore, I said that I was curious to see the Widow McCormack's farmhouse, where Young Ireland made its one and only stand, and the celebrated Battle of the Cabbage Patch took place. It's no longer celebrated in Ireland, it seems, and Bobby and Moira were vague about it; they'd never seen the house themselves, but offered to take us there. They seem to enjoy such expeditions, and have plans for others in the days to come.

We're nearing a little village called Mullinahone, to the east of Cashel. The Golden Vale lies all around us, bathed in late sun: this huge expanse of farmland on the plain of Tipperary that's the richest in Ireland, breeding prime dairy cattle, and stretching away into Limerick. Long shadows cross the road, and these gold and green pastures of plenty extend in a dreaming brightness, ordered and empty and at peace, marked out everywhere by lines of blue-green trees. They dwindle, in summer's tinted haze, becoming minute on the horizon. Nothing mars the beauty of the Vale; nothing breaks its perfect stillness. The gardens of the cottages beside the road are blazing with summer flowers.

We stop beside one of them, where a white-haired old man and his wife are digging in the garden. He comes across to the car. Moira and Bobby are not sure of the route to Ballingarry, and ask him the way. He screws up his face into a sly smile.

'Turn right,' he says, 'and follow the telegraph poles. Ye can't miss it – God bless ye.'

As we drive off, Bobby says: 'I think he's paid by the Irish Tourist Board to put on that act. Are you any the wiser, Moira?'

'Not really,' Moira says placidly, 'but I'm following the telegraph poles.'

'You do that, Moira. We'll come back to Mullinahone later,' Bobby says. 'There's a very special pub I want to show Chris, that's just near here. It's called the T'atch.' He chuckles mysteriously at the thought of it, and Brian joins in.

Mullinahone: I'm remembering what happened here.

This was the village where the Young Ireland rising began to falter – led as it was by a man who had never believed in violence, and who disapproved of the methods of revolution. Poor Smith O'Brien! Upright, utterly honest, worthy and somewhat humourless, this handsome aristocrat with the firm and well-cut features and luxuriant head of hair was stiff-necked to a degree. Not to be bought or sold, he was an idealist in the true sense of the word. But he was the wrong man for the moment: a fastidious, highly-strung intellectual. True, he was a descendant of Brian Boru, king of ancient Munster; but he was also a Protestant landowner, a product of Harrow and Cambridge, and a member of the House of Commons. He was not even disloyal to the Queen. All he wanted – as he had said in a speech in the Commons – was an end to rule through the Commons, and self-rule in Ireland granted instead, through a local legislature. But if England continued to deny Ireland this through force, he said, then Irishmen had the right to arm – as citizens all over Europe were arming, in this momentous year of revolutions, when the old order was being challenged every-where, and new nation states being born. Yet even now, with habeas corpus suspended, and the charismatic firebrand John Mitchel exiled in a prison hulk off Bermuda, and with a warrant out for O'Brien's own arrest and that of his comrades, he did not fully believe that the time for a rising had come – or even that a rising was wise.

Thomas Meagher and John Dillon also knew the timing was wrong. It was too soon; there was no proper organization or communications; and the Catholic priests were warning the people against a rising before the harvest, telling them truthfully that they were in no state to fight. Yet Meagher and Dillon and others realised that there was now no turning back; the British Government had forced their hand, and they were determined to give the rising their best efforts. They insisted to Smith O'Brien that he must lead the people, since he was the leader the people looked to. Reluctantly, he agreed.

But William Smith O'Brien was a Hamlet. He wandered from

village to village in Tipperary, attracting armed followers everywhere, in a saga that began by seeming confused, and which ended in tragic farce. With Patrick O'Donohoe at his side – one of the few Young Irelanders who was a man of the people – Smith O'Brien had drawn crowds of peasants who were ready to follow him anywhere, seeing him as Ireland's saviour. But before he consented to revolution, he said, he wanted 'to test their disposition'. And so, in Mullinahone, in that warm July, with two pistols in his belt, wearing a cloth cap trimmed with gold lace, he addressed the crowd of men who crammed the street, many of them armed with muskets, pikes and pitchforks. Although their local priest spoke against a rising, they were ready to follow Smith O'Brien to the death, they said.

But his speech would dismay them, as it had dismayed the people of other villages. He spoke of Ireland's wrongs – but he also warned them against any attack on private property. There must be absolutely no plunder, he said. This was an Ascendancy gentleman speaking; not a revolutionary activist. Starved by the Famine, hungry for a leader, thirsting for revenge against those who had so long oppressed them, the people began to be confused. Was this the language of revolt? Smith O'Brien had been hailed as a deliverer of the people, Patrick O'Donohoe wrote later; now, as O'Brien spoke, their vision of deliverance and freedom vanished. They began to melt away.

But O'Brien was convinced of the rightness of his position. He next led a group of six hundred wildly enthusiastic followers to Ballingarry, six miles off in the hills, riding in a jaunting car. They were ready for anything; but he addressed them in the same vein. No plunder – and only those men who could provide their own bread could take part in the rebellion. Having said that, he ordered them home to see to it. When it was suggested that if Carrick were taken, its bank should be seized for funds, he was horrified.

Ballingarry, when Moira at last finds it, proves to be very small and pretty, with a few houses, long stone walls and stone barns, and a snug yellow pub at a crossroads. She pulls the car over, and we all get out. The village can't have changed much, since that other momentous July of 1848. It looks down onto the plain, over miles of green and tawny flatland. To the south is the round and perfect blue breast of Slievenamon: the magic mountain where the Young Ireland leaders hoped to make their headquarters, and where Thomas Meagher holed up, before his arrest. Here at Ballingarry, on Saturday July 29th, William Smith O'Brien was forced to make his stand.

He did so at a time when things had grown desperate for him. The other Young Ireland leaders – gentlemen like himself, who had little or no knowledge of the peasantry they wished to lead – had fallen out with one another the day before. Discontent over O'Brien's Quixotic leadership had brought things to a head. John Dillon told O'Brien that his refusal to seize property was 'an act of fatuity'. Some even spoke of shooting him. But they finally cooled down and agreed to disagree, like gentlemen. They then scattered to different parts of the country, intending to carry on the struggle in their own ways. Terence MacManus and James Stephens remained in Ballingarry with O'Brien.

On Saturday, just after midday, they were drilling their ragged peasant force in the roadway, and had set up barricades. Then, at one o'clock, a detachment of armed police was seen, marching towards them in the distance. But instead of advancing on the barricades, the police turned off into the countryside, making for the Widow McCormack's farmhouse, which they occupied and made their fortress. O'Brien and MacManus and an army composed of enthusiasts and idlers followed, bent on attack.

We all go into the bar of the yellow pub, to ask where the farmhouse might be found. Over a round of Guinness, the matter is discussed with the half-dozen people here. At first, no-one seems to have heard of it. Then a middle-aged man in a cap comes in, and listens. 'That's the War House you're wanting,' he says, and gives us directions on how to get there.

We have another round of Guinness and some sandwiches before leaving; when we come out, the shadows on the road have grown longer, and a thick, brassy tinge has entered the light. The War House – a name I've not heard before – proves to be hard to find: not as close to the village as the accounts of the incident seemed to indicate. We drive up and down a number of narrow, empty little roads running between hedgerows, but the directions given us by the man in the pub don't seem to work. Twilight creeps in, and Bobby and Brian are for giving up. But Moira, still driving, is determined: we must find the Widow McCormack's house.

Finally, coming up a road onto the top of an empty hill, in a darkening, open landscape of far-flung, patchworked fields, under a sky where giant silver rain clouds are beginning to move, we come upon a lone local builder, about to get into a truck loaded with timber. We ask about the War House.

We've found it, he says, and points to an open farm gate.

We drive through, entering a deserted field, and here in front of us is the house, which I recognize from drawings reproduced from the *Illustrated London News* of the day. Moira is delighted we've found it; without her persistence, we never would have done so. 'Men are terrible at finding things,' she says.

It's a very plain, two-storeyed house, slate-roofed and faced with peeling stucco. Its windows are dark and empty: two on the ground floor at the front, three upstairs. Not derelict, but vacant, sombre and neglected. Though the house bears a plaque signed by Taoiseach Bertie Ahern, stating that the War House was acquired by the state in 1998, it scarcely looks like a shrine, moping on its empty hilltop. And indeed, it's forgotten and unknown, even by most people in the area: Smith O'Brien and his Young Irelanders, once seen as towering heroes in Ireland's long struggle, are now seen as romantic failures, and irrelevant. Perhaps the revisionist historians of whom Tim Pat Coogan spoke to me have had their effect.

We move towards the house. A copse of dark fir trees stands behind it, adding to its gloom. In front is a low stone wall, with an old iron gate open at its centre. Inside it is a tract of grass that's overgrown with thistles and tall, flowering weeds. This, from the newspaper pictures, was once the widow's cabbage patch, which gave the battle its name – and which was a source of much amusement to the *Times,* and other English newspapers.

When the armed police burst into the house, the Widow McCormack was out, collecting two of her children from a nearby school. But five more children were at home, and now became prisoners. The police barricaded themselves in and waited by the windows on the upper floor, carbines at the ready. The mob arrived close behind them, led by Smith O'Brien and Terence MacManus – some carrying guns, most armed with pikes and pitchforks. But the police held their fire. At this point the Widow McCormack came home, and rushed to the window on the right of the front door, which was open. She pleaded with the police inside to give up her children; then she turned to Smith O'Brien and appealed to him.

O'Brien climbed onto the low stone sill, and began to negotiate with the police. 'We are all Irishmen, boys,' he said. 'Give up your arms, and we shall not hurt a man of you.'

There are conflicting accounts of what happened next. It seems likely that stones were thrown from the crowd through the windows – and according to MacManus, they were thrown by idlers and ruffians who had joined them simply to make trouble. In response, the police at the upper windows opened fire into the crowd with their carbines. This was at about two-thirty. The rebels took refuge behind the low stone wall at the front, and an exchange of fire went on at intervals for the next two hours.

Concerning O'Brien's actions there are also conflicting accounts. One constable claimed that he retreated into the cabbage patch – enabling the *Times* to concoct a fanciful account of a cowardly Smith O'Brien weeping and crawling on all fours through the cabbages. This was fairly typical of the anti-Irish propaganda of the day. All the other eye-witness accounts portray a man who appeared neither to be in control of the situation nor willing to run away – and who exposed himself to fire in an almost suicidal manner. Even the *Illustrated London News* reported that O'Brien would have been totally exposed to fire in the cabbage patch, and would hardly have gone there for cover – and that he actually took up a position with his men behind the stone wall. It also reported that his behaviour from a military point of view was 'censurable' for its indiscreet daring. He is said to have stood there, refusing to crouch down, while the bullets whistled around him. James Stephens wrote later of his 'splendid bravery', and called him 'the truest and best of men', while dismissing 'the scum of journalism known as the press of England'. MacManus, who was wounded in the leg, said later that O'Brien refused to get out of the line of fire, and had to be forcibly led away: the last to leave.

Sixty-five additional armed police had arrived. Outgunned, the rebels had dispersed – persuaded to go by two priests. Two of their number had been killed; the police had suffered no casualties. O'Brien escaped on a horse which Stephens took at gunpoint from one of the police. The Ballingarry rising was over. Smith O'Brien, who had never wanted to see blood shed, would be arrested trying to catch a train in the nearby town of Thurles a few days later, on August 5th. He would be convicted of high treason and sentenced to death; but his sentence would then be commuted to transportation for fourteen years. Along with his comrades, he would be sent to my native island as a political exile: a prisoner of state. He would never be confined there as a common convict: London had decreed that the exiles were to be treated as gentlemen. He would be free, as his fellow-exiles were, to mix in the best society on Van Diemen's Land – such as it was – and to live as he pleased.

At first, though, he endured a period of house arrest in two penal stations: Maria Island, off the east coast, and Port Arthur, on the

Tasman Peninsula. He had no direct contact with other convicts, and was given a small cottage of his own, where he lived in isolation, under military guard. This was a situation of his own choice: unlike his comrades, he had refused to give his parole to the Governor not to try and escape the island. Stiff-necked to the end, he pointed out that it was not a promise he could honestly undertake to keep.

He did make one attempt to escape. Friends arranged for a ship to pick him up from a beach on Maria Island; but someone betrayed him, and he was dragged from the longboat by his attentive guards, and carried up the beach in a state of collapse. He made no more attempts, and eventually signed the parole. After many years, he would gain a pardon and return to Europe. But his health and spirit were broken, and he would end his days, at odds with his conservative family, wandering about the Continent, prematurely aged. Although he was honoured as a patriot, both in Europe and the United States, his life would seem to have been wasted – his struggle for his country's freedom having ended as a pointless fiasco.

But there is another way of seeing him, I believe. He had ruined his life for a cause he believed to be just. He had given up a position of privilege, wealth and comfort when he had no need at all to do so; when he'd suffered no personal wrongs. The mean and envious bitterness that is the secret force driving so many radical activists wasn't in him. He had no lust for power; and his lack of such a lust brought him down. His romantic gamble which he knew to be a gamble – was carried out purely on behalf of his country and his people; not for himself. And despite the petty defeat at Ballingarry, the exiled Young Irelanders would give inspiration to generations of patriots to come; until the Fenians, more ruthless than O'Brien, would take the cause of freedom to its ultimate, bloody success.

So there is perhaps more tragedy than comedy about Smith O'Brien's story, in the end. Impractical idealism and stubborn, unbreakable honesty are surely more endearing than ruthlessness, and cunningly contrived success. As for his refusal to permit plunder and pillage: many a Napoleon has gone down that other road, and left little but a legacy of wretchedness. Patrick O'Donohoe, the self-educated man of the people who stood by O'Brien to the end, put it best:

A scrupulous conscience frustrated his undertaking. A vicious man with the talents and prestige of O'Brien's name would have overthrown English dominion in Ireland. A man of such virtues could not and never will succeed in Ireland.

We drive down off the hill through a shower of rain. This soon passes, but the sky remains overcast, and darkness is coming on quickly, in the empty countryside.

The War House lingers in our minds, together with that set of romantic and impetuous Irish gentlemen who condemned themselves to a life of exile, and are now dismissed or forgotten, in the Ireland of the European Union. Forlorn, absurd and unsatisfying, scarcely earning a place on the stage of history, the Ballingarry incident resembles instead those small yet piercing failures and joys that mark out the course of an ordinary human life. Perhaps that's why it's haunting. It was so odd and hopeless and confused, for all the wild hopes of the people, and for all the grandiose dreams of Young Ireland: so sadly unlike those momentous confrontations that earn themselves niches in history. 'A nation once again'! No; not here, not yet; Thomas Davis's promise must wait. The widow's bare grey house is no monument to an historic victory, or even to an historic defeat. It sits brooding on its hill like a building in a bittersweet dream: one whose final meaning eludes us, but in which people lurk who trouble us, and to whom we've given our hearts.

We are all silent for a time; then Bobby begins to talk.

'I once read a little piece written by Oscar Wilde, which talks about Smith O'Brien. It's called *The Apple Woman of Thurles*. Have you heard of it? No? Wilde tells in it how his father's house was one of the few that Smith O'Brien visited, and that O'Brien greatly admired his mother, Lady Wilde. She was a member of Young Ireland, you know: she wrote poems for their newspaper, the *Nation*, under the pen-name of 'Speranza'. Smith O'Brien used to call on her, as the other Young Irelanders did – and he came calling again after he'd served his sentence in Australia. This was at a time when his life had become very dreary. Oscar was just a boy of nine or so then, and O'Brien treated him as a favourite. Wilde describes him as a fine, brave soul – a patriot who gave up everything for his country. And he tells how he was reading some old book one day when Smith O'Brien was there, and O'Brien told him to put it aside, and he'd tell him a better story. Would you like to hear it?'

We would, we say.

'The story Smith O'Brien told him,' Bobby says, 'was about being on the run in the town of Thurles, just after the Ballingarry rising. There was a price of ten thousand pounds on his head, and he was walking alone through the streets at night in the rain, and had decided to give himself up. He passed a poor, bedraggled old woman selling apples, huddled in a doorway. And he thought: if I'm going to give myself up, why shouldn't this poor old woman have the ten thousand pounds? A fortune, in those days! Then he would at least have helped one suffering person. So he told her who he was, and suggested she take the reward. And guess what she said? "Betray ye, Smith O'Brien? Curse the one that'd do it – and shame on ye that ye could think of an Irish heart untrue to ye, and an Irish woman that wouldn't give her life, and her children's life, to help ye!"'

It's full dark now. Little clusters of lights appear on the plain like showers of sparks, then disappear into the black. We're on our way back towards Mullinahone, and the pub Bobby and Brian call the Thatch – or as they pronounce it, 'the T'atch'.

'This is a very special pub,' Bobby tells me. 'You have to know where it is, or you'd never find it. It doesn't look like a pub at all – and there's no way of getting in at the front. That's because there *is* no entrance at the front. And there's no sort of sign up anywhere. In the days when you drove a horse and cart there, that made sense. Now it makes *no* sense – but you still have to do it. You drive around the back, where there's a farmyard. *That's* where the entrance is!'

I feel somewhat bewildered. 'So the T'atch is really a farm?'

Bobby nods triumphantly. 'Of course! the T'atch is a farm, as well as a pub. Here we are, Moira – turn in the gate here.'

Moira takes the car up a short, rough drive in the dark, and brings the car to a halt in what is certainly a farmyard, with stables and a barn on one side, and a dark, rambling old house with a low thatched roof on the other. A man is sitting quietly at a rough wooden bench by the door of the house, drinking a beer and smoking. He greets us with an amused smile. A cow lows in the barn. There's no-one else here; but a low, steady murmur of voices comes from somewhere in the house. As Bobby has said, there's nothing to show that this is a hotel. Nor is there very much light; the yellow-brown glow from the windows seems extremely dim, as though there's been a power failure.

This is explained when we stoop through the low, narrow doorway. We've entered a large, semi-dark space like a stables, and it's lit only by candles. Rough wooden pillars support the ceiling, and clusters of candles are fixed on these. Candles also flicker on long, rough-hewn, medieval-looking tables, where people sit on benches. There are perhaps thirty people in here; no more. A simple wooden bar at the far end is lined with bottles and more candles. A curly-haired barman pours drinks there: the only indication that this is a public house. The feeble flames do little to lighten the darkness, and very few details in the room can be made out. It's like the meeting place of some secret organization – an effect compounded by the fact that the people here are all talking in low, indistinguishable murmurs. They appear to be perfectly ordinary men and women; but their faces are difficult to make out, unless they're very close to one of the candles. There are no other sounds here but their muffled voices, and occasional low laughter. The flickering darkness is hushed, and our voices become hushed in response.

'So this is the T''atch,' I say to Bobby.

'This is the T'atch!' Bobby whispers. His eyes flash, reflecting the candle flames, and he smiles at me triumphantly. 'You see? No electric light – there never has been! No TV. No piped music. And everybody's *quiet*! This is the way it's *always* been, in the T'atch!'

Brian goes across to the bar to buy drinks. Moira follows him, and Bobby and I sit down at one of the tables. He leans close to murmur in my ear, his hushed voice eager and confidential, as though imparting secrets that it's important for me to remember.

'You see that bar up there? The top of it's all eaten away by woodworm. I remember one time they put in a wooden box there: a box to hold electric fuses. They thought that they'd put in electric light. But that was when rural electrification was just starting – early in the game, when it took the electricity people a long time to do things. It took *so* long, that the box was eaten away by woodworm too! So they never did put electricity in the T'atch. It's still a place of candles and cows. Do you see?' His hushed voice is elated; his sharp eyes seek mine, and he raises a finger, and smiles. '*Listen*. There's no sound here but these people murmuring to each other. Isn't it lovely? We've gone back in time – two hundred years. And that's very hard to find these days.'

Brian and Moira are back, and set our drinks down in front of us. Then they sit down on the other side of the table, resuming a conversation they've been having at the bar, murmuring as the T'atch requires, too low for us to hear. Bobby drinks a little of his Guinness, smooths back his mane of white hair, and leans towards my ear again.

His voice, half-whispering, takes on the Irish storytelling cadence: the bardic cadence, whose rhythms are compelling and hypnotic. He wants me to see the disappearing past, and the rhythm helps me to do so.

'There used to be so many old pubs like this one, Chris. They were all around the country here: in Tipperary; Kilkenny; Waterford. Now they're almost gone. In the days when my brothers and I were young – before the Clancy Brothers group was formed – we'd go out to those places all the time, especially across the border down in Waterford: in Ring, where it's still Irish-speaking. There's a pub there called the *Seanachie*, near Dungarvan, which I'm very fond of: that means "the old storyteller", in Irish. It goes back to the eighteenth century. It's full of tourists now, but it wasn't then. You'll see it in a couple of days, when Moira and I take you down there. And the brothers and I would go there often, in the old days. It had a little parlour as dark as this, with only a kerosene lamp on. A flagged slate floor, and a fire in a bloody great black fireplace, twelve feet wide. A big black carved settee, two hundred years old at least; straight-backed chairs; a barrel where flour was kept. And dark old stairs going up to a landing overhead, and a door there leading to a bedroom where the owners slept. When we came in, the locals would all be sitting there with their pints: all the men with their caps on.' He laughs. 'And the caps were pulled low over their eyes, so that all you could see in the dark was their mouths, moving as they talked. And people would sit snug in front of that fire and sing – *anybody* would sing, you know what I mean? The brothers and I would sing too: we were always welcome. And that's the sort of setting that's going so *fast* : it's sad.'

It's sad. His voice has an elegiac note; but it's not maudlin. It manages to combine elegy with a brisk matter-of-factness: with a hard-headed acceptance of things. The twenty-first century is advancing like a tidal wave, carrying its computers, piped music systems and video games; and soon the traditional world Bobby loves will be gone. He knows this, and no doubt he mourns a little; but he doesn't dwell on it. He enjoys what's left to enjoy.

He's been staring into the candle; now he turns and looks at me. 'The music's still here, if you want to find it,' he says. 'It's still in places like Shirley's. It was good there last night, wasn't it?'

I agree that it was.

He smiles; his eyes grow brilliant in the candle flame, and his voice is tender and caressing. 'Sure: nicest sing-song you could ever want to hear. That's what I *love* about all this!'

III

Down in the old stable yard at the back of Clareen House, Martin Feeney is playing in the sun with a tortoiseshell kitten. He's seated on a bench beside a shed there, and is trailing a long blade of grass for the kitten to pounce on. It makes a short rush; he pulls the blade just out of reach, and smiles cunningly.

I stand at the window of our attic room, looking down at him. It's ten in the morning on Saturday: we've been here in Carrick for over a week, and must leave the day after tomorrow. Next Tuesday, we fly home to Australia from Dublin. I want to catch Martin to tell him this, and decide to go down to the yard.

When I come out there and greet him, he's nursing the kitten on his knee. He looks up with a childlike smile, slightly abashed, as though caught out in something.

'You've got a new kitten,' I say.

'No, no,' he says. 'It's *not mine*.' He puts it down quickly on the ground, and it begins to lurch off towards some bushes by the shed. He points to the bushes. 'The mother cat's got a litter in there. *She's* not mine either – she just settled in here.'

We both go over to the bushes and peer in: a lean tabby cat is lying behind them, with her four lively kittens tumbling about her. She looks up at Martin complacently, and he sighs.

'I should discourage her,' he says. 'Shouldn't have cats in a B and B. But she just stays.'

I somehow doubt that he tries very hard to discourage her, but I don't say so. Instead, I tell him that we must leave on Monday. It makes me sad, saying this: I'm deeply reluctant to leave Carrick-on-Suir.

But Martin, who sees guests off every day, looks professionally cheerful. 'That's a pity,' he says. 'But you'll be getting homesick, no doubt, and glad to be getting back to Australia. I hope you've enjoyed your time here. Bobby Clancy's certainly kept you busy: so many nights carousing! He must think a lot of your friend.'

He does, I say. Brian and Bobby have known each other a long time.

Martin's sly gaze rests on me. 'And they're both musicians,' he says. 'Two of a kind – of course. But you're not like your friend: you're more of a scholar, I think. You've had a sheltered upbringing – am I right? Not like me: I led a rough life, when I was young. You seem a well-*preserved* gentleman.'

Down on the coast of Waterford, a short drive south from Carrick, is the *An Rinn Gaeltacht*. This is an Irish-speaking district which is Moira Clancy's native place; and Irish, I've discovered, is Moira's first language. Yesterday, she and Bobby took us down there, in a final expedition across the border.

An Rinn – or Ring, in English – turned out to be a little farming district of about 1500 people, tucked away in the countryside only six miles outside the fishing port of Dungarvan: Waterford's major coastal town. And Ring was elusive. It has no centre, which makes it baffling to tourists. There's not even a village. Hiding away among its fields and pine woods, it's simply a community of farms and little pubs: a community left over from the nineteenth century, and scarcely belonging in this one.

Many of the people there are friends of Bobby's and Moira's. And

Moira's family, the Mooneys, have run a pub in Ring for generations: a pub which is famous for Irish music.

Mid-afternoon at Dungarvan. A bright day, with high white cloud. We've eaten a lunch of shellfish, in a pub on the quay. Moira and Bobby have some shopping to do; they go off for half an hour, leaving Brian and me to loaf along the waterfront.

Dungarvan Harbour is beautiful: a vast, blue-green bay, dotted with yachts and fishing boats, enclosed by the long, thin fingers of far-off headlands, and opening on to St George's Channel. Its long stone quay is thronged with tourists from all over Europe: the scene is Mediter-ranean, and sparkles. Tall old warehouses have been converted to tourist pubs and chic restaurants, and are painted in bright colours, with names like 'King John's Patisserie' and 'Grab & Go'. But down at the end of the quay, near the town centre, in front of a set of genuine warehouses, front-end loaders speed about: this is still a working port.

Four middle-aged German men, clad in the baseball caps and checked trousers usually worn by touring Americans, are sitting at a varnished table on the quay. A pretty young waitress who looks no more than twelve hurries across to them with a tray of Irish coffees. A blond, six-year-old boy with the face of a brutal businessman sits eating an ice cream. Laughing, big-breasted Irish women in tight singlet tops and brief shorts eat pastries outside a cafe; a sparrow hops after crumbs. A moustached man in a white t-shirt walks a corgi. A bald, middle-aged Briton with one earring and a shoulder bag and unhappy eyes stands rolling a cigarette, alone. Pleasure boats ride here at anchor; tubs of flowers are placed at intervals. Dungarvan, like Dublin, is part of the Ireland of the Economic Union, and vibrates with tourist money.

Brian and I emerge from the quay and walk south around an esplanade that curves beside the bay. Tall new yellow apartment blocks have been built here, in a style to match the nineteenth century ware-houses: but they have the basic, functional look of most modern build-ings. Esplanades always draw me: highways to enigmatic distances.

This esplanade has a new look, and is handsome, with fine brick paving, a bitumen road for cars, young trees, and black and gold lamp posts in the nineteenth century style. Below its wall, dark-hooded sea birds catch sand worms. The tide is going out: light green water and long ripples. A gull rides sideways on the air. Distant voices of children, calling from a sports ground; few other walkers. Two young men in well-cut dark suits pass by, talking intently; men of the new business class: real estate agents, perhaps.

At our backs, enclosing the northern side of the bay, is a distant stone sea wall with rows of guesthouses behind, and an old square church tower, small on a promontory. In front of us, as we walk, out on the horizon beyond the esplanade, is another promontory, enclosing the bay in the south. Very long and low under the big sky, it extends for many miles, ending in a lion-shaped headland on the Atlantic. It's a place of far, coloured fields and trees: a promontory of dreaming beauty. A second neck of land extends from it towards us: treeless, sandy, and clothed in dry grass, coming right across the bay and into the harbour, like a yellow ribbon. At lunch, Moira told us that her grandmother used to walk across this peninsula each day, to take a little boat to the quay.

But it's the main, distant promontory that holds my gaze, with its patchwork of fields in every shade of green and tawny yellow, and the microscopic trees on its top almost black, stamped against the sky. It glows behind sea-mist and the hazes of afternoon; it dreams outside modern Ireland, and is surely much farther from Dungarvan and its bars and patisseries than can be measured in miles or kilometres.

I point, and ask Brian its name.

'That? That's Helvick Head,' he says. 'That's where Ring is – the Gaelic-speaking area. That's where Moira's grandmother used to walk from each day.'

An Rinn – of course. Ultimate land's end; territory of the nineteenth century. It's difficult to believe that we'll actually go across there, to those pastures outside today.

Driving west out of Dungarvan, on a road that passes through pine woods, Bobby takes us first to the *Seanachie*: the ancient pub he described to me in the T'atch, where he and his brothers sang and were happy in their youth.

It's a long, white, studiedly quaint cottage, catering now for tourists, with a thatched roof and deep-set, aged little windows and hanging baskets of flowers. The parlour at the back is exactly as Bobby described it; but it's dark and empty, in the late afternoon: a place of shades, with a print of the Sacred Heart on the wall above the fireplace. We go out into the bright, narrow front bar, where a number of tourists are gathered, and order drinks there. Four locals are seated at a table: a young man in corduroy trousers, who looks like a farmer, a young woman with long copper hair, an old man in a cap, and a thin old lady with very pale eyes. They are speaking quietly in Irish. We're in Ring.

As we drink, I notice on one wall the print I first saw in Powell's in Oughterard: the Kennedy brothers, heroic in profile, like icons to be prayed to. Moira, standing beside me, follows my gaze, and asks what I thought of them.

I admired them greatly, I tell her. I was in America when John Kennedy was elected, and he meant something special to me. Like many other people, I can vividly remember the day he was killed, and what I was doing, and my disbelief. Then I say how disillusioning it's been, since their deaths, to discover how corrupt the Kennedys were. I assume as I say this that Moira will be of the same mind.

But she stares at me blankly. 'What do you mean?'

'The connections with the Mafia,' I say. 'The sexual scandals.'

Still she stares, and it dawns on me that for many people in Ireland there's been no revision of the Kennedy myth, and never will be. Moira shakes her head.

'No,' she says. 'I don't believe all that. It's lies. The Republicans have enough money to get people to say anything – and put it in books, too.'

'There's something in that. You could be right,' I say.

Bobby has driven us to Ardmore, a little way down the coast.

To be with Bobby and Moira is to be always moving through late afternoon into an evening without limits; and the unlikely summer weather continues. In bright six o'clock sun, the four of us are walking down a path called St Declan's Walk, on a high green hill above Ardmore village and the sea. St Declan, Bobby tells us, was a missionary bishop who came here from Wales in the fifth century. He arrived before St Patrick; so this is perhaps the oldest parish in Ireland.

We've come here having visited the ruins of St Declan's Cathedral, on another open hillside nearby.

Built in the twelfth century, on the site of Declan's original monastic community, the massive Romanesque building was now a shell. It stood close to a survivor from a more remote time: the tall, intact Ardmore Round Tower, which was the refuge of the Gaelic monks when the Viking raiders came. The strange, faceless stone cylinder rose to nearly a hundred feet; there was no door in the base, and its high, slitted windows looked out over the wide blue vista of Ardmore Bay below: still scanning the Atlantic for the Northmen in their longships. The monks would retreat from them into the tower, Bobby told us, pulling up a ladder to a door too high to reach, and taking their treasures with them. On the sun-gold stone facade of the cathedral, scenes had been carved showing the fall of man, the weighing of souls, and the adoration of the Magi. A modern cemetery crept right up to its wall: Celtic crosses and stone slabs, and a white statue of the Virgin gazing inland over miles of many-coloured fields. Moira showed us the grave of one of her uncles there. This was the land of her family; many of them were buried here, she said, in various little graveyards in Ring.

Now we're on our way to St Declan's Well, which is reached by St Declan's Walk, and which stands by his ruined oratory, or hermitage. Moira has urged us to come here: the well is a very holy place, she says. And oddly enough, today is St Declan's Day: July 24th, his feast day, known as Patron Day. That must mean something, she tells us; and her smile is only half-joking.

We're walking in the direction of the sea. No-one else is coming down the path, at present. St Declan's Walk is narrow, winding and pebbled, going between a hedge on our left and banks of low green bushes on our right: bushes that run uphill to the summit of the ridge. Long and high, falling away to the sea, the ridge is bare of trees and clothed in straw-pale grass: massive and open and empty, under a wide, milky sky. We turn a bend, and here in front of us, with the long blue bar of the sea beyond, is a tall, gabled, Romanesque stone remnant: a single remaining wall, with a little window at the top and an arch at the bottom. This is what's left of the hermitage.

We walk on, and come soon to another section of ruined wall, with a doorway in it leading nowhere. A spring feeds a little pool here, in front of more fragments of stonework, below a crude stone cross. This is St Declan's Well.

It's silent here, under the long slope of the ridge, and the sky that curves over to the sea; and the atmosphere is ambiguous. Not quite melancholy, it seems to be one of hushed and gentle gravity, containing the half-heard droning of a mystery too old to be identified. Is it entirely Christian, this little well of St Declan's? These rough stone structures were built to honour a Romanized evangelist and scholar who came here bringing Latin Christianity, at a time when the Roman Empire was in the final stages of its long collapse, and when illiterate barbarian chieftains were taking over Europe. Like so many of his missionary brethren, Declan would have been obliged to mingle his new doctrine with the myth and magic of Irish paganism, so that its seeds would sprout here; and this, perhaps, is what makes the atmosphere at the well so enigmatic to me: the presence of ancient magic, as well as ancient piety.

We stand for a time; then we turn to make our way back, Bobby and Brian leading, Moira and I walking behind.

The path runs in a circle, around the well. Two men are coming towards us: local farmers, one old, one young, the elder in thick, heavy-framed glasses. They are carrying rosary beads and bottles.

After they've passed, Moira says to me: 'Because it's Patron Day, they've come here for water from the spring. It's supposed to cure sickness, if you drink it. They'll take some water in their bottles, and then they'll walk in a circle here and pray. It's a very special place, don't you think?'

I agree that it is. Something can be sensed in the air here.

She smiles; St Declan's Well is clearly important to her. 'Just think,' she says. 'For hundreds of years, people have been coming here and walking in a circle and praying, just like they're doing now. And nothing modern's been done to it – it hasn't changed. *Nothing's* changed here. Think of all the prayers that have been said here: that's what you feel in the air. The Rosary is said here in Irish. You'll know what Rosary beads are?'

'I used to have some,' I say.

She glances at me quickly. 'Of course – you're a Catholic.'

'And *does* the water cure sickness?'

She is silent for a moment, walking. Up ahead, Bobby and Brian are laughing together.

'I had a friend who had stomach cancer,' she says. 'She came here and prayed for a cure. When she came back from the well up the path here, she saw a bright light ahead of her. And then it was all around her, wrapping her in a sort of whiteness.' She pauses. 'She was cured of the cancer.'

We pass through the little door in the wall, to go on towards the road. As we do so, I surprise myself by making the sign of the Cross. Out of the corner of my eye, I see Moira do the same.

We catch up to Bobby and Brian. The four of us walk on together, leaving behind this shrine from the beginning of the Age of Faith: the grim and shattering fifth century, when the shrunken Roman Empire had lost its common beliefs and its power; when the East German barbarian Odovacar would sit on the imperial throne; when Germanic tribes would carve up the Empire between them, while Christendom waited in embryo, ready to supplant Rome and to reinvent the West.

Now, on the rim of the new millennium, as we four move up St Declan's Walk, Christendom is dead, the West once again without common values, and the Catholic Church foundering in Ireland. But not in Ring: not in the land of St Declan's Well.

Anne, Moira's sister, is singing in Gaelic. The air is beautiful, strange and antique; I've not heard anything that resembles it.

It's ten o'clock at night, and we're sitting in the crowded bar of Mooney's pub – which goes by no other name, and is the great Gaelic singing pub of Ring. It's owned by Anne, Moira tells us, and Anne and her husband Tom Gough manage it together. 'The pub's always been passed down through the women of the Mooney family,' she says, 'as far back as the Popes.'

Mooney's is on that long, many-coloured promontory which I saw from the esplanade at Dungarvan, and which ends at Helvick Head. We're sitting on stools near the windows at the front of the bar: the pub looks north-east over Dungarvan Harbour and the sea. It's a rambling structure, divided into two sections: a big lounge-bar on the right of the entrance, and this smaller bar on the left which is reserved for traditional singing. It's a long room with a snug bar counter at the top where Tom is serving drinks: a quiet, slim, friendly man, smoking a cigar. The place is so packed that there's scarcely room to get to the counter. Some of the voices around us are speaking in Irish, some in English, while others veer constantly between the two. On the walls are many original paintings and drawings: the leaders of the 1916 Rising; folksingers and musicians, including the Clancy brothers, and sketches of old men and women of the district. The crowd is of all ages: middle-aged, elderly, and a scattering of young people in their twenties, some of whom will prove to be singers.

Singing unaccompanied, Anne is sitting on a stool quite close to us, wearing a plain black dress. She's a handsome woman with straight blonde hair, a broad face, and the oblique, faintly Slavonic blue eyes that recall the ancient Celtic stock. Her song ends to resounding applause, and shouts for more.

'Ah no, I've sung enough,' Anne says. 'It's time Deirdre sang. Deirdre! Come down here and help out, now.' Then she breaks into Irish, beckoning vigorously to a small, slight blonde woman in jeans and a grey t-shirt.

Deirdre makes her way down the room, carrying a glass of whiskey. 'I'll not sing on my own,' she tells Anne. 'I've a hoarse throat tonight.'

'Ah, don't give us that!'

'I have. But I'll do a duet with you.'

People clap and shout in encouragement, and the two women begin, side by side on their stools. The room falls almost silent: people watch, with expectant eyes. Again the song is in Gaelic, of a far and wistful beauty that enters strangely into the rumbustious bar, and yet which seems as natural here as the air. Sometimes, at the beginning of a verse, Deirdre forgets the line, and looks at Anne, who prompts her with a murmur in Irish. It doesn't matter; the song is sung to the end, to everyone's satisfaction.

Next to me, Bobby Clancy chuckles with pleasure. 'Lovely. *That's* what it's all about.'

Anne and Deirdre join us, squeezing onto stools next to the windows, and Bobby and Moira introduce them. We are joined soon afterwards by a friend of Bobby's from Carrick: Seamus McGrath, a stocky, broad-shouldered, balding, blond man, down here in Ring for the evening. Seamus is a carpenter, Bobby tells me, but also a talented singer and composer of songs. After more drinks, when the evening has revolved a few times, a number of different conversations are proceeding at once, and I find myself talking with Deirdre. I ask her about the song that she and Anne sang.

'Ah, don't ask such questions,' she says. 'I just sing the songs, I don't explain them' She is vivid and quick, and her voice has a humorous edge to it. 'A while ago some academics came down here and asked us questions about the music,' she says. 'Anne and me. One of them even asked me to give a talk. Well, what a joke *that* would have been! Academics! What would *they* know about anything?' She laughs. 'Academics know nothing at all that matters.'

'I'm inclined to agree with you,' I say.

She looks at me quickly. 'So you're an Australian, then. And what do you think of Ireland?'

I tell her how much I like it. She nods and then sighs. 'Yes, we've a lovely, lovely country,' she says. 'But government and business between them are doing their bloody best to ruin it.' She turns to Anne, who is listening. 'Isn't that right now, Anne?'

'That's right, all right,' Anne says. 'Look what they're doing here in Dungarvan. Look at this superdump of theirs.'

Brian, Bobby and Moira are listening now, and Deirdre and Anne proceed to tell us about a superdump which is to be put in above Dungarvan. I remember now seeing notices by the roadside this afternoon, protesting against it. It will take the garbage of three counties, Deirdre tells us – despite the fact that experts have claimed that its poisons will enter the streams that run into Dungarvan Harbour. Superdumps are to be outlawed in Europe next year, she says – but both Waterford local government and officials in Dublin want the dump, and are pushing it through quickly. And when local councillors were persuaded to vote against it, one bureaucrat in the county corporation was able to dismiss the decision, she says.

'Jesus, they're so *corrupt*!' Deirdre cries. She is now in an ecstasy of outrage, looking around the circle and seeming to coil herself in readiness for a spring. 'We've a corrupt government in Dublin, taking millions behind the back, and now this! And it's not the corruption that matters so much, it's the *dictatorship*! Everything's about bloody money. Was *this* what the Republic was for? Was *this* what the heroes died for?'

It's one o'clock in the morning. The Guinness continues to flow, and the music to be sung, and the pub shows no sign of closing. A very pretty girl with a mass of bright auburn hair has just sung in Gaelic, her voice as electrifying as Enya's. Bobby has sung, and so has Seamus McGrath, with a composition of his own.

Now Seamus and I sit talking together in a corner. This stocky, solid man with the large head and thinning fair hair has an infectious friendliness, and an extraordinarily happy smile. I've seldom met a man so instantly likeable. He proves to be extremely cultivated: widely read, with a deep interest in Irish history. He's lived all his life in Carrick-on-Suir; like Bobby, he loves his native town. He talks to me of the moods of the river, and of the past: of the days under British rule in the nineteenth century, when soldiers were billeted there, and often made friends with the people. Not all of them were brutal, he says.

'The British were great organizers,' he says, 'like the Normans. You've got to give them that. But they saw the Irish as a quaint, comical people. It was Michael Collins who knocked *that* out of their heads.'

He says this without any resentment or hostility, his round face and wondering blue eyes lit with good humour. We've talked for at least an hour: he's a fine conversationalist, and his voice, with its soft Tipperary accent, is extremely musical: I could listen to it endlessly. Unlike most dedicated talkers, he's never boring, and not given to monologue. Instead, he has a gift for genuine two-way exchange, and an interest in everything. *To be interested*: the older one gets, the more this capacity becomes precious. I seem to have always known Seamus, perhaps because we had very similar boyhoods, at our opposite ends of the earth – both of us having served time under the Christian Brothers. Quoting some of their rebukes and homilies, and exchanging anecdotes about our encounters with the strap, we fall into helpless giggling. Perhaps it's the Guinness.

Brian is now singing 'The Wild Colonial Boy', to general enthusiasm. People are joining in, but Seamus and I go on talking, leaning to each other's ears, shouting happily above the din.

'You know, I'm still a Catholic, but I hate the old Church for its repression,' he says. 'It *ruled* Ireland until now. The priests told everyone what to do – and what gave them their greatest power was the Famine. All the best and bravest people emigrated, then: they jumped ship. And those that were left were broken. They wanted to be looked after; they wanted authority; and the Church gave it to them. You see? They *wanted* to be told what to do.'

I ask him if memories of the Famine have come down through his family.

'Some,' he says. 'Not many. My grandmother used to tell stories about her grandparents eating a yellow meal that was doled out. They called it "gold dust": it used to make them sick.' He finishes his Guinness. The noise in the bar is very loud now, and he says: 'Let's go out the front, and get a bit of air.'

We stand up, and I look at my watch. It's nearly two o'clock, and I ask Seamus about closing time. Doesn't it exist, in Ring?

He laughs. 'Sure it exists, but no-one takes any notice. The *gardai* come around and make a raid sometimes, as a matter of form. If they do, we'll all go out and hide in the garden. It's a convention, you might say. Both sides are happy with it.'

We stand outside, in the dimness on the steps. The music and the voices are muted, and the air is pure and limpid. We're silent for a moment, looking out over the harbour, beyond the dark trees across the road. There's a bright moon, and the scene is remarkably clear. A radiant, mauve-grey mist hangs low above the sea: a mist whose colour seems unreal. Far orange lights go off around the coast in a long, beckoning arc, like the lights of another country – the Many-Coloured Land, perhaps. Smaller lights are glimmering on the sea: the lamps of fishing boats, out after mackerel and pollock.

Beside me, Seamus speaks softly, picking up our former conversation and continuing with it, as though there's been no interruption.

'Back in that time, you see, the best people went to America – and they took their memories of the Famine with them. So the memories and the tradition stayed pure – a bit like your Aboriginal songlines in Australia. That's why the IRA did so well collecting in America – all that hatred burned *pure,* after three, four generations. Whereas here it was diluted. And now we've moved on; it's all in the past, and we know it.'

He smiles at me, making another Irish conversational leap, and picking up a thread we dropped an hour ago. 'Your great-great-grandmother *might* have lived in Carrick, Chris – who knows? But what does it matter which town she was in? She was a Tipperary girl, that's what matters – and you found your way back. It's a pity you're not staying longer. You've got to come back again.'

Inside, Brian and Bobby and Anne are singing 'The Parting Glass'. Drunk, happy and sad, I gaze at the arc of lights and the haze above the sea, saying goodbye. Am I truly leaving a strange country? Or will the country I go back to now seem strange?

Author's Note

Most of the people portrayed in the journey section of this book appear under their own names. A few, however, are semi-fictitious.

My sincere thanks to Richard O'Brien, former Ambassador of Ireland to Australia, who has been a warm friend to my work over recent years, and who gave me valuable introductions in Ireland. My thanks as well to the Irish Tourist Board, which assisted me with the journey, and in particular to Sandra Willett for her help with background information.

Two books by Australian historians were of special help in filling out the background of Margaret O'Meara's story. *Convict Women*, by Kay Daniels (Allen & Unwin, Sydney, 1998), yielded much information that was new to me concerning the female factories of 19th-century Van Diemen's Land. And in picturing the departure of a female convict ship from Kingstown Harbour, I found rich detail in Patrick Howard's *To Hell or to Hobart* (Kangaroo Press, Sydney, NSW, 1993).

Michael Coady's poem *'Na Prátaí Dubha'* is from his collection *All Souls,* published by permission of The Gallery Press, Loughcrew, Ireland (1997). The quotation from 'Becuma of the White Skin', in *Irish*

Fairy Tales by James Stephens (Macmillan, 1924), is by permission of the UK Society of Authors. The quotations from *Bowen's Court & Seven Winters*, by Elizabeth Bowen, are by permission of the Curtis Brown Group, Ltd, London, on behalf of the Estate of Elizabeth Bowen, copyright Elizabeth Bowen 1942, 1964. The story concerning Joe O'Reilly's recollection of Michael Collins is from *My Father's Son*, by Frank O'Connor (Macmillan, London, 1968). The lines from *The Hosting of the Sidhe*, from the Collected Poems of W.B. Yeats (Macmillan, 1950), are quoted by permission of A.P. Watt, Ltd, London, on behalf of Michael B. Yeats. The composer Pete St. John has given permission for the quotation of the verse from his song 'Dublin in the Rare Ould Times'.

This book is also dedicated to the memory of Bobby Clancy, who died in Waterford in September, 2002.

Sydney, 2002